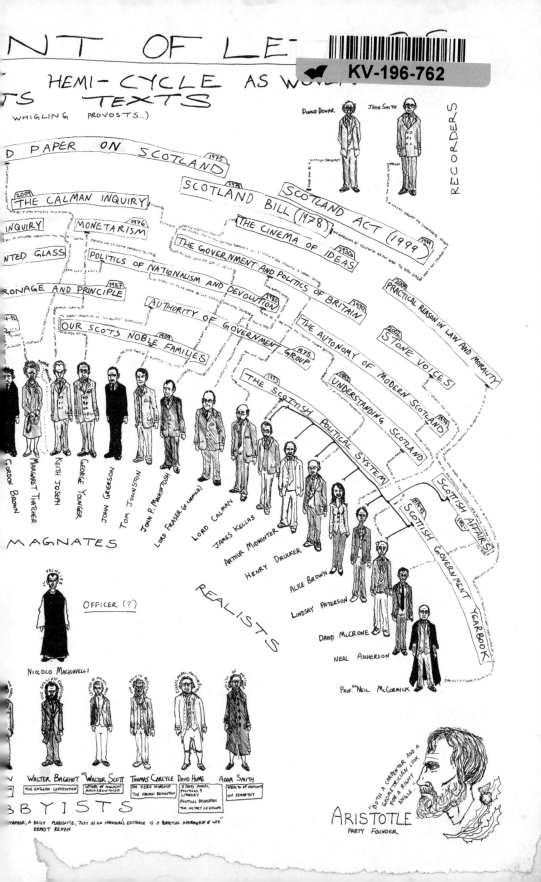

TARTAN PIMPS

GORDON BROWN, MARGARET THATCHER, AND THE NEW SCOTLAND

MITCH MILLER, JOHNNY RODGER
& OWEN DUDLEY EDWARDS

ARGYLL✠PUBLISHING

First published in 2010
Argyll Publishing
Glendaruel
Argyll PA22 3AE
Scotland
www.argyllpublishing.com

British Library Cataloguing-in-Publication Data.
A catalogue record for this book is available
from the British Library.

The publisher of *The Drouth* acknowledge subsidy from the
Scottish Arts Council towards the publication of this volume.

Scottish
Arts Council

ISBN 978 1 906134 50 1

Printing: Bell & Bain Ltd, Glasgow

Thanks to
British Film Institute, Viven Carvalho, Glasgow City Council,
Dorian Grieve, James Hunt, Craig Laurie,
Professor Nigel Leask, *Private Eye*, RMJM Architects,
Scottish Screen Archive, Scottish Television, Catherine Stevenson,
Claire Schlitz and Gavin Wallace.

Image Credits

1 *A Parliament of Letters* Mitch Miller
2 *The Red Paper for Scotland* Gordon Brown (ed.) Mainstream Publishing 1975
3 *Dear Bill* Courtesy: *Private Eye*
4 *The MacDunciad* Norman Buchan
5 *The Leviathan* Thomas Hobbes
6 Hugh MacDiarmid Courtesy: Dorian Grieve
7 Harry Lauder, Courtesy: James Hunt
8 from *Seawards the Great Ships* Courtesy: Scottish Screen Archive
9 STV logo (1980s), Courtesy: Scottish Television
10 Billy Connolly's banana boots, Courtesy: Glasgow City Council
11 Electoral Map of Scotland 2007, Courtesy: GNU Free Documentation
12 from *My Childhood* (dir. Bill Douglas), Courtesy: Scottish Screen Archive
13 from *Trainspotting* Courtesy: Universal Pictures
14 UCS Shipbuilders demo 1971, Courtesy: Herald and Evening Times
15 Rosie Kane swears, Courtesy: Associated Press
16 Ravenscraig Steelworks, Courtesy: RCAHMS
17 Oil Rig, From a Private Collection
18 Blair/Dewar/Steel, Courtesy: *The Scotsman*
19 The Holyrood Opposition, Courtesy: Associated Press
20 A Scottish Leviathan, Courtesy: Alasdair Gray
21 Kilbryde Covenanter Flag, Courtesy: Kybo Theatre Co.
22 Playfair Graph, William Playfair
23 Plan of Holyrood Parliament, Courtesy: RMJM Architects
24 Plan & Section '79 Scottish Assembly, Courtesy: National Archives of Scotland
25 Holyrood Parliament and Royal High School, Courtesy: Andrew Lee

Contents

INTRODUCTION

Notional Independence?

There shall be a Scottish Parliament.

Donald Dewar, *The Scotland Act*, 1998

THESE words – the first six of the most important work of Scottish existential non-fiction in 300 years – were given a certain incantatory power when, as Frankenstein to the monster, Donald Dewar spoke the dead Scottish Parliament back to life. Against the advice of a small but vocal anti-devolutionist core within his party he steered the document through Westminster and inscribed the words on the Scottish Parliamentary mace. The same words were carved on the plinth beneath his statue. At the opening of the new parliament in 1999 the words were declaimed by Winnie Ewing.

But the ramifications of there *being* a Scottish Parliament would cast the Labour Party into a narrative it could barely control. As with all who create monsters (and every Leviathan is) Dewar's cohorts would be surprised and appalled at what would happen to their creation. Their election defeat to the Scottish Nationalists in 2007 was the most obvious 'Pandora' moment, but even in the previous election of 2003 a palpable sense seeped into the collective conscious-ness of Scottish Labour that, far from consolidating their iron grip on Scottish public life, their actions presented new opportunities to old enemies.

As Labour First Ministers came and went with alarming rapidity the Scottish Conservatives regained their sense of purpose and even independence from the London centre. Aspects of Labour Militant re-emerged in the form of the Scottish Socialist Party; the Liberal (Democrat)s, previous overlords of Caledoniashire who had gouged their share of power out of the devolved coalition government, began to make it clear Labour should take nothing for granted; and the SNP demonstrated they were – at least numerically – the official opposition in Scotland.

Labour's response to this last threat was to take great pains to pretend the Nats did not exist, speaking at every opportunity of the threat of the *Tories* (the opposition in Westminster) and thus reminding the electorate that while Scottish politicians could count the 'sweeties', real politics, politics that mattered, that changed things, was still limited to the British level. Insofar as it diminished the Nats, this was something the other unionist parties and the mainstream Scottish broadcast media seemed largely happy to comply with. But in the past, even to attempt such a manoeuvre would have been unthinkable – staunchly Unionist Scottish Labour mandarins such as former labour Scottish Secretary Willie Ross could hardly have conceived the need.

Though they tried not to twitch, it was obvious to even the casual observer that this parliament was not quite what the Labour establishment in Scotland had expected, and that in the face of less than predictable democratic forces chipping at their powerbase, the party seemed less sure of its footing. According to that oddity-by-definition, Tory Home Ruler Michael Fry, writing of the 1988 Constitutional Convention, in which Scottish Labour effectively committed itself to Home Rule, they had envisaged the new Parliament as 'the portal of a participatory socialist paradise' dominated for here and hereafter by the intricate and massive Scottish Labour apparatus that had dominated Scottish politics at grassroots, council and constituency level for most of the twentieth century.

If Fry is correct then we can see the Labour apparatchiks' dream as having been initially perfectly plausible; that nothing changed in Scottish Politics – or rather, that there was no real, *contested* Scottish Politics – was a given and is arguably reflected in the 'consensual' design of both the Calton Hill and Holyrood debating chambers. To the aforementioned casual – or perhaps more provocatively, the non-aligned observer – the post 2003 Parliament brought a new sense of excitement and unpredictability to Scottish politics as the electorate gradually realised it was no longer required to act as a negative pole to London's positivism. This necessitated a change in the way the Scottish political classes thought and acted, as articulated by Jason Allardyce, politics editor of *Scotland on Sunday*, writing in 2003:

> . . . [T]he fragmentation of Scottish politics derives from the fact many want to break Labour's stranglehold on Scotland and are interested in the potential for experimentation, new thinking – at last, perhaps a genuinely new politics.

In 2007, the electorate's wishes extended not just to bringing new issues into debate (in particular, by the Greens and the SSP) but new structures in the power relationship between Holyrood and Westminster. But 'new' in relation to what?

Let us recall what John Galt would refer to as 'The Member', the MP dispatched to Westminster largely to join the lobby fodder for their party drawn from the various constituencies of the United Kingdom of Great Britain and (Northern) Ireland. Imagine them stepping off the coach and sniffing the smoggy air of the Imperial capital, their papers and petitions clutched in hand, they would, through a series of adventures, find that the impolite issue of distinctive Scottish needs, or its lacklustre public life would never even be an issue. We sent oor lads (and lads they so often were) southwards armed with the conviction our democratic rights would be redeemed. When they got there, they quickly realised how little interest the English capital had in the northern deputies. Their main duty to Crown and Mother parliament was to learn the rules of the club and then, and above all, be quiet over anything to do with Scotland.

What they must do instead, was to pay attention, realise that patronage aplenty was flowing from the leather armchairs to be grasped by the keen and energetic – but only after a necessary disabusement of the place of Scottish Affairs in this system. Their local connections won them a seat in this system and an opportunity to access its treasures; but that was all. The validity of this ticket was entirely dependent on this system being preserved and guaranteed, a point rarely lost on the bulk of mainly Labour MPs who headed south. In the case of Labour, the party was in the unique position of providing so many such tickets that the UK electoral mandate became dependent on it. Scottish Labour MPs were thus in a kingmaker position, yet could only be so if they disavowed any inkling of their home 'region' as a separate political entity in its own right. Their acquiescence to Westminster culture while in London served as reassurance to the political centre that they shared a vested interest in the union, and that they would keep Scotland quiet.

And when they came home to their constituencies these Scottish MPs regaled their electorates with tales of derring do at (or near) the dispatch box, reassuring their constituents they were an essential facet of a great empire and that its system of governance not only worked, but it was entirely appropriate and enriched them all. Especially the Rt. Hon. Member for Godknowswhere.

Of course this set-up was often unconscious, which made keeping these dirty 'secrets' much easier. It was in effect, a Scottish political (dis)establishment of considerable longevity and durability, whose reign was further eased by the generally benign relationship between a Scottish identity, lingering despite nearly 300 years of union, and the 'British', buttressed by interdependent economic and industrial infrastructures, what was left of the Empire, Consensus Politics, the internationalism of the socialist left and the shared experience of World War II.

The ideologies of left and right of the late fifties, the eve of the period covered in this book, carefully denuded the nationalist questions of the Celtic peripheries, and class treachery, be it Tory or Labour, was rarely more arch than when a Scot suggested their respective ideological goals might be better achieved under self-rule. The one-nation Tory could barely conceive of the idea while their Scottish Labour counterpart, as typified by the late former Foreign Secretary and Leader of the House, Robin Cook, was disgusted that any left-leaning Scot could 'abandon' their needy brethren in England and thus fail, to paraphrase John Burnett in *The Red Paper for Scotland,* to square conduct with intellect. Even were you not of either camp, the lingering spectre of fascism, and the super-sized corporatism of the Soviet Bloc made home ruler aspirations seem even more eccentric, or indeed scurrilous: witness Labour MPs' attack on the Scottish Nationalists during the 1978 Devolution debate, as 'Allies of Doctor Goebbels'.

Back at home, where the implications of Westminster legislation had to be enacted in line with local conditions, affairs were conducted in committees that while not secret, were obscured, and through deals and arrangements brokered in places the average voter would struggle to identify. The exceptions were the council chambers, to which distinctively Scottish political activity was restricted, and which by consequence were somewhat parochial and technocratic.

Scottish politicians became adept at manipulating what Fry called an atmosphere of 'jovial conviviality' that had reigned in Scotland, under left or right, for centuries. This amounted to a number of obscure-sounding committees and working groups as described approvingly by Midwinter and Keating, participating in a distinctive administrative system, where the fruits of either London or local politics were interpreted in a fashion that while not secret, was certainly secretive, and while not closed, was certainly inaccessible to the average citizen. The most adept Scottish politicians, waiting for their train ticket to London thus learned to work the table rather than the chamber, which could explain just why Gordon Brown had so much trouble as front man when communicating to wider audiences.

There were of course, institutions, separate from politics and classified as 'civic' which sustained a sense of Scottish exceptionalism; the waning Kirk, the Scottish press, its legal system and at the centre of all, its school and education system. To this we could also add more nebulous elements, in particular, its literary culture, expression of a general faith in documents, words and covenants. Through action and reaction these sustained a separate Scottish culture, an alternative Scotland that existed independently within the British state that could articulate a demand, at times weak and at others very strong, for a Scottish response to social and political problems. These could – as in the body of the Kirk – be conservative in nature, but they almost unwittingly provided a rallying point when a notional 'Scottish tradition' felt itself to be threatened.

This notional Scotland did find ways to express itself. One of these was at the ballot box which, (with the exception of 1951) returned primarily Liberal, then Labour representatives to the House of

Commons. Scottish and English voting patterns were demonstrably different; whereas in England voters frequently varied their vote at council and Parliamentary constituency level (voting Labour for one, Liberal another, for example) Scottish voters returned the same votes in both types of ballots. The result, in Scotland, was an extraordinarily long-lived and seemingly unassailable Labour hegemony at local council and parliamentary level.

Nevertheless, the reign of Mrs Thatcher demonstrated that Scots could overwhelmingly vote in one direction and be dictated to from another. More importantly, perhaps, Labour seeped into every aspect of Scottish politics and public life. For forty years or so the country was effectively represented by a single party system at Westminster, and arguably ruled by one at local government level. This had its consequences, good and bad, for both Labour and the country it presumed to 'own'. It meant that while the party was resistant to nationalism, the notion of Home Rule, and a redemption of the firm support given to it by the Scottish electorate became increasingly attractive to an influential faction within it. David Hume, who had never heard of the Labour Party, describes it well in his 'First Principles of Government':

> But where the original constitution allows any share of power,
> though small, to an order of men who possess a large share of the
> property, it is easy for them to stretch their authority, and bring the
> balance of power to coincide with that of property.

It may be cynical to suggest, as does Fry, that if the Labour Party had not regarded Scotland as their exclusive property – a valuable commodity that underpinned their periodic control of the Commons Chamber – they would never have approved the devolution of power from London to Edinburgh. But for various complex reasons, many of which resemble Fry's analysis, this element of the Labour power base made the case for constitutional change that would 'coincide with that of [their] property' increasingly compelling. It also (as such men of property would learn, whether in 1688 or 1999) led to new and unforeseen, distinctly 'Frankensteinish' problems for the Scottish (dis)establishment.

Tartan Pimps examines the writers, thinkers and analysts that have fed, nurtured or scorched the institutions, ideologies and 'civil society' that have sustained a distinct, if subsumed, Scottish political identity. It originated in the *Suns of Scotland* series that started with an analysis of Gordon Brown's literary career in issue 21 of *The Drouth*. This first instalment set both the tone and the format of the series and much of this book; it appreciated the efforts of the future Prime Minister in ring-mastering the ferocious exchanges of *The Red Paper on Scotland* in the seventies (described by many who participated in its making as a continuation of the worldwide 'war' of '68 by other means) and investigated the technical and ideological frameworks Brown set for New Labour in a series of social and political treatises published during the eighties. Finally, it analysed the transatlantic prudences of his Chancellorship, before the weight of the world was plonked on his slightly hunched shoulders.

At the time, gossip and innuendo over what transpired at the meeting between Brown and Tony Blair at a restaurant in the mid 1990s, where they divided the dead John Smith's kingdom between them, was at its height; *The Drouth*'s response was to eschew soap opera (aka the Blair-Brown deal in Granita in Islington) and consider the actual substance of the then would-be Prime Minister through the books he had published. It may be a prejudice of whatever passes for literati at *The Drouth*, but is it not arguable that without these books by Brown et al., Scotland as it exists today would be, if not unthinkable, certainly less likely?

To say that is of course to embrace an example of what Tom Nairn calls 'symbol operation', a potent conceit of ourselves as a country founded on the word – a written republic of declarations, trumpet blasts, Covenants, Letters, Disputations, Parish Records, Red Papers, Claims of Right and Scotland Acts that may be just as mythical as the notion that all Scots are basically 'Calvinist'. Conceit or not, we will entertain it. In the beginning was the Word, and in the midst of it all were the wordy.

Whether through the contestable notion of the Republic of Letters, the codification of Scots law, or the estimated 600,000 signatures marked onto the National Covenant, the *document* has been fundamental to Scottish public life and political consciousness, expressing a notion of what the aforementioned document describes as 'the corporate right of the people to resist a lawful king who threatened to become tyrannical'. As a path of resistance it might seem overly delicate and meandering compared to the most recognisable, and iconic moments of Scottish political thought – think Jimmy Reid and his nae bevvyin speech on the banks of the Clyde. Then again Fry (not of Reid's tradition mind you) notes in his *Patronage and Principle* that literary groups, as in the venal corporations of early nineteenth century Dundee and Edinburgh, were often the chief source of resistance and critique against corrupt and insensitive political establishments. This is suggestive as to why the works of the Italian political philosopher Antonio Gramsci, who conceived the intellectual as organic, an organiser with the responsibility for dispersing intellectualism among the broadest and most pluralistic social base possible, should have proved an animus to Scottish writers post '68 (whether they knew it or not).

As a founding myth of a modern Scotland, the power of the word and the covenants it articulates, with Kirk or Crown or Capital or Labour or Volk, has been enduring. It was noticed even by the English, such as the seventeenth century poet Abraham Cowley, who in 1638 celebrated the success of the covenanters with these lines

> Others by war their conquests gain,
> You, like a god your ends obtain,
> Who, when rude chaos for His help did call
> Spoke but the word and sweetly ordered all.

Dewar's inheritors in Scottish Labour may look at the Scotland Act and wonder where all the 'sweet order' got to, but Cowley's poem articulates a powerful Scottish conceit about the power of the word (backed with the moral authority of God *and* the community). But it fudges the very precariousness of this particular tradition (not least that the Covenanters soon after took to arms and pressed their agenda through a string of military successes). The legendary texts of Scotland were all shaped by successive crises of the Scottish state, Scottish society, Scottish religion, and Scottish political culture; typically, they have responded to deficits of democracy that shift political and economic power elsewhere, in favour of crown, Parliament or global capital.

This book examines how in response to this, the Scottish political system was *written* into being and how, since the devolution settlement of 1999 a recognisably new Scottish polity has been formed. It contends that the political infrastructure of this new system and its relation to the people was a long time in gestation, and that said gestation – ostensibly with no express forum or political space for its progress – took place in the work of the nation's political and cultural thinkers. In that sense, where there was a rapid velvet revolution bringing democracy to Czechoslovakia, in Scotland we might see the present political system as brought about by a long, slow literary and academic revolution. In effect, writers and thinkers took stock of the nation's political temperature, and the symptoms of its social malaise, and made of their prescriptions a public debate. This being so, we apply the methods of literary survey and criticism in understanding the political development of Scotland over the last ten years to ask how this theorising fed into the specific structures of the new political system, and in what way have they affected its particular legislative successes and failures?

We'd also argue – hence the title of this book – that for at least 200 years, Scottish politics had operated through a process of 'pimping the tartan', where a political elite has regarded Scotland primarily as political capital, failing to concede its own democratic rights or traditions. If we had to define a Tartan Pimp it might be one of those aforementioned Scottish MPs – what Tom Nairn might call a 'peripheric elite' – arriving at Westminster only to realise how diminished they are once they leave their nursery pool. Subsumed yet undeterred, they compressed their Scottishness into a costume, a comic licence to invoke and revoke an idea of Scotland or Scottishness in the theatre of Westminster as they saw fit. And thus, they kept right on, to the end of the road.

While the Pimp as a type suffers of myriad and variegated manifestation, nonetheless the most in-your-face exemplar of the phenomenon is indeed our first star here, Gordon Brown. Brown may have been a protégé of 'why-don't-they-[the-English]-just-realise-we're-better-than-them' John Smith, but he didn't waste time uploading an entirely different set of baggage when the opportunity presented itself. Not long installed as Prime Minister and Brown was extolling the virtues of 'Britishness', declaring, in a mode reminiscent at once of 70s Labour *and* National Front, 'British Jobs' were for 'British Workers', and identifying – with a dagger to his sporting compatriots' collective heart – his favourite footballing moment as when Paul Gascoigne's goal for England put Scotland out the European Championship.

Brown admittedly had profile ultimately which kept his every move magnified under the political jockoscope, but there are many more ornery manifestations of the trope. Take London Labour MP George Cunningham, a Scot who insisted on the 40% rule which scuppered the devolution referendum in 1979, and George Robertson, who declared that 'Devolution will kill the Nationalists stone dead'. In the light of the 2007 election results, the only really surprising thing from this latter man of the People's Party bearing titles such as Baron of Port Ellen, Knight of the Order of the Thistle, and Knight of the Grand Cross of the Order of St Michael and St George, was that he didn't have the nous to decorate his own petty remark with the wean's world retro-sarcastic suffix 'Not!'.

But the Pimp is far from a merely manyheaded Labour Party monster, and for an extreme Tory example we need only look at the tricks turned (including the hated 'poll tax') by Michael Forsyth (now Baron of Drumloan) for Thatcher in Scotland. And as for ex-Westminster manifestations, Winnie Ewing's self-designation as 'Madame Ecosse' (for our ears only – the French had never heard of her!) in Brussels is surely only a revamp of the Scots penchant for gaily mythologising the tartan where there's no global reality check to haud ye back. Of course with all this vamping around in ermine, garters, skirts for men, and the French language, we might imagine that once our representatives get beyond our grey shores that they're understand-ably just dying to get in some sort of identity drag and sauce it all up.

Yet only a century ago it seemed all so different and all so serious (Harry MacLellan Lauder notwithstanding). In the early 1900s the Independent Scottish Labour Party had yet to make any significant impact and Scotland was the province of the Liberal Party. Yet in the course of a hundred years Scottish Labour would establish a lasting hegemony, a parallel government devolved to the town halls and district offices that would take over the once-Whiggish Scottish (dis)establish-ment and continue perpetuating a very Scottish exceptionalism. This (dis)establishment seemed solid until, as the century turned, it began to waver, as a combination of global trends, Anglicisation and a correlative desire for greater autonomy forced it into reforming itself. Now, for the first time in decades, it finds itself in opposition. All of these changes, including those that led to devolution of power, took place in a political arena subsumed into Westminster and relegated to 'Scottish Business' – so where was the debate joined? The answer lay in words, of books that essayed the matter of identity, authority and sovereignty in Scotland, and contributed to a growing consciousness that a political expression of 'Scottishness' or 'Scotland' or 'Scottish Affairs' was both valid and desirable.

This consciousness has, we would argue, been developed through an ongoing 'conversation' pursued in Scottish literature, academia and political documents. In 1909 Tom Johnston published *Our Scots Noble Families*, one of the first books to frame class, social and national issues in terms that were distinctly and uniquely Scottish, rather than the concern of a northern portion of Britain that was assumed to follow the patterns, logic and tendencies of the whole island. Since then, 'Scottish Labour' held the joint potential to move the country towards greater separatism or to entrench its unionism, a schizophrenia that dominated Scotland's disaggregated national ideology ever since.

What happened next has been fairly well documented and is in effect, the back story to this book. The 1960s saw the decolonisation of the ex-Empire, a fundamental realignment of both left and right towards respectively, the new left symbolised in the uprisings of 1968 and the new right founded upon the American monetarism of the Strauss-Friedman school. British governments issued loans to bail out heavy industry such as shipbuilding on the Clyde, and regional accents began to appear on the telly. The devolved state of Northern Ireland, a constitutional anomaly born of expediency and blackmail, descended into chaos. At home, the democratic deficit between Scotland and Westminster gradually became more and more apparent as an entire generation of thinkers and writers gradually drew their attention to the nature of an increasingly bedraggled British state. In exasperation, many among Scottish Labour came to the opinion that if the English working class were blind to the evils of Thatcherism, then it might be time for a more enlightened Scottish working class to go it alone – as proclaimed by *A Claim of Right for Scotland*; 'The Scots are told that their votes are lying; that they secretly love what they constantly vote against.'

It was the rise of Margaret Thatcher that drove home the point about democratic deficit, but even before that, the rumblings of the late 1960s led to the 'long '68' that lasted a decade until the failed devolution referendum of March 1979. As suggested in its subtitle, the main characters of this book are two political magnates. Gordon Brown, a man who has described himself as Heathcliff in *Wuthering Heights* is, *au contraire*, clearly a nightmare of Pip from *Great Expectations*. It was he (pre-eminent among many others) who instigated the great 'rethink' in the Scottish then British Labour movement of the early 1970s, even before its traditional modes demonstrably fell apart in 1979. In the wilderness of the 80s he conceived the intellectual bases for unified political resistance to Thatcherism, dealing, in ideological terms, with the various militant and nationalist heterodoxies within the Labour ranks.

At exactly the same time Thatcher was heading a cabalistic and initially highly successful reordering of British conservatism, and what is so interesting about it, given its impact on Scotland and Thatcher's ultimate destiny as Scotland's *bête noir*, is how little attention they paid to Scotland's constitutional position. Their ignorance on this matter persisted right up to 1997 and it was only the realignment of the Scottish Conservatives as a credible force in Holyrood that freed them from the legacy of the panglossing, otherwordly Tory centralism as typified by Scottish Secretary, George (Lord) Younger, a Pimp extraordinaire who reassured his Margaret that he could always deliver Scotland for her.

But entwined as their destinies were, Brown and Thatcher were not the real antagonists here; Brown *thought* Thatcher was it, but his real nemesis was the theorist Tom Nairn, whose conversion from standard new left internationalism to Scottish nationalism opened up a new intellectual and political space in Scotland. Whereas for MacDiarmid, communist nationalism presided in loftily eccentric mode, Nairn offered up a logical and credible reason to support constitutional change that could be reconciled with social democratic values. He was thus, wittingly or not, followed by a series of Caledonian merry muses; the writers, thinkers, poets, politicians and academics who engaged directly with the question of democracy in Scotland.

The character of this group is telling. They are a diverse and eclectic bunch (though not quite as diverse or eclectic as they perhaps might be). Most are white and Scottish, a few are English, Irish, or from the ex-colonies and the majority are men (relate this to MacDiarmid's infamous remarks on women in Scottish history as you will). Most came from within the established structures and institutions; academics such as T.C. Smout and James Kellas, not to mention Arthur Midwinter or the journalist Fry who were also pre-eminent in the major political parties. With the exception of Chris Harvie and Neil MacCormick, influential writing from out-and-out nationalists was surprisingly rare. Direct action and activist political groups, including the militant left were also wary or disinclined to play much of a role, though many more 'established' figures such of course, as Tom Nairn, had radical pasts. There was in short a civic character that fed into the mythology of the word that sweetly ordered; the revolution would be kept off the streets. . . except of course, that it *wasn't*; there were poll tax demonstrations, CND Peace Camps at Rosyth and Faslane, strikes and work-ins woven through the history of these times that fed the popular imagination and doubtless informed the thinking of those writing at the time.

For this book we reviewed a range of texts from the past fifty years that we believe have played an instrumental role in the development of Scottish political thought, and complicated the routine operations of the 'Tartan Pimps'. It is, by necessity, a selective list, and many readers will likely be perplexed and perhaps annoyed at what has been excluded. The books, essays, letters, speeches and pamphlets we did select were chosen because the authors felt they had a particular importance and influence, or were at least representative of an important aspect of Scottish political thought. They are intended as a prompt and a hint for further reading and exploration, as suggested in the bibliography included at the end of the book.

The restrictions on writers and works included are necessary for reasons of space, but also because it was felt there was a recognisable period during which this development of political consciousness took place, and when it had direct and observable effects on the political system(s). This means for example, that some readers might take exception to the exclusion of writers Reginald Coupland and H.J. Hanham whose seminal works on Scottish Nationalism are nowhere mentioned, yet whose influence, we concede, is strongly present. It also means the prominent historian Tom Devine is missing because he is such a great synthesiser and compiler of Scottish history, rather than a picker of fights with other protagonists in the field. Another hugely important writer of this generation, James Kelman, although politically and civically committed and a true 'purifier of the language of the tribe', is missed perhaps because writing as he does in the Scottish high-minded and critical tradition of popular fiction – inherited from a long tradition including James Hogg – he has specifically avoided public engagement with generalities about 'the nation' and with the party-minded. That this avoidance of debate over union, devolution or new institutions represents an equally authentic, alternative strand in Scottish political thought is of course, acknowledged.

Each section deals either with a specific individual (Brown, Thatcher or Nairn) or group of writers of similar type. The first chapter in each section by Miller and Rodger sets the context and describes the general environment, followed by a second chapter from Owen Dudley Edwards, himself a key figure in the movement to secure home rule for Scotland, mainly through his editorship (with Hugh MacDiarmid) of *Celtic Nationalism*, and later, *A Claim of Right for Scotland*. His take is often highly personal, fuelled by a densely rich series of associations and experiences that balance the 'cold readings' of the other two authors.

As a whole, this book could be said to be a 'primer' in Scottish politics, digesting texts that few might now choose to read, to establish a 'narrative' of Scotland's political existence as it was argued into being. Or perhaps this motley assembly, united by its thin, oft-fragile thread is proof of E.H. Gombrich's maxim, to paraphrase – there is no politics, only politicians – or perhaps, more accurately; there is no prostitution, only a succession of pimps constantly reworking the rules of 'the game'.

GORDON BROWN

THE RED PAPER ON SCOTLAND

Edited by Gordon Brown

The Red Paper for Scotland Gordon Brown (ed.) Mainstream Publishing 1975

I. BECOMING GORDON BROWN

Castruccio assumed this office with great pomp and circumstance, and donned a brocaded toga with an inscription embroidered on its front, reading 'God wills it', and another on the back, reading, 'What God wills shall be'.

Machiavelli, *Life of Castruccio Castracani*

LIKE Machiavelli's perfect *condottiere*, Brown made his anointment as Prime Minister seem not only palatable, but natural, unfinished business; an overdue reward for his Herculean labours at Number 11; an entitlement, even a redemption of the sordid final years of the Blair Administration. As his father, the Rev John Ebenezer Brown might say, it appeared predestined. In popular folklore Brown's baptism as once and future king took place over dinner; in reality, the minister's son had courted Fortune for many years before sharing a table with Tony. In 2007, in those last days when the PM teased him, and us over when exactly, he would go, Brown stood impatient, brooding, breathing loudly through quivering nostrils, desperate to snag the sash over his head and lead. We can only imagine what thoughts and emotions moved beneath that Saturnine brow. Excitement? Fear perhaps, that the careful work of years would by some dastardly circumstance, fail to bear fruit? As with Castracani, God's will or the natural order of things had little to do with Brown's purported triumph and he knew it. His elevation had come through his works, not divine Grace. If he fell now, God would not catch him.

It was natural for someone like Brown to further those 'works' through the written word. If Castruccio's blessing was delicately embroidered, Brown's output as a writer and scholar of the changing face of British labour politics and the Thatcherite project was pulp-printed in between his exertions as a political organiser and prospective Parliamentary Candidate. Like Machiavelli, his intellectual activities were activist in nature, and so the best analogue of Brown's becoming is textual. A 'text' is woven, so are webs, and we frequently find Gordon Brown at the centre of both. Brown's political capital was invested in a latticework of adherents marbled throughout Scottish (and to some extent English) public life, and in particular, the machinery of the Labour Party. He published, up to the eve of his chancellorship, some nine books, and in the period of transition from Numbers 11 to 10 Downing Street published a few more – *Courage, Britain's Everyday Heroes* and *Visions, Values and Voices*, and collaborated in the publication of his collected speeches.

This chapter deals primarily with the more 'formative' earlier texts, books that shaped his emergence on the wider political scene and commemorate significant moments of his gradual 'becoming'. They are, by and large, also much more substantial in both ideas and significance, whereas the last clutch, dealt with in the epilogue, are merely the residue that explain his 'present' and hint perhaps at his future.

In a sense, the development of Brown's politics form around a relatively simple core, a redress of Labour's history (the subject of his graduate thesis) that coolly assesses various traditions at the heart of his political movement and attempt to synthesise them into new, politically workable alternatives. In 2006 he saw fit to eulogise this life's work in the chapter in *Courage* on Robert F. Kennedy.

> We know a great deal about the years of the John F. Kennedy Presidency – and perhaps little more that is new can be written of those years. But one unanswered question that continues to fascinate revolves at root into one of personal courage; how, after his older brother's death, did Robert Kennedy – best known for his genius as a political operator – become transformed into a political revolutionary, and how did he become the leading evangelist for a new politics that took on not just the old right but also the traditional left?

How indeed? Hubristic or not, Brown's self-association with RFK (can we really think it is anything else?) was surely an attempt to explain himself and his role in the New Labour project up to 2006. If RFK took on Southern bigots and Jimmy Hoffa, then JGB (James Gordon Brown, that is) critiqued – on paper – Thatcherite depredations and intruded upon and appropriated Bodhisattvas of Labour Militant such as James Maxton. Writing these words was an act of agency on his part. Brown's wielding of his pen as a political tool in this way has addressed some very specific aims, against some even more specific threats, and in the early days at least, with considerable subtlety.

David Stenhouse has pointed to Brown's grounding and involve-ment in the wider Scottish and indeed European intellectual life, with literary figures like Hamish Henderson and Owen Dudley Edwards bearing influence; and of the *Red Paper* Stenhouse says 'the influence behind all this was Gramsci, the Italian socialist thinker', who likewise influenced Tom Nairn and a disparate array of intellectual and literary figures. This cluster (group is too strong a word) echoed Antonio Gramsci who was himself, an avid reader, and re-worker of Machiavelli's activist-as-writer approach. Brown and others grappled with Scotland's past and present in order to imply its future. A Gramscian scholar will recognise that the younger Brown conformed strongly to the template of the 'organic intellectual'. While some of his generation, like Robin Cook, believed that the traditional leftist soapbox techniques – argument and debate – could win the way forward to a rejuvenation of Labour politics, Brown used his writing to cultivate supporters and to furnish them with the intellectual tools to fight these specific battles, via Gramsci's idea of the scholar as organiser.

The book was his site of struggle and for a long time, he was the only prominent Labour politician who showed clear mastery over it. In his oeuvre, Brown addresses the three great challenges presented to the Labour Party – from both the inside and out – in the 1970s to 90s. On the inside Brown/RFK faces down the Militant, extra-parliamentarian and allegedly Trotskyite challenge to the moderates, and on the external front he provides the faithful with the tools for combating both Thatcherism and nationalism.

Brown's editorship of the *Red Paper on Scotland* (1975) can be fitted to this pattern, being published at a point of crisis for Scottish Labour – except the threat came not from the longitude but the latitude in the form of the Scottish Nationalist Party. Labour were down, the Nats were up, the economy was in crisis; enter the Edinburgh whiz-kid to reinterpret the flickerings on the cave wall. As with Machiavelli, Brown was a historian with active and imminent political interests; for him politics could be no abstraction. He was eager to gain access to power and the apparatus of state to put ideas into practice. First stage of course, was not the greater Italy (and Antipope Blair) but Scotland, where he could lay his foundation.

The *Red Paper, Where there is Greed*, the *Politics of Nationalism and Devolution* and *Scotland: the Great Divide* are the tools of this literary activism, a record of movement (his) as much as an analysis of the substance of the social and political issues faced at the time. Brown's role in two of these three books was primarily as an organiser and facilitator, a central figure who could coax his peers into speaking out as his mind ticked over. He was, to paraphrase his introduction to the *Red Paper* (see below) in the transcendent.

If this approach was bookish (a feature of Brown so amazing to the English press the *Guardian* dispatched Stephen Moss to write a feature about a Prime Minister who reads. . .) then it made sense in a country where historically speaking, as politics has failed so spectacularly to secure the state and status of the people, the text and the web have worked in concert to mitigate London's vampiric advances. Think the *Solemn League and Covenant* and the Conventicles, Lord Stair's *The Institutions of the Law of Scotland* and its Advocates, or *Das Kapital* and the Scottish Labour Party (or for that matter, the writings heavily influenced, or even produced, by leading political and intellectual figures in the Soviet Union). For Brown, North America via the likes of John Kenneth Galbraith is also clearly a source, and would become more and more important to him as his chancellorship, and subsequent tenure as Prime Minister, wore on.

There has of course been endless debate and disagreement about the significance of Brown's writings: where does the long trail lead to and where has it come from? The political spoor has been scratched and sniffed at, turned over in the muck, and thrown to the several prevailing critical winds. Many on the left claim that the trajectory of Brown's writings exemplify nothing but a long and dastardly betrayal; starting from the anti-Thatcherism espoused in *Where There is Greed*, and culminating in the neo-liberal apologetics of the likes of *Global Europe*. But has it really been as simple as that? In a long article in *International Socialism* (July 2007), John Newsinger claims that in 1986, Brown's biography of the Independent Labour Party leader ends 'with a strong endorsement of Maxton's socialist vision', showing Brown was still, at that time, a socialist (although not a Bennite, Newsinger points out) on the left of the party.

But that's not how we read it here. Newsinger quotes Brown, saying, 'Maxton's journey through the politics of the twenties and thirties must be read in context.' And just so, surely, must Brown's journey be read too, with his timely biography of a 'failed' leftist giving spiritual comfort and practical advice to the moderates' philosophy and praxis in the imploding Labour Party of 1986. Of course this makes the history and development of his political beliefs much more complex, and renders it difficult to put the texts in context. But this contextual complexity is inevitable with someone who has a long pedigree as a 'political operator' *as well* as one as a writer and thinker. And is there anyone else in this book quite so involved in all the fields we attempt to cover?

All of which goes to say that there is no straightforward or obvious way to read his texts. Not even when they are inscribed – cross my heart – across the front of his teamshirt. So if, when he writes on RFK, JGB assumes the clan colours himself, and steps onto the stage in that costume, from out of the smoky committee rooms of his political operation, then that self identification with his protagonist is emphatically absent in the Maxton case. (How can we really think Brown identifies with the man that walked out on the Labour Party and into impotence on points of political principle? Does he not indeed admit that he does not understand some of Maxton's motives?)

Gordon Brown's trajectory through public life divided the population as Moses did the Red Sea. But it was not simply a case of believers to one side and sceptics to the other. For the dry land of

Brown's rocky patriarchy had more tides of strife to deal with than the Mosaic path: the threatened engulfment came, that is to say, not just 'on his right, and on his left', but from the nationalists too. When Brown finally came out as leader of men and women towards – and not just as writer about – the Promised Land, critics and indeed former allies from all three sides were not slow in showering him with dispraise for his alleged failures, incompetence, unsuitability, backsliding, and hypocrisy.

On the left hand Tom Nairn, who had topped the bill of Brown's 1975 *Red Paper*, bottomed out (in *Gordon Brown 'Bard of Britishness'* 2007) with a redefinition of Brown's former protégé status as a 'courtier of self-abasement'. On the right, Michael Fry, claiming to have spent chummy 'old times' in Brown's flat, punts the picture of the patriarch become a boorish authoritarian in an article in *The Herald* (Nov 16th 1999). 'Control remains the major theme,' writes Fry, and totting up the instances he can find in *The Red Paper*, he notes, 'Brown uses the C-word like Kelman uses the F-word.' And from the third, nationalist, wave, Christopher Harvie (now SNP MSP), a former Labour faithful who co-authored a guide to the 1979 Assembly with Brown (*A Voter's Guide to the Scottish Assembly*) was arguing already in the *Guardian* on 27th May 2004 that the patriarch's economic 'miracle prove[d] to be a mirage.'

If as Irn Broon, the erstwhile 'most successful Chancellor since Gladstone', he was the champion and crowned leader of the backroom boys (several of his former female colleagues have also made allegations of misogyny), the private genius with a back-catalogue of publications and ideas of his own, directing all the public operations from offstage; then ultimately, for the politically cynical, his fall deep into the void via a trap door from centre stage has to be seen as a public relations failure. Is it possible to face the corporate mobsters of the British media as a figurehead of secretive and authoritarian British Government without a smooth running public relations interface? Both Thatcher and Blair were armed with an understanding of the 'value' of insincerity here. Yet in such given conditions surely the only possible honest approach for a British leader would have been to radically change the nature of that secretive and authoritarian government; and many hoped that Brown was the man with the intellect, compassion, political nous and moral courage to do so.

But as it happened, he did not do so. And thus, having no Machiavellian front man like Thatcher's Bernard Ingham or Blair's Alistair Campbell to manage his image (at least not since Charlie Whelan left him in 1998), Brown could never get beyond the fact that he became our onstage and actual political leader, and was a sovereign reality, in Hobbesian terms, not by institution but by acquisition. The *civitas* or commonwealth, that is to say, got him not by agreement and the vote (he did not come to the position of Prime Minister through winning a General Election as leader of the Labour Party), but through the party machine, or 'as when a man maketh his children to submit themselves'.

His fortune had been that Britain has no Presidential system but a party system. But he would so play the president, even when his party was over. He was alas, in the end, as we conclude below, the nation's Paw Broon. He became the Emperor with no civvies on. And the bairns were not for submitting to that.　　　　❏

THE RED PAPER ON SCOTLAND
GORDON BROWN (ED), (1975)

'. . . what this Red Paper seeks to do is to transcend that false and sterile antithesis between the nationalism of the SNP and the anti-nationalism of the unionist parties.'

Gordon Brown

This was in fact the second *Red Paper*, (the first being 1970s *Red Paper on Education*) the spectre of the SNP leading to a reorientation of socialist debate from the technocratic to the national. The book's contributors are largely built around a unionist core that give a cautious endorsement to limited Home Rule (a Labour policy that had previously been safely buried with R.B. Cunningham-Grahame) but seem doctrinally terrified of the 'slippery path' to independence. A smatter of nationalists (Tom Nairn and Owen Dudley Edwards being the heavyweights in this camp) are included as antibodies within the Labour Kirk (Jim Sillars' contribution on land reform comes long before his famous defection) but it is the core group of Ronald Young, John Foster, Ray Burnett and John McGrath who tellingly, steer the anthology into a Stuka-dive against the ranks of the Scottish National Party; their remit, to cast the SNP as 'no place for a socialist'. In doing so no corpse was too mouldy to disinter. 'Can a socialist really justify his membership of the SNP?' asks 'Socrates' Burnett, swaddled tightly in his Red Flag, 'and yet at the same time stand with John MacLean and say, "I have squared my conduct with my intellect"?' (p 122)

Clearly, dialectical materialism need not mean that romance is dead. But misty eyes soon clear as the *Red Paper* gamely tries to land the rabbit punch that will knock the SNP out of the constitutional ring. The cunning of it is that as an anthology encompassing various shades of opinion, the match *appears* to be boxing when it is actually a form of wrestling. Nationalism is given its time on the canvas, but always as the 'heel'. Fixed by the limited opportunities for a forum and the electoral system, the game was initially won by Labour's devolutionists. The subsequent publication of the Scottish Government Yearbooks between 1977 and 1992 gradually shifted the constitutional agenda firmly towards limited devolution of power, understood within the framework of Scottish Labour politics. Labour identified itself as the best hope for Home Rule, as shown in the final Constitutional Convention of 1997, dominated by Labour and boycotted by a stroppy SNP.

A reasonable argument could be made for Brown's introduction to the *Red Paper* as a first, major step in this process of ideological realignment. His analysis of nationalism permits both a cultural and a class-based socio-economic understanding of the phenomenon:

> 'Scotland's social condition and political predicament cries out for a new commitment to socialist ideas, policies and action emerging from a far-reaching analysis of economy and society. . . searching for a new social vision for Scotland which begins from people's potentials, is sensitive to cultural needs, and is humane, democratic and revolutionary.'

Brown's understanding of Scottish identity expertly finesses the role of both culture and class in fomenting Scottish national feeling, and does so with far more delicacy in 1975 than Vince Mills in his introduction to his *Red Paper* of 2005:

> 'But if it is accepted that creation of a national identity is a sine qua non of a nationalist movement, and given the complexities and contradictions of the Scottish peoples, then the definition of what it is to be Scottish has to come in contradistinction to what we are not – English.'

But Brown must not escape with all of the credit for this adjustment of constitutional politics. An entire generation of Scots were writing Scottish politics back into existence. Tom Nairn had realigned the concerns of 'New Left' thinking into a more sympathetic relationship with Scottish nationalism. James Kellas, whose seminal *The Scottish Political System* was published in 1973 floated the idea of a distinctive Scottish politics that already existed, and this spurred others into replying, among them Henry Drucker, Alice Brown, Lindsay Paterson, David McCrone,

Michael Keating and Arthur Midwinter, the latter having discredited the 'subsidy junky' myth then peddled by London.

For his part, Brown shows a sound and indeed sympathetic understanding of the nationalist position. As the 'referee' of the *Red Paper* he is able to make his own posthumous political appropriations (see *Maxton*, below) that show such breadth of vision but simultaneously gradually undermine Nationalist territorial claims. He quotes C.M. Grieve's own grievances with the SNP over economic policy, the latter in his view, 'having no concern. . . with the great spiritual issues underlying the mere statistics of trade and industry,' and thus, subtly, questions the exclusivity of MacDiarmid as a Scottish Nationalist totem.

And what of Brown's 'spiritual issues'? The introductory essay to the *Red Paper* competently argues a broad socio-economic case against nationalism, (a symptom of 'Scotland's uneven development', solved if that development can only be evened out – pretty much the tack of the Scottish Executive between 1999 and 2007) consistent with the materialist traditions of his party. Scotland is not so much a culture seeking to be free as an aggregate of socio-economic stresses that must be addressed. The 'Iron Chancellor', the volatile First Lord of the Treasury and the Saviour of the Free World has yet to be forged. Instead, there is a distinctly Scottish political sophisticate both moderate and moderator, able to trash the opposition in the most collegiate fashion – redolent with all the ambiguity and inconsistency such terminologies imply.

THE POLITICS OF NATIONALISM AND DEVOLUTION
GORDON BROWN AND HENRY DRUCKER (1980)

In this book, written together with Henry Drucker, Brown focuses attention and brings a much more detailed scrutiny to bear than is to be found in the *Red Paper* on the phenomenon of late twentieth century nationalism in the British Isles. By this time (1980) hard lessons have been learned in the failures of the 1979 Referenda to find desired solutions to the constitutional problems, and in the second half of the book Drucker gives us a close study of parliamentary political manoeuvres which led up to those apparent failures.

In the first half, however, Brown gives us an extended essay (some fifty pages) on the history of nationalism in Scotland and Wales in all its forms culminating in the electoral successes of respective nationalist parties in the 50-70s. There's a lot of interest here for the casual reader: lay Scots might be unaware for example, that the Anglican Church was not disestablished in Wales until 1920, and that the Welsh Office came into being as late as 1964. The short study is not only detailed however, but also disinterested – almost to the point of supermagnanimity. Brown goes as far as describing the former leader of the SNP, Billy Wolfe, as 'the nicest man to lead a political party', and of that party's various members he says Donald Stewart is 'avuncular', the left wing intellectual doubling as a press officer, Stephen Maxwell 'a great asset', and George Reid 'important'. While on the one hand this is welcome as a humane and mature departure from the sort of petty party political bickering as we may observe any day in the Scottish Parliament, on the other less kind hand we may read it as an attempt by a would-be patrician parliamentarian to show that his 'real people's party' can not only understand, but comprehend in its widest sense these nationalist sentiments. As such, of course, this magnanimous tack can be seen merely as a more urbane extension to the earlier, and at times, somewhat crude attempts at *Red Paper*ing the nationalists out of the picture.

Perhaps the most interesting and provocative aspect of this essay is its siting of nationalism in a fully British context. Given that the Scottish newspapers take an unavoidably local view of the issue, and the English dailies have almost completely ignored the phenomenon, this is a most enlightening approach. Brown makes two very important points here. The first is that, following a study by Ivor Crewe, he demonstrates that through the 60s and 70s one can detect a de-alignment in British electoral politics, such that there appears to be a weakening, caused by social and economic changes (which again he details) of traditional class attachments to one or the other of the two main parties in the mid twentieth century British political arena. He observes that where in England this resulted in the phenomenon of the floating voter, in Scotland and Wales nationalism offered a different but ready-made basis of allegiance in which the Celts could drown their affiliative sorrows.

The second point is that by charting the expansion of administrative devolution (ie to the Scottish and Welsh Offices prior to political devolution) Brown claims that this can be understood more clearly not as a result of nationalist pressure, but as a dilemma in British government – exacerbated by twentieth century wartime conditions – over whether governmental administrative differentiation should be done by region or by function (ie transport, education etc.).

Much of this – in particular the first point – may by now seem axiomatic, but the value of this work surely, is that Brown was able to take an uncommon and unexpected view of a political situation bogged down in cosy, familiar, proverbial and conventional polarities.

SCOTLAND: THE REAL DIVIDE – POVERTY AND DEPRIVATION IN SCOTLAND GORDON BROWN AND ROBIN COOK (EDS.), (1983)

'What some people call the problem of poverty, others call the problem of riches.'

The best quote in Gordon Brown's introduction to this volume is in fact borrowed, though it shows the sound literary touch that underpins this valuable study of Scotland's grim social and economic predicament. Brown's self-conceived shibboleths tend to be much less poetic, but are effective appeals to an aspirational ethic beyond Thatcherism based on collectivist (but not entirely Marxist) principles, calling for 'An egalitarian ideology that argues people are by nature, more co-operative than appetive'.

In looking inwards to the mechanics of Scotland's uneven development this forms a natural companion to *The Politics of Nationalism and Devolution*. Here, Brown pairs off with Robin Cook to swing at the Thatcherite head of the Labour hydra (the other being Labour Militant, dealt with by proxy in *Maxton* – see below). *Scotland: The Real Divide* is a sophisticated rejoinder to the newly returned Thatcher government, marshalling sociologists, political scientists and economists to provide the necessary poundage. As might be expected, Brown apportions a great deal of blame to Thatcherite policy and legislation as 'ensuring that the poor cannot enjoy the benefit of any increased prosperity that may come to the nation.' But he also sees the problem as structural, stemming from severe design flaws within the British welfare state.

This book achieves a much better argued, more coherent synthesis than Brown's first edited collection (the *Red Paper* that is, which as another mass sortie against a rival political ascendancy it in many ways resembles). The editorial role in such publications can in some instances take on a kind of ceremonial redundancy (surely tempting when one's energies are embroiled in trying to secure your first parliamentary seat. . .), but Brown's introductory essay demonstrates a growing personal authority reflected in the higher profile of his contributors (drawn from the top flight of the Scottish social sciences – Kay Carmichael, David Raffe, G. M. Norris and Stephen Kendrick) and his own command over the material. Brown's career rise from Rector Gordon to Chairman Broon is reflected here in the confidence with which he sets the ideological agenda.

Read in tandem with the *Red Paper*, *STRD* reveals several consistencies that marble all of Brown's political thought. The first of these has been mentioned already; that nationalism is a symptom of Scotland's uneven development (implied in 'The Real Divide' subtitle) but Brown whittles this down to specifics, identifying a low wage culture and the poor industrial and occupational structure of the economy. He very quickly moves to rule out any ethnic, cultural or colonial reasons for poverty

North of Tweed familiar to Irish history; 'Scotland's poor are therefore not poor because they are Scottish: they are poor because, if they are not unemployed, they are in the wrong job, generation, sex or class – and because our welfare state fails to compensate them for it.'

Secondly, Brown argues that the Welfare State is not only under-resourced and mismanaged (the standard crossbench rejoinder), but that its design makes it inadequate to the task of alleviating the worst stresses of capitalism.

Thirdly, he makes the case that Thatcherite policy merely salts the wounds.

Through 'Margaret P___', an elderly breadline widow in Glasgow we are appraised of a depressing array of social ills – low benefits, high costs, decaying housing, frail health. Brown's analysis of these, and their roots in the Welfare system is cogently argued and insightful. He is unafraid to point out the flaws in Beveridge's original plan though a little coy perhaps, in addressing the 1945 Labour Government's role in implementing it:

> 'The Beveridge Report of 1942 did not recommend a social security system that rectified the injustices of the market economy. Quite the opposite. Benefits, the report argued, should be lower than wages in work; otherwise they make as a disincentive to take on paid employment.'

For Brown, the preconditions of 1942 are at the root of the conditions of 1983;

> 'The economy of 1983 cannot guarantee work at decent wages, the

welfare state of 1945 has never guaranteed adequate family support, pensions or protection against sickness, disability, handicap or unemployment.'

In his own way, Brown follows Thatcher in calling for a break with consensus politics, albeit for apparently different reasons. Citing the entries by Raffe and co-ed Cook, he proposes a re-evaluation of the working assumptions on which public sector spending is organised; Raffe shows fairly convincingly that more public spending on education invariably favours the middle classes – a pattern repeated throughout the public services.

Whatever the inadequacies of the system, Brown's central argument is that the monetarism of the Thatcher government threatens to remove all compensation to the depredations of the market economy. He demonstrates that the purpose of the Thatcherite moral programme and its 'grimly deterrent poorhouse' is to pave the way for lower wages and lower benefits. This is the point where Brown's theory becomes a campaign ticket, proposing five initiatives to end mass unemployment, set a minimum wage, redefinition of the poverty line, targeted public spending and a progressive income tax.

Those of us with oversight can recognise some of the early manifesto commitments of the Blair government – the minimum wage, the redefinition of 'the poor' into the 'socially excluded' and opening the possibility that some cherished Labour beliefs may have to be ditched; is Brown's acceptance of Raffe's view of public spending on education the first inkling of tuition fees and other 'modernisations'? Then again, we can also see the inklings of the more 'classic' social democracy that would be attempted by the Dewar, McLeish and McConnell administrations. But north or south, we might wonder what became of the progressive income tax – was this just a youthful passion? Still, Brown did eventually nationalise the banks, and may have done more to destabilise capitalism than any Labour Leader before or since.

In any case, as time told, the 'problem of riches' were contagious, if not downright pathological. . .

MAXTON, GORDON BROWN (1986)

Workmanlike is the description that most immediately comes to mind on encountering this political biography. In forty round, widely researched chapters, each of a neat three thousand or so words, and each dealing a blow-by-blow account of the buffetings of the career of a charismatic radical socialist, the impression we are left of Brown himself is of a young politico as a hungry dog – a Scottie dog, right enough. Published only three years into Brown's own career at Westminster, we can, indeed, imagine the young MP for Dunfermline was putting down another new short chapter to this work every time he sat through the long train journey to London. (And it just shows that it can be worthwhile after all, sending our brightest brains down to Westminster!)

It may on the face of it seem surprising however, that any ambitious young politician should choose for his subject another politico described in the author's blurb as an 'ultimate failure'. Maxton never held any political office, nor did he manage, in Brown's words, to 'capture the Labour Party for a programme of socialist change.' Why then, we might ask, did Brown not choose someone like Maxton's fellow Red Clydesider John Wheatley for a subject? Apparently a more effective politician, Wheatley was instrumental in bringing about real change in fields like housing and education, while Maxton spent over twenty years speechifying gloriously on these topics and arguably achieving nothing substantial. But then Wheatley of course, had a working class labouring background and was Roman Catholic . . . It is often said that the Labour Party in England is the Methodist Church at prayer; just so, is Brown, son of the Manse, in this biography of a son of a dominie, asserting the credentials of the Presbyterian Party in the political pulpit?

There is for sure, in Scottish Labour circles – as they say there is in the north of Ireland – more than one tradition here. That's not to suggest this book is in any way sectarian in its approach, and besides, in that year of its publication there were even more vital territories in the broad church of the Party over which Gordon Brown wished to stake an early strategic claim.

1986 was of course the year when at Conference the 'moderated' Kinnock attacked Derek Hatton's policies in Liverpool, and the internal disputes between the Militant Tendency and the right wing of the Labour Party collapsed into open warfare. It's almost impossible not to read this story of Maxton and the ILP (who saw themselves as 'a propaganda party' within the Labour Party, and as 'an advanced guard for socialism') as an allegory for the so-called Trotskyite entryism of the Militant movement in the 1980s Labour Party.

The genius – if it may be termed such – of Brown's scope is that he is able to impose his own historical framework on the how, where, when and why of this tale. His telling of it, that is to say, demonstrates a sophisticated appreciation of political history, theory and practice which at once establishes new paths and brings old traditions to life. On the one hand it shows the way for moderates of the 1980s Labour Party to claim themselves as heirs to the radical nature of the ILP, in terms of developing social consciousness; while on the other it requires and justifies the rejection of an allegedly radical irresponsibility that goes with the separation of political, industrial and municipal spheres of action (and thus of course, the Derek Hattons and 'Red Robbos of the 80s world are shown the door). It is moreover, strangely enlightening that Brown in 1986 even goes as far as ascribing what we now know to be a proto-Blairite agenda to Maxton, when the welding of these different spheres of socialist action into one coherent approach in the 1920s and 30s is described as the 'Third Way'.

Of course we cannot forget that this

work is a political biography and not a personal nor intimate one, and thus it is debateable if Brown ever truly puts a finger on Maxton's heart. Does he ever reveal to us the real human crux of Maxton's political motivation? Brown confesses for example, that he does not understand the dynamic of Maxton's close political relationship with John Wheatley, saying 'The precise chemistry of the their political partnership is unknown in detail.' Nonetheless it is strongly hinted that though in theory and practice Maxton proved to be more often than not on solid ground, it was the non-conformist, maverick drive in his personal make-up, and his consequent inability – telling for Brown – to be a Party-man, that led to his ultimate failure to be politically effective.

The important point that we take away from Brown's writing however, is that he understands the general picture and broadbrushes it in so well that the case always seems paradigmatic. Why, even the difficulties of our recently most famous fallen maverick, the erstwhile leader of Militant in Scotland, Tommy Sheridan, might be summed up by borrowing a few choice quotations Brown cites from Maxton's contemporaries. The man is described as having 'a grotesque and infatuated egotism' and an 'irresponsibility' that 'was part of his charm', while he was said to have only preserved his 'purity at the cost of impotence'. 'Nuff said – although to be scrupulously fair, impotence does not seem to have been a part of Tommy Sheridan's personal problem.

JOHN SMITH: LIFE AND SOUL OF THE PARTY GORDON BROWN AND JAMES NAUGHTIE (EDS.) (1994)

If a reader picks up *John Smith: Life and Soul of the Party* in the hope of enjoying, vicariously, the raucous exploits of the late Labour leader they are to be sorely disappointed. There are no tales of spin the bottle philandering, no-one photocopies any body parts and the hors d'oeuvres are tastefully arranged but taste of cardboard. Altogether too stodgy for a coffee table book (too long, too grey, entirely the wrong shape), altogether too lightweight to be a work of political history and timed altogether too closely to the Labour leader's death, it sets a mood comparable to a rigidly formal

school Qually, where dominie Broon sternly lines up the boys and girls into a decorous and sombre Strip the Willow – or, even worse, that dourest of soirees, the at-the-desk-birthday-celebration in the office, where the encomia are not only dull but mandatory. In short this makes for an inevitably poor and unsatisfying treatment of the man who drafted the first devolution bill of 1978 and who spoke of 'The Settled Will of the Scottish People' fully aware of what he meant when he said it. More fun and enlightenment can be gleaned if we read JSLASOTP as a cod-psychology of its editor and his then associates on the eve of the Blair revolution/coup de diner/apocalypse (delete as applicable).

The book is sectioned into three acts – Smith's politics, Smith's personal life (much hillwalking, many Munros), and lastly, the press eulogies which vary greatly in calibre; Ruth Wishart's tries too hard to jerk the tears, James Naughtie's is a bumbling tangent while Neal Ascherson's prose runs deep purple. Helen Liddell merits attention as a sterling example of the dutifully sycophantic political panegyric, telling us that Smith could 'spot fools at ten paces' (but how then did he miss one of Maxwell's more ghastly molls?).

And then there's Alistair Campbell, who offers an interesting and today wholly incredible insight into Smith's Europeanism:

> 'Smith painted a picture of the day when Rocard [leader of the French Socialist Party] was running France, their mutual friend Rudolf Scharping was running Germany and Smith was running Britain. One day, he vowed, the whole of Europe might be run by democratic socialist governments.'

We now know of course, that Campbell's many twists of the lip helped to inter that dream as surely as Smith himself. Not only did none of this Eurosocialist dream team gain office, his political master/instrument (take your pick) romanced such nauseating discharges of the European Right as Silvio Berlusconi and Jose Maria Aznar. As gravedigger, Campbell proceeds to incorporate Smith into the 'lost leader' mythology of British and especially Labour political tradition –

a 'shouldawouldacoulda' axiom of almost impossible expectations of probity and deftness and infinite jest and most excellent fancy is marbled throughout this book and especially Brown's keynote essay.

Interesting perhaps, that Brown should at this point be associated so strongly with a lost leader so similar in outlook and sensibility. Editor Brown (assisted by James Naughtie) must finesse such critical encomia with a truthful (or at least convincing) account of Smith's political and historical importance. These requirements are not very compatible. The book is too reverent, too 'of the party' to penetrate, critique or challenge the late leader; whatever it has to say about the post-Smith interregnum that was to usher in New Labour (Blair is not to be found among the contributors) can only be said indirectly while the jostling was underway or through close readings of what is not being said. This is a book of surfaces whose weighty pretensions only serve to imbalance the whole.

Brown's contribution is nevertheless, interesting as putative intellectual ballast (it certainly gives little clear indication as to his personal feelings). It is somewhat mis-titled as 'John Smith's Socialism: His Writings and Speeches', the last half being an accurate enough way of describing this thematic summary of Smith's Hansard entries. Inevitably, such an approach tends to focus on the spectacular over the substantive, statements over policy over the development of theory. It's called socialism – but is it? It has neither the incisive intellectual currency of Brown's earlier books or their disinterested scope that reached out to many different traditions and callings (all contributors have the red rose pinned firmly to the lapel). A hymnary written for the faithful, it avoids theology beyond emphasising Smith's firmly Christian Socialist credentials.

On the subject of economics as an engine of social justice, Brown and Smith are in synch, and we pick up many of Brown's favourite themes, through Smith; 'For me [Smith], economic progress and social justice are intertwined and inseparable. That is why I want to see economic policies that encourage growth, employment and investment in people.' The speech continues by linking skills, workforce and training as the engine of economic prosperity, which has since become orthodoxy within the Labour administration, especially in the early Labour (largely Brownite) Scottish Executive.

Brown is not so good in affecting what would become synonymous with Blair-style 'informalidy'. He is never quite comfortable in commencing his paragraphs with 'John' though it appropriately keeps the proceedings informal and apolitical. Smith's moral purpose is emphasised over his ideology: 'John's politics were not born out of envy, but from a strong desire that everyone should have a fair chance in life.'

On one level, this reiterates Smith's transcendence of party and province into a potential English premiere, but is also, more sincerely, a tribute from the minister's to the dominie's son, an acknowledgement of shared pre-socialist roots deeper than those laid down at Party conferences. Traced here then, is Smith's trajectory from lad o' pairts, to King of Hearts – and to an extent Brown's too. Life and soul, Smith was an advocate, effective in manipulating convention and precedent. Furthermore, Brown's close identification of his own thought with Smith's public face suggests a symbiosis of sorts between the academic and the Scots lawyer – the Demiurge to Smith's Metatron, or rather, the fabricator of small 'n' new Labour teamed with the ideal front man.

Significantly, both men would pass through the Shadow Chancellor's brief but Smith won a leadership election, while Brown demanded and secured a succession. It certainly adds a new dimension to our understanding of Brown's career, tasked with redeeming the hopes of the Scottish Labour establishment to take the centre, its natural course was suddenly diverted towards centre stage, a calling ill fitted to the ultimate backroom boy, whose only real mandate was his claim to substance.

New Scotland New Britain
Gordon Brown & Douglas Alexander (1999)

This short book (47 pages) – or pamphlet as the authors call it – is not only written some twenty years after the other two works above which dealt with the challenge of nationalism, but it is apparently for a very different readership. Strictly for the rosebuds, one might say. But this is no Shorter Hymnary. Who indeed, could the short, 2-3 sentence long, querulous paragraphs be aimed at but the hacks of partial journalism and the party faithful eager for enemies?

And nor do we find here any Brown as lofty statesman or disinterested and inquisitive potential parliamentarian such as seen in his 1980 publication. But it's not just a matter of speaking to a different audience, for there is indeed something shrill and vindictive about the tone of this prose. Where there was magnanimity in the earlier books, with generous leeway and understanding given to others' beliefs, here an incessant train of short quotations from an implausibly diverse set of individuals (William McIlvanney, Neil MacCormick, John Maxton, Eric Hobsbawm, Linda Colley, Mario Cuomo, Tom Nairn, John Stuart Mill, Trevor Phillips, George Kerevan – and even George Galloway and Jim Sillars, to name but a few. . .) are all forcibly yoked to the New Labour juggernaut.

The literary method here is one of the oldest and dullest: if you say something often enough people will believe it's true (the alleged Weapons of Mass Destrction in pre-war Iraq was a later example of this method). But are we to find any small relief in the fact that the 'Smith Institute' which publishes this diatribe is named not after the eighteenth century Fifer but the twentieth century Argyllman?

The evident culmination of this book's argument, found in the last couple of pages, comes in the form of a veiled threat as 'the real question is what is the point of the SNP?' And the irony here is, of course, that if you want a real considered and serious answer to that ostensibly rhetorical question all you need to do is look at Brown's pages in the 1980 book, *The Politics of Nationalism and Devolution.*

In fact the real question for any reasonable reader is –why did Brown ever put his name beside Douglas Alexander as co-author of this stuff? The realpolitik of the situation may well be that in his uber-busy role then, pre-PM, as the Most-Seniorist-But-One man in the State, Brown – for so long an authentic operator – had to accept that by signing off such work he not only gets to nourish his reputation and currency amongst the minions, but can keep his own terriers like Alexander on a short and very eager leash.

But ultimately, while for a time (now lost deep in a history of shame and inexplicable incompetence) it was difficult to imagine anybody wouldn't get at least a secret thrill at the thought of the dream ministerial ticket – Brown as Prime and *Wendy* Alexander as First – surely in a real and honest democracy no- one who ever read anything by the charmless (and ultimately, traitorous) teacher's pet who really wrote this book would put an X anywhere near his name.

GLOBAL EUROPE: FULL EMPLOYMENT EUROPE GORDON BROWN (2005)

One might have expected that the pressures of the Chancellorship would leave little room in the schedule for further literary adventures. And yet, this pamphlet is Brown from skin to muscle (the latter being the considerable bulk of HM Treasury) offering more substance than the average New Labour tract. The titular couplet may well be an exemplar of glib Blairism, but is from the get-go 'My [Brown's] argument'. The sweeping statements of the introduction are tempered by a great deal of substance – many tables, a short but sophisticated historical analysis of European integration and a useful comparative summary of the Chinese and Indian economies.

Global Europe formed the policy statement of Britain's EU presidency – and judging by appearances it is to be a Eurocentric Brownite rather than a Transatlantic Blair administration. If the title is oxymoronic (especially as we're all, apparently, putting that nasty Imperialism behind us now) it is more likely an exercise in the calculated Patrician vagueness perfected by the PM than sloppy thinking. If he speaks the language of Tony, Gordy at least keeps his accent, the better to distance himself. He is fluent enough to deliver what could be a barb over the Rumsfeldian 'New Europe' that so crucially backed Bushblair's Mesopotamian adventure:

> 'The issue now is not just how Europe integrates as it grows from 15 to 25, but how all 25 – soon to be 27 – reach out to the rest of the world.'

Indeed. But whether or not Europe is to be an amputation of the US ('partners, not rivals') or retain its own sense of agency, Brown is in fact looking inward, to how 'Europe' 'reaches out' to our own rocky archipelago, and what it takes to turn this reach into an embrace rather than a half Nelson. Brown's most audacious move is to recast the European ideal not as a single market (which presupposes a single currency) but an 'integrated market zone' within the larger global super-market that includes China, Southeast Asia and the North Americas. This dour-sounding quasi-neologism effectively describes a gaily-decorated supermarket shelf, made welcoming by the two-for-one deals and points on the loyalty card. When he calls for the 'completion' of the single market he is bound to have Europhiles and sceptics rolling in the aisles for entirely different reasons. Brown's trick is to suggest that this 'completion' is in reality a terminal point, an act of containment rather than capitulation. But before the paper is wafted at the crowd, he might consider whether making such a call in the first place is a tacit admission that the current position of countries such as Britain and Denmark is selfish in impeding the fruition of the single market as originally conceived.

Brown manoeuvres via his first love and discipline – history – using it to deflect the 'single market' (and all moral obligations to fully realise it). It is, he writes, the last unfinished business of a 'trade-bloc era' Europe to be surpassed.

Such smoke and mirror virtuosity reminds us too of Brown's murky role in the genesis of 'Blair's' Third Way. In *Global Europe* he makes an implied counterclaim to Blair's appropriations of the term, in a very Brownite idiom.

There is much emphasis on 'enterprise', skills, limited deregulation and knowledge economies. Yet he is clever enough to console traditional labour constituencies with the prospect of Europe-wide full employment.

In any case, as these short commentaries argue, Brown had laid the basis of the Third Way as far back as 1983. In *Scotland: The Real Divide*, Brown made similar arguments tying social justice to economic growth, particularly skills and workforce development. The 'skills' imperative in social, educational and economic policy is now orthodoxy, a culmination of Brown's long-term effort to tie economic prudence to traditional labour values. This is to be opposed to Maggie-Maggie-Maggie-out-out-out-low-skill-low-wage orthodoxy. Implied in phrases such as 'higher skills levels' are more educational programmes, rising wages and an expanded role for government and the public services. In short, through his own central tendencies, Irn Broon finally gets to show the Lady how it's done.

Global Europe: full employment europe • Gordon Brown

II. AN OPEN LETTER
TO GORDON BROWN

My dear Gordon,

I DOUBT if you will ever see this; your minders have too much at stake. Nevertheless, as the Wee Free minister said when in response to his announcement that Marie Macleod would now sing the *Bonnie Banks of Loch Lomond* a voice from the back affirmed that Marie Macleod was a whoor: 'Nevertheless, Marie Macleod will now sing the *Bonnie Banks of Loch Lomond*'. Thirty years ago we were friends – you were, in fact, one of the gentlest, kindest and most appreciative friends I have ever had – and the personal business of writing a letter, however open, has no justification for presuming a change. We have not seen each other for ten years, but we never broke; I was concerned with students, you were concerned with Exchequers, and they overlap less than the days when the state gave you the education in which as a student you triumphed so well; and to which – as a student – you contributed so much (intellectually and polemically as opposed to the way students are forced to contribute now).

Of course we wrote when you lost your daughter, and you sent me her picture in reply; Bonnie and I were among thousands who wrote, and probably among millions who grieved for you. Your political ambition to represent the people is great: but I hope you will never again face circumstances such as these, which made you dearer to countless people than public life is ever likely to do again. At that point the horrible plague of spin-doctors, publicity-hounds, gutter journalists, political acrobats, and electoral manipulators froze whether they knew it or not and there were only two bereaved parents and a sea of sorrow for your tragedy. In such a moment the people's love was real and turned towards the human heart it so rightly saw in you. May you never know a sorrow equal to that; and yet you never can be so widely and deeply loved as in such a moment. I doubt if any politician in the UK was so much loved since Churchill died.

If my perception is right, the people had diagnosed beneath your habitual austerity of manner the generous heart that I knew so well from your student days. This would be to question a great deal of the conclusions drawn by so-called opinion-makers and reporters, and in my view you would be right to question it. The Government of which you form part has placed ludicrous confidence in such dubious augurs, and for your own reasons, perhaps including humility, you seem to have subscribed to much of it. It is ironic that you have been caricatured as the Iron Chancellor (a cliché whose absurdity is demonstrated by recalling its initial identification with Bismarck, to whom you bear as much resemblance as St John the evangelist does to John Reginald Halliday Christie). You were distinguished for me by your receptivity of mind, your readiness to admit you were wrong when so convinced, your courageous insistence on putting to rights what could be righted when you were persuaded mistakes had been made. That was a truly great quality in you: but insofar as it led you to accept and practise political conduct and credulity foreign to your nature, it became tragically misused. Today what divides you from your Prime Minister? And why should anyone support you as an alternative if you are no alternative? And yet all I know of you proclaims an integrity now apparently invisible.

Between the new masters of make-up, and their frequent products the media anatomists, politics has become virtually meaningless, pursued by individuals above all determined to conceal themselves. Machiavelli has become unacceptably honest by comparison. The Blair Government was initially disembowelled by a Tory confidence trick and has since been flapping its remaining innards into enslavement by thug upon thug, Rupert Murdoch, George W. Bush among others.

These be your gods – can you imagine the contempt in which the giants of the labour movement in history would have held them, you who have a historical mind rather than the joke mirrors that enthral your colleagues? There was a time when it was no wrench of the imagination to think of the ghosts of Hardie, or Maxton, or Attlee, or Bevan, or Shaw or Wilde or any of that admirable galaxy of Socialists represented in your inspired anthology *Values, Visions and Voices* taking your hand and acknowledging your brotherhood. How many would do so now? Admittedly, when it appeared in 1995 it bore thanks to names that even then rang tinny notes in a preface supposed to usher in the values and visions of great voices: you thanked Blair, Blunkett, Hain, for instance, any one of whom would be more likely to silence the voices upholding such values and visions. Blunkett would have sneered at the lot as bleeding heart liberals as he locked them in his dropsiacal prisons; Blair would find them inferior company to Berlusconi. Hain would pile them in a pyre to light as he ratted.

The Tory confidence trick was the Tories' last splutter as the bubble of Major's government burst in clouds of expectoration, and having lost then ceased to believe in it, or themselves, or anything else except directorships and douceurs, but they hung around the necks of Blair and his creatures the taunt, that their lack of government experience made them unfit for it. Any sane observer of the Major government might have argued with more truth that participation in it made most of its inhabitants unfit for future government, but all of you visibly fell for it, from your own honest self to the cringing George Robertson. (I remember when Thatcher left remarking on the BBC that she lacked one single decent contribution to the betterment of human life, for which George reproved me although unable to supply an alternative: that was your party's shadow Secretary for Scotland when you were denouncing Thatcher in *Where There Is Greed* (1989). If the English seriously want to celebrate Scotophobia, they should exhume George as a slur on British self-respect – no wonder the Americans openly greet Blair as their poodle after hearing George in NATO.)

You as a historian had what almost all of your colleagues lacked and lack: a sense of historical perspective. But you let the Tories lure you into ignoring it. Perhaps the only Major minister of any stature was Ken Clark, and how well he exemplified it by remarking, 'I don't think I'm infallible, though Gordon Brown does'. In other words, he saw you as the innocent swallower of Thatcherite economics. In some ways it is a pity you didn't continue to regard him as infallible; on the Iraq War he is far to the Left of you now. Similarly, Scots who equated your hatred of poverty with that of Robin Cook would tell themselves that you were ultimately the man of principle, where Robin seemed likely to capitulate to opportunism: the laugh is on us now, and Robin is alone in his glory. Blair having conned you into thinking you could not defeat him for the leadership of the Labour Party has carried on conmanship with some success in his own ranks. You know as well as I do that either John Smith or you would have won the General Election of 1997, and quite probably with bigger totals than Blair, just as the Blair babes lied when they claimed the Scottish results a vote for him when they were clearly votes for devolution, defeating Major candidates by the strongest party against them in each constituency You know the election of 2005 was a vote for any Labour person but Blair, to judge by the number of Labour candidates who ruthlessly kept his name from their election literature, and his person from their constituencies. He may be entitled to the middle election, and to that alone, just as his pal Bush is entitled to the 2004 result, and to that alone (though I have some doubts even there, about either).

But if there is one person who showed from the first that he had no confidence in himself, and thought in his heart nobody else should, it was Blair. Having seen his party win a clear and decisive mandate for change from the Tories, his prompt reaction was to prostrate himself before Murdoch. He clearly felt nobody would have voted for him had it not been for the prompting of Murdoch the magician. Murdoch had no more to do with the result than *Old Moore's Almanac* – people do not read the *Sun* in order to digest its politics, they read it to excite themselves sexually, for which Blair is most unlikely to furnish the necessary pulchritude. But Blair believed in Murdoch because he could not believe in himself. Nixon, similarly, incredulous at his own popularity resorted to Watergate.

And how Nixonian proved to be the creatures among whom Blair wallowed. Preference for the company of Bush or Berlusconi was natural to a man who turned continually for direction to the foul-mouthed Alistair Campbell, whose language perpetually recalls the worst of the Nixon tapes and whose self-love was ready to sacrifice British broadcasting to his vanity utterly indifferent to its unmatched services to British prestige across the world. Its impartiality may not be equal to its own estimates, but it is good enough to be a shining light to so many countries all too grimly aware of the failure of their own radio and TV transmission by comparison. Yet his readiness to take a vendetta in Blair's cause or further it at any cost was ultimately turned against you only after you had thanked him for aid in the making of *Where There is Greed*. . . Perhaps he had explained to you where his own greed differed from that of the Thatcherites, a difference which if visible then is now beyond any discovery. Nor did he – or the Blairites in general – differ much from the Thatcherites in their readiness to cheapen British international stature for petty personal gains. Knowing as they did that Lord Hutton's Northern Ireland background led him to equate any criticism of government with aid and comfort for the IRA, they chose him to whitewash which simply made a laughing-stock of British pretensions of independent inquiry. Did you applaud such false coinage?

It might seem that Peter Mandelson, an obvious candidate for the Haldeman-Ehrlichman (Nixon's co-conspirators in Watergate) stakes, was another (an ominous precedent that Nixonian one, for pragmatists no less than for idealists, these people inevitably destroying those they purport to serve – who, one wonders, will be Blair's John Dean?). Mandelson was of course trying to build Watergate in England's green and pleasant land, with his incessant intrigue – networking at John Smith's funeral, for instance – his aura of awful vigilance, his supposed architecture of New Labour peddled with all the delicacy of the investor/purveyor of New Lavatory – or New Nixon, invariably the package intended to ensure indemnity and oblivion for all preceding Nixons. It was a little gerontophagous, since it implied that his sacred grandfather, Herbert Morrison, was to be rebranded as of some earlier leper colony labelled Old Labour and consigned to new sewage, and one might wonder whether Mandelson would have made any mileage without the nostalgic leverage from said grandfather (just as one wonders where Blunkett would have been without bleeding heart liberals ready to help him forward in sympathy with his blindness). And yet Mandelson, like so many self-styled hard men, was little more than soft, pulpy, self-interest fed by startling stupidity. After Blair's victory, when Mandelson was everyone's candidate for Richelieu behind the arras, he high-tailed it to Germany, of all places, for the valuable purpose of suggesting democracy was outdated and we needed another system of government. The Germans, who had tried one (and in the east, two) in the recent past, were unimpressed. Britain shuddered a little – would 1997 be one of our last elections? – but all it amounted to was proof that Mandelson scarcely knew where he was going, let alone Blair. His two falls from power were not so much signs of corruption as of further folly. His tour of duty in Northern Ireland united all sections of political society against him, an achievement in its way, but instead of profiting by his unpopularity all Blair could do was to proclaim him a cul-de-sac embalmed in roses and myrtle. He is now the George Robertson of the EU, a Present from Tony: I suspect that if only he would oppose Giscard's interminable bore of a Constitution he could get it ratified. Young Ian Paisley, asked to say a word in obituary of Mo Mowlam, gave himself space for unexpected charity by saying one saw her stature in comparison with what preceded and followed her. Thereby he showed more leadership than Mandelson, and we may yet find him no less than his sainted father the stumbling block in the way of the Blair-Adams future envisaged for Northern Ireland.

How deeply were you contaminated by that world? Apart from your thanks to them, which may have reflected real if trivial and thin obligations, how much did you echo their style, and with it their empty minds? (Blair in himself has become virtually the embodiment of Empty Sound.) You were, after all, for a time the supposed beneficiary of the services of Charlie Whelan.

I have broadcast with Whelan, and found him someone utterly indifferent to the idealism which took you into politics and made you the charismatic student leader of Edinburgh in the 1970s. It was also fairly evident that in his company even Blair might shine as an intellect. What on earth such a creature was doing among your advisers baffled description. The only explanation was that in fighting your foes inside and outside the party (and I know the Blairs were your enemies from the formation of Blair's first government, a private but certain knowledge), you felt it necessary to employ your opponent's weapons.

Thatcher had her Ingham. Major had I forget whom – or what. Blair had his Campbell. Your entire career should have taught you that your whole political *raison d'être* was the disavowal of any such repulsive artists in hatchetry or manicure. Instead you chose Whelan. On such a precedent, I shudder to think to what depths you have lowered yourself since losing him, however strengthened you must have been by his departure.

You might say that this reproach has been commonplace in politics since politics began; Caesar had his Clodius. Goldsmith, in his masterly portrait of his friend Edmund Burke in 'Retaliation', saw him:

Tho' fraught with all learning, yet straining his throat
To persuade Tommy Townsend to lend him a vote.

Trollope, in *Can You Forgive Her?*, showed his supremely noble Plantagenet Palliser dependent on the odious presence of Mr Bott. And the analogies are not absurd. You could be as magnanimous as Caesar – and as hard-bitten. Your intellect may not be Burke's, but in relation to the present Commons, it is: I doubt if anyone equals you apart from Ken Clark, Alex Salmond, and – just possibly – Gove, the Tory. You were always a noble figure in your student days, making the enemies among the higher echelons opposed to you seem dingy by comparison. So why should you not have your Clodius, your Townsend or your Bott? One answer is the contagion of such figures. The horrible spectacle of Campbell instructing Robin Cook to divorce his wife and announce it in an airport is symbolic. Caesar's wife was defiled by Clodius; Palliser's was spied on by Bott. You think you separate all that is dear and sacred to you from subhumans like these, but they wriggle, claw and knee their ways into every portion of your lives. They are in their way the heroin and cocaine of public life: you take them only for some slight uplift, some minor tactical fillip and discover, too late, that you are hopelessly hooked. God help the addict hooked on Alistair Campbell!

They begin by morally bankrupting you, they continue by implicating you in schemes increasingly befouling all in which you believe, they end as the usurers they are, entrapping you in obligations whose mounting interest nullifies all your attempts at cancellation. In his way, Campbell is a metaphor for his own infection of politics: his foul language begins as an amusement and ends as the only vocabulary left to his associates.

The politician, sequacious of reputation as a statesman (cf. A.P. Herbert: 'By statesmen I mean members of my party. By politicians I mean the members of yours.') will deny such creatures have as much influence as the supermarket clerk and leave us in little doubt that their immediate influence is less than the supermarket owner (has any government prostituted itself to business more than yours, my dear Gordon?). True enough – Labour apparatchiks are directly less able to sway individual issues when in government than when they sell themselves from it to employers who know how best to put their government-earned knowledge to use. You may point out that the Malcolm Rifkinds and Ken Clarks – to go no lower – have hired themselves out at high pay. Blair, who notoriously hesitated on the brink of a political career as to whether to join Tories or Labour, may reasonably ask why we should expect more from him, and to do him justice anyone who expected ethics superior to the Tory variety was hardly likely to apply to 10 Downing Street 1997-2006. But the author of *Where There is Greed* got where he did through supporters and voters who believed him. You put it in very clear moral terms in accurately pin-pointing Thatcherism:

> For the rich, there is the rationalisation and sanctification of greed;
> the few, in the absence of any moral justification or empirical
> economic evidence, will continue to increase their advantages over
> the many. (p 132)

How far can you declare your nine years at the Exchequer has changed such attitudes? How far do you still care?

And this gets us to the heart of our question. In 1960 the fanatical Democrat Arthur M. Schlesinger Jr confronts the US voter with a pamphlet, *Kennedy or Nixon, Does it Make Any Difference?* Forty-five years later I found myself listening to American liberals telling me that it did not, and if it did, that a Nixon Presidency would have been superior in 1961-63 to a Kennedy Presidency. Kennedy might have been a shade more liberal than Nixon on civil rights, a touch more bellicose on Cuba and in Vietnam. The real contrast was with Lyndon Johnson who did care passionately about racial equality and about the erosion of poverty, and blunted his great work on both by obsession with winning Kennedy's war in Vietnam. All of them, like Blair and, I fear, you, were fool enough to think political cynicism clever as a form of humour: it is in fact suicidal not simply to individual politicians, but to politics and democracy in general, and far greater damage is done by supposed idealists like you than by self-evident opportunists like Blair when you give way to it. To the extent that you indulge in it, and are known to indulge in it, Blair must be preferable to you; was there ever anyone initially credulous enough to be disillusioned by him? The real bankruptcy of faith in democracy ensues when politicians accepted and respected for their idealism turn their back on their beliefs with an air of sophistication and a Peter Pan 'Oh, the cleverness of *me*'.

Many people genuinely were moved by the working-class evangelism of David Blunkett, by the Marxist intellectualism of Jack Straw, by Robin Cook's war against racism and prejudice, by your own campaigns for devolution and against poverty. The supporters of all were left wondering whether they were merely new versions of the parody of the Red Flag:

> The working class
> Can kiss my ass:
> I've got the foreman's job at last.

Power has seldom seemed to corrupt quite so blatantly. You may feel that you have done nothing to equal Blunkett's transformation into Fascist playboy, or Cook's and Straw's apparent indifference to a moral foreign policy (although Cook certainly and Straw, just possibly, may not have been entirely indifferent to it). But you tried the patience of old admirers fairly badly when you revisited the University of Edinburgh and remarked that when you were leading the student revolutionaries the choice was between those who wanted to burn the university down today and those ready to wait until tomorrow. It was a miserable betrayal of the comrades who had believed in you, and it was probably uttered on the instructions of Campbell or some other Labour hierophant of cynicism. That day, you crossed a filthy Rubicon.

But was the Rubicon that wide? Could you not leap back, drycleaning your breeks en route? Are you to be condemned for one damn foolish attempted witticism (and God knows how many I have made)? Will you not still redeem Labour from Blair's pollution, when given the opportunity? Well, how far have you held true to your indictment of Thatcherism: 'There is no right to privacy, or anything approaching it, in Britain' (*Where There is Greed* . . . p. 176)? You are reported as supporting a strengthening of the ID cards beloved of Blair, certain as it is that these draw us closer to the 1984 state: the difference is apparently that you will do it cheaper and less catastrophically. Well, it is not hard to improve on a Blair proposal, but you are hardly prettified by cut-price concentration camping-up. You complained (ditto, p. 177):

> 'Britain is significantly further from having a free press. The Monopolies Commission did not intervene when *The Times* and then *Today* were taken over by the Murdoch empire and only belatedly has an inquiry begun. Ten companies control most of our newspaper industry.

Today such sentiments are hardly linked to you. You may be less promiscuous – or less obscene – than Blair in his courtship of the most successful pornographer of our times, but you are on the *Qui vive* for an invitation to Palace Murdoch where Blair made his grovelling obeisance the other day. What your government should be doing is taking steps against non-resident non-national control of organs of public opinion and penalising those attempting it; a tax of £1 per copy of the *Sun* would greatly improve public health in the UK.

If it be said that this interferes with freedom of the press, the answer is that a foreign-ruled dissemination of mindless filth, orchestrated with utter ruthlessness, has nothing to do with freedom save for that of an utterly selfish capitalist proffering pestiferous poison against British values. Already this plan has done enough to justify warrants against him for conspiracy to break the law such as by instructing employees to defraud and deceive individuals by disguise, false claims of identity &c. for no other purpose than the enrichment of himself. How right you were to condemn his increase in power over Britain's media, and how do you justify your volte-face? I grant that there is scope for fear: Murdoch's means of discovering or inventing solecisms by persons targeted are probably superior to those available to your own government, and he evidently has persons on his payroll in countless institutions who are there to supply information (however confidential) to his minions on demand. But that is no reason to grovel; it is reason to stand up to him. I never saw any lack of courage in you when you faced your critics in the University of Edinburgh, however threatening their legal rumblings.

Your critics, my distinguished co-authors, differ from me to the extent that their indictment does not suggest much of a sea-change in your doctrines. Equally, Neal Ascherson remarked that your contribution to the *Red Paper on Scotland* was a much more gentle tocsin than most of the other essays. My own recollection is somewhat different. I recall the student Rector, thrilled with the excitement of Gramsci's writings in and out of prison, fascinated by the new meaning for national identity which he offered. Your inclusion of me in the *Red Paper* I remember as sheer good nature; you had no intention of bringing SNP people (one of whom I then was) into the collection.

Tom Nairn was much more hostile to Scottish Nationalist politicos than he subsequently became, although his perceptions were, as you so rightly saw, well worth pondering wherever his diplomatic loyalties might lie. You greatly admired Nairn's internationalism so well expressed in criticism of Labour or Tory chauvinism against a European identity for the UK. All of this may seem a long way from your pursuit of press coverage of your expressions of enthusiasm for the English team in the World Cup, but they are not incompatible. There was actually a charming naive eagerness about it, which at least left it more sanitary than the Campbell cynicism (although he, too, apparently likes to show himself as football enthusiast, however much his vocabulary may rob nearby solicitous parents of their pleasure in taking their children to cheer their team). At least no one can say that you have taken the usual route of deScottification for supposed Britification: Anglifying the accent, &c. Your somewhat fevered attempts to celebrate a British identity may actually do more to strengthen the cause of disunity than you realise: such concern may lead more people to feel there is a problem about British unity. And a UK identity which proclaims Britishness has to reckon with the horror of one part of Northern Ireland, and the glee at another, that such an identification removes the UK from Ireland.

It is hardly encouraging that Hain is supposedly your disciple, and that he ratted on his long CND record when you made Trident your new icon. Northern Ireland is littered with broken promises and abjured convictions, and for Hain so to parade his indifference to his own past rhetoric is as rotten a credential as a Secretary for the place can have. What has destroyed the place is an absence of trust, and yet it is such creatures who have left no room for trust.

In your own case I realise that you never were a bomb-banner in the way the rest of your friends and supporters were. You have not ratted on this, whatever about your sacrifice of Socialist for neoliberal economics. But your championship of Trident brings back even more forcibly the doubts as to your difference from Blair. If you are pledged to this disgusting retention of weapons of mass destruction at abominable cost and atrocious principle – that you are ready to murder innumerable human beings the moment somebody else does something – why should anyone accept you as alternative to Blair? Your constant calls for the end of poverty in Britain and in the world are noble in the utterance, but become mocking ridicule when you thus wantonly sacrifice the UK financial resources which could otherwise be put to anti-poverty use. The holding of such weapons of death, certain to destroy non-combatants if ever used, is in itself a foul offence against morality, but for what purpose do you wish to hold them? To enrich armaments-makers whose repulsive trade has proved all too lucrative as it is? To posture as the pistol packing poodle of George Bush? To assume that in some impossible way the nuclear powers would scrap the UN Charter to exclude you from the Security Council to show independence of the Americans, without whose permission you would never dare to use nuclear weapons?

If your use of moral rhetoric means anything, it means that the UK can take the international lead in ending world hunger and disease and the only way to achieve such leadership is by ridding yourself of hypocrisy. To be ready to kill countless thousands while campaigning against human suffering is hypocrisy on a grand scale. You are about the last person against whom I would have expected to bring such a charge.

The speed in which you are now tumbling into such latter-day

Cold War ethics with so little evidence of serious reflection (save for political ambition) is horribly reminiscent of poor Lyndon Johnson, with his genuine hatred of racialism and his conviction that poverty must be eradicated and all went by the board to further a foreign entanglement in which he had shown not the slightest interest before seeking the Presidency. Equally, you endorse the illegal war on Iraq, however self-distanced from the lies used to justify it, and you did so more or less by monosyllable. You may be complimented on your taste in distancing yourself from the quagmire of lies from which Blair so piteously demands to move on; the deeper he sinks and the wilder he stinks. But you will be the heir to this and all other follies of Blair's foreign policy, including the very doubtful question as to whether it is Blair's foreign policy. The signs are perfectly clear that he gave full support to Bush on Iraq from the first, without the slightest pause, lie as he might about it afterwards. Do you know why? Does it interest you? Are you similarly committed? How and why?

Evidently, for all of your pleasure in English football, or British national days, you have acquiesced in the Blairite removal of independence from the United Kingdom such that the country is now at last 'Airstrip One' as Orwell bitterly forecast in *1984*. The loss of sovereignty in a European Union (where the UK has countless rights of dissent) is nothing to the loss of sovereignty under the American umbrella (where clearly it has none, apart from an occasional space to allow the poodle to pee).

This would seem to have made the mythical 'special relationship' a stranglehold where the UK has all the room to manoeuvre given to Poland under Gomulka, with the USSR under Brezhnev. That analogy may be apt in terms of personnel: Brezhnev became an alcoholic and Bush appears to have the intellect of the kindergarten he was visiting when the news came through of the 9/11 horror, after which he ran to save his skin, knowing at least that much. What a contrast he formed to the courage of US Presidents in former years – Washington at war, Jackson and Grant at war, Lincoln under fire, Teddy Roosevelt insisting on speaking after an assassin had wounded him apparently fatally, Woodrow Wilson and Franklin Roosevelt forcing their crippled bodies into inevitably destructive campaigns, Reagan wisecracking in his best MC manner after an assassin had wounded him. Bush's place was in

New York at that moment, or at second best in Washington, DC; the American people were never more in need of Presidential paternalism. But he, first in war, first in peace, first in protection of his hide, took best care that whoever was in danger it could not be George W. Bush. Blair had Queen Elizabeth compliment him on his courage on that occasion – or perhaps in a moment of dazzling irony, she said it herself. Royalty, like contemplative monks, can sometimes startle by the appositeness of their few moments of personal comment. Blair, of course, would have meant it for sycophancy.

Bush now seems to have proved himself the worst President in America's history, distancing Nixon, Harding, &c. by increasing lengths. From your point of view he has made the condition of the country's poor worse, their numbers greater, and their environment more hazardous that any predecessor could claim. Equally he has the scoundrel's instant recourse to professions of patriotism, thoughtfully providing himself with the undeclared wars whence to do it. Blair jumped to attention and support for Bush's adventures, notably Iraq, with what we now know to have been Pavlovian promptitude: all the miserable concoctions of investigation, determination and then – and then only – declaration, on the British side, are stripped from the truth they sought to cover, and which decent persons were forced to aid in covering or traduced for questioning. Blair jumped, since his subservience to Bush has now been made obscenely clear in the 'Yo, Blair' dialogue refusing permission for Blair to undertake the pretence of an independent initiative in the present Middle East crisis, we may want to ask why and since when?

The UK is entitled to know at what point it gave up its independence, and for how long. You may yet have to answer the last point, but to take the first, we must be clear that it is new. Harold Wilson was much abused for undue subservience to Lyndon Johnson over Vietnam, but compared to Blair he seems a Tito. The UK did not participate in the Vietnam War (although Australia and New Zealand did, and Franco sent an ambulance), Thatcher was notoriously goofy about Reagan, having graduated from the Grantham-shown movies, but did her own thing in the Falklands: it's clear that Reagan was actually startled by her war, possibly because he had informed her that US intelligence anticipated an Argentine invasion (which almost certainly they did, and almost certainly he did). Major responded to Papa Bush's Kuwait war but that had some rags of legality; Blair's canine fidelity to Bush seems his own, but you are now so close to him on major policies – and so anxious to have that closeness acknowledged by man and beast – that we are left to wonder if you envisage such a Pavlovian future for yourself. American observers give you the credit for rather more independence: a fine play here at the Edinburgh Festival Fringe by Nick Salamone, *Hillary Agonistes*, purportedly sets itself in 2009 with Hillary Clinton as President and you as a Prime Minister refusing to involve the UK in US war adventures. I wish to God its diagnosis might be true.

Actually, the profundity of the play shows itself here. Because Senator Hillary Clinton has supported the undeclared and illegal war on Iraq, many of her former admirers have discarded her as potential leader against Bush and his Republican heir. There is no use in an opposition which will not oppose the incumbent government on its greatest crimes. I agree with the criticism, regretfully; Hillary Clinton's autobiography in its family and personal details make its authorship by any other hand extremely doubtful, and the same details, notably regarding her father, show her to be a great and a good woman. But her virtues alas, be she as pure as grace, as infinite as woman may undergo, shall in the general nature take corruption from this particular fault; she is pro-war, therefore she is unacceptable to anyone wanting a US regime-change.

The same point also applies to the ridiculous Cameron, despite the Tory's Darwinian assumption that Haig becoming Duncan Smith becoming Howard becoming Cameron = *Homo Sapiens*. You might nevertheless take cognisance that if Cameron is ludicrous cycling through London streets pursued by the secret service, flourishing a St George's Cross from his behind, you are lowering yourself comparably – and you have, of course, much farther to fall – by certain of your adman-inspired exposures. You must also recognise that as with Hillary, and as with Cameron (if anyone was fool enough to want him in the first place), so with you; there is no value in a new broom whose bristles will not sweep clean.

I wonder how Blair became the lackey of the Bush administration.

He certainly was out for whoever would pay the best price for him from the start, and he had a wife who would want such a price to be a high one. The CIA is notoriously ready to play Santa Claus with the US taxpayers' money in winning hearts and minds of what are taken to be useful protégés. There is evidence now that Hugh Gaitskell received some of its bounty. We all know that Osama bin Laden did (and when did the payments to him stop? – the UK would do a service if it got the US to release a little more information about its former beneficiaries while turning the Middle East into a bloodbath when it can no longer control them). David Owen's career invites some attention on the matter. And Blair came from nowhere very fast. Once he had taken CIA money, the CIA were in a perfect position to blackmail him into support for specific policies, if he ever showed signs of jibbing. 'Play up or we tell *Private Eye*.' It would be necessary for Blair to appear judicious, giving time for the Blix mission to find anything to be found, using the UN for an authorising resolution. I have reason to suspect that you took such matters seriously, and were anything but sympathetic to the hell-bent Gadarene swine-run led by Bush to war. In the event Blair would only be given so much time, and the effect was in fact disastrous for any pretence of legality. The Blix mission was aborted before completion, and the failure in the UN high-lit the insufficiency of existing resolutions as authorisation for war. So the USA was clearly marked as an international outlaw employing terrorist war, and the UK, as Scots would say, was art and part.

Even the miserable *ex post facto* excuse that the former American and British ally/customer Saddam Hussein was a nasty man with a hideous totalitarian regime collapses in the face of the apparently endless slaughter that has succeeded him. Nor is there anything academic about all this. The signs are clear that Bush wants to go against Iran, by nuclear methods if necessary. Israel would never have dared commence its offensive against Lebanon (and whether it likes it or not the slaughter of another country's civilians and economic bases is action against it, Hizbollah or (however much we might wish it) no Hizbollah), unless the Bush administration gave it the go-ahead. Nor is it likely that the initiative came from so weak and inexperienced a premier as now suffers in Israel: in all probability, the Bush administration told Israel to go to war, partly in the hope of winning back US voter support on the plea of beleaguered and endangered Israel, partly to bring Iran into conflict on the side of Hizbollah thus affording excuse for another patriotic war intended to help win the November Congressional and state elections. The performance of Condaleeza Rice in denouncing a cease-fire in the initial stages resembled nothing so much as Madame Defarge urging on the guillotine. I suspect that the thin peace into which international pressure (as opposed to Yo, Blair) has forced the US may be wired for self-destruction if the US can ensure it, and that hope of nuking Teheran before November is not yet dead. If so, will Blair make one genuine move to stop it? Would he dare?

Now, Gordon, I will take you at your word in your demand for the eradication of world poverty. I have always known you to be a man of utter integrity, admirable courage, genuine humanity and – if you will – justifiable prudence. You know perfectly well that your record as a prudent Chancellor of the Exchequer was besmirched only when the lunacy of the Iraq adventure drained the billions for which your careful betting had not foreseen murderous prodigality. It's possible, of course, that the UK is so inextricably held in the US grip that neither you nor anyone else dares to extricate it. On the other hand, there are clearly enough Americans hostile to the Iraq war and its potential ghastly sequels that your pro-American sentiments can find allies there of whom you need not feel ashamed.

I know your liking for the USA; I so far anticipate you there that as the husband of an American and as an Americanist trained in America I hold my anger against President Bush an American anger. The wretch dishonours great traditions and predecessors' names in which I take every pride. I think you could do with a little reflection on the American past to deepen your affection; history is your true profession, your natural distinction and, I hope, your ultimate salvation. To salute Alan Greenspan as the greatest American financial statesman was an ignorant and silly compliment as he will have well realised; the greatest American financial statesman was Alexander Hamilton, and will always be Alexander Hamilton – if Hamilton had not possessed that inventive and innovative genius, there would not have been a lasting USA for Alan Greenspans to grow up in. In your use of the USA – assuming that you are not simply No. 2 Boy, hoping to inherit Blair's stool as No. 1 – a sense of the American tradition, a knowledge of ways in which be USA ticks is essential. You may be ready to sacrifice much, including independence of international action, and including morality in the ownership of weapons of mass destruction, for your aim of eradicating world poverty. You will not do it by handing succulent hostages to the Wolfowitz at the door. Equally you will not accomplish the UK's part in eradicating poverty by tying up the money that could play part in that eradication, and instead consigning it to the worship of Trident.

Small wonder the Cardinal Archbishop of St Andrews and Edinburgh and the Moderator of the General Assembly of the Church of Scotland condemned Trident and its proposed replacement, and censured you for its worship: they at least know false gods when they see them. Trident and its successor are the weapons of Antichrist.

I remember when you were brought back by your own beloved Edinburgh University Student Publications Board to move the vote of thanks to the great Socialist reporter James Cameron when he gave the first Kenneth Allsop Memorial Lecture, and we got Principal Sir Hugh Robson to chair it. Unlike his predecessor Lord Swann he had borne no part in war against you, and with a charming smile he remarked that most Rectors had been politicians in the initial stages of their careers and Rectors later, but Gordon Brown had very sensibly done it the other way round. I remember smiling grimly in appreciation of a good debating hit. I did not of course believe it. I knew you to have become Rector to benefit humanity, to which your political career was also secondary. I liked Robson, but I very much wanted him to be wrong. Your life was surely not going to spend itself merely on self-advancement.

The hope is much thinner, almost anaemic, by now, but I still hope Robson was wrong.

My love as always goes to you and your family.

OWEN

POST SCRIPTUM: As We Go To Press . . .

Finales are seldom if ever final. An author may end the story by talking to himself, if, like Karel Capek, a 'him' deciding thus to end his *War With the Newts*. Or after Alice wakes up from Wonderland her sister hears rural phenomena whose noises have inspired the dream. Nature, in fact, was telling the human race, via Alice that humans lived on illusions induced by environment (of which Progress has evidently been the greatest). *Through the Looking-Glass* finalised itself by declaring Alice and the Red King to have dreamed one another into apparent existence. Scotland, the Once and Future country, exists in dreams initially diagnosed by the prophet Nairn whom Nationalism then dreams into a great role in the dream he grew out of his diagnosis. Christopher Harvie grew into the culture historically evolving under his cartography. Are we our own Frankensteins or the monsters they have tried to make? And the monster is surely a far more likeable being than Frankenstein.

And beyond these comforting metaphors there is the hard unreality of the Political Stage, supposedly what History will Remember if only to argue about the meaning of what existence it pretends to have. Gordon Brown did become Prime Minister soon after the date of my 'Open Letter' and amongst much to regret and a little to cheer in his premiership he unfroze the problem of Scottish Calvinism in peculiarly horrific ways. The whole premiership seemed predestined to follow an agenda dictated now by a disintegrating environment, and then again by the incomprehensible somnambulistics of an undead ruler. The boy Rector of Edinburgh University had begun his travels as a Red Pawn and now found himself trapped in a White Queen's nightmare whose limits seemed dictated by the mare's Knights. Whatever he knew about economics turned itself inside out and spat in his face. The Marxism he had so carefully sloughed away from his proximity gleefully announced itself in determinist control: capitalism would writhe itself into cataleptic agonies, as he had been told long, long ago, and now the dream came true when he had repudiated it. Because thou hath rejected thy Red Books, O Brown, thou shalt suffer and die from their laws.

The historical consciousness feeding Brown more nutrition than was given to any premier since Churchill told him the United Kingdom existed as a sovereign state, with civilian control of its armed forces, and had done since Marlborough: but the armed forces sank politicians at their will by leakages, disclosures, statements in retirement, lobbyists and every sign of ensuring perpetual war for perpetual peace. The grandeur of Parliament mocking down the time dimension left shades of Pitt and Fox, Disraeli and Gladstone, miraging while their heir sat shackled to a Front Bench inescapable from public school snobs shrieking mindless epithets.

And the United States, having enslaved him to a moron almost killing him in a golfcart, subjected his powerlessness to even greater humiliation: a President intellectually, emotionally, artistically and charismatically his superior. The myth of a special relationship had in practice kept itself going by implications of a superior British *gravitas* won by experience over more centuries, however ostentatious the wealth and power of the juvenile. One could hint if not say too loud that Churchill was really greater than Roosevelt (cigar over cigarette-holder), Attlee than Truman (LSE lecturer over failed haberdasher), Eden than Eisenhower (not completely demolished by Suez), Macmillan than Kennedy (senior member of the same clan), Wilson than Johnson (Oxford over Texas Teachers' College), Heath than Nixon (Europe over Watergate), Callaghan than Carter (strikes over hostages), Thatcher than Reagan (patronise your pop-idol), Major than Clinton (Edwina over Monica), Blair, Brown or even the Prince of Wales than G.W. Bush.

And Obama towered over Brown, in every sense. Brown could claim authorship of better books than any premier since Macmillan, perhaps since Churchill, but neither he nor any other politician of our time has anything to rival *Dreams from My Father*, and it is small consolation that neither has any President of the United States since Ulysses Grant posthumously published his *Memoirs*, perhaps since Lincoln delivered his Second Inaugural.

The implication of British moral superiority in rulers also crumbled. Ethnically Obama means that for the first time the USA has decisively pulled ahead of the UK: slavery and Jim Crow hit viler depths institutionally than the Empire could offer. Militarily Obama may also be heavily circumscribed by what Eisenhower (its product) called the military-industrial complex, but he shows far more interest in demilitarisation than Brown does. The UK looks decidedly worse than the US in nativist victimisation of non-white immigrants, asylum seekers, and refugees from countries suffering from US-UK military invasion. It resembles Stalinist Albania making the USSR seem liberal. In electoral future prospects Obama hopelessly eclipses Brown. Both are persons of intellect and quality facing ludicrous opponents: but where nobody is likely to bet on Sarah Palin (as of now Obama's most obvious opponent for election in 2012), everyone bets on David Cameron, although Cameron is small improvement on Palin in intellect, rhetoric or manners. And while under the US system of checks and balances between executive, legislature and judiciary Obama cannot at the present time hope to deliver all the reform his supporters crave, he remains firmly to the Left of all Republicans of consequence; Brown is now to the Right of the Tory Front Bench on certain questions – bonuses (or bribes) for bankers, ID cards (still retained as an objective in principle (!) by the Brown Government), erosion of civil liberties (especially favoured by Labour's ex-Communists many of whom regard civil liberties as contemptible bourgeois softness).

The UK still retains a Health Service which despite international Right-wing cascades of mendacity continues great service for the population while the USA is literally being lied to death on the issue. But the American Medical Association and all their filthy allies hell-bent on the last cent from a plague-ridden people, have been forced to expose themselves in all their indecency. We have too much reason to believe that the real influences on the Brown Government are unknown to the public.

Otherwise why has Brown wandered so far from home, and why with all his loathing for Blair has he fought for Blair's policies, prejudices and power-grabs? His honour rooted in dishonour stood, and faithful unfaithful keeps him falsely true, but to what? Seldom to the impulses that drew him into politics. Even to think of the Labour Party as what drew him into politics will not answer: after Blair, loyalty to Old Labour is like loyalty to an old car every nut and bolt of which has been replaced, together with all the body parts.

The yearning to qualify for power in the world beyond Scotland led Brown to invent new loyalties: Britain, for instance, and the artificiality of that construct (for him, anyway) drew him into such horrors as 'British jobs for British workers' grabbed to become a foot-warmer for the BNP. What a way to defeat the SNP, call up the real horror that calls itself nationalism. Similarly the supposed desirable heir to Brown, Alan Johnson, deplores Labour failure to have been sufficiently xenophobic about immigrant exclusion. Yet even when the Brown Government was driven tactically into agreement with the SNP, as over the release of the so-called Lockerbie bomber, it could not accept the watchword once prized in common between them – compassion – but instead sent its latest moth-eaten toy dog, Iain Gray, to piddle on pavements in the path of the Scottish Government in hopes the police will shoot the wrong hound.

Where Scotland must differ from Brown's Britain is that England may see Brown as an outlet for bile and no more, but anyone who remembers the Edinburgh University hero of the 1970s knows they are witnessing the last scenes of a real tragedy of ancient Greek or Shakespearian proportions. If Brown had simply been another solipsistic Wilson, another jobsworth Callaghan, another elocutionised Thatcher, mechanical Major or empty Blair, the thing could be dismissed as a Punch and Judy show without a supporting cast as entertaining as Denis the Secret Teetotaller or Michael the Murderer Manqué. But it isn't the usual tawdry tinsel however miserable the mummers from Mandelson to Murphy. Scotland may well decide at the next election that Gordon Brown is a Cause as hopelessly Lost as Charlie after Culloden. But it will still contemplate the tragedy with sublime regret for the Boy It Left Behind It. ❐

MARGARET THATCHER

I. PRACTICALLY PERFECT IN EVERY WAY

A WOMAN arrives from nowhere. Her attire, smart suit, handbag, hat, and her pinched, scrupulous demeanour mark her out as of slightly lower class than those presently in charge. Nonetheless she confronts them head on, as it were. She speaks in clipped epigrammatic phrases. She seems to be just what the gentle folk needed, just what they were waiting for, and soon she has the run of the household. She holds out a vision of a practically perfect future encased in the bright, solid relief of the past: a thoroughly Victorian architecture of the mind.

Only the relative nowhere in this schema of a fabled political coup is not the windy ethereal skies, but Lincolnshire, and Our Lady of Perpetual Succour does not arrive blown in by umbrella as Mary Poppins, but by chauffeur-driven car as Margaret Thatcher.

It would be stretching credulity in the influence of Disney films to say that the 1964 classic feature had paved the way for Margaret Thatcher's election as Prime Minister in 1979. But somehow, nonetheless, England was ready. Thatcher, that is to say, could not be described as a carpet-bagger: but the best joke in the film is exemplary – when the boy notices that Mary calls her large bag a 'carpet bag', he exclaims 'a bag for carrying carpets in!'.

'Not for' responds Poppins drily, 'made of.' It is a most Thatcherite moment in its display of complete self–possession and absence of self-irony. Yet we can of course, say so only in retrospect: or to put it in another, interrogative and non-anachronistic frame, was Thatcher expressly Poppinsesque? It may seem a ludicrous question, but we must remember that Thatcher's ruling time mode of speech did not come naturally to her, she had spent her earlier political career losing her Lincolnshire accent, taking lessons from a voice coach, and advice from, amongst others, Laurence Olivier. She had deliberately slowed her enunciation, and lowered her tone – in line, we might say, with the Poppins way. And the Poppins fable of a commonsensical miracle – so popular and so dear to the English heart – was, as demonstrated in our first paragraph, substantially the vision that Thatcher had mapped out for herself. Fine for England, but what of Scotland?

In *Tartan Pimps*, we take figures, writers and politicians of the last thirty or forty years or so, and examine in what way their writings have influenced the political path of the nation. The problem we face with Thatcher, as a political figure of great importance over the period, is that the only books she has published were written after her period of wielding direct power and influence had come to an end, and as memoirs they only have an illustrative or anecdotal value rather than an analytical or theoretical influence on ongoing political life.

There exists nonetheless an organisation – the Thatcher Foundation which was set up in the early 90s to propagate her ideas. It was modelled on the Konrad Adenauer Foundation and although it was refused charity status by the Charity Commission, it has published on a website and on CD all Thatcher's speeches from 1949-91. By exploit-ation of this excellent resource, we have been able to identify and isolate letters, minutes, individual speeches (such as the 'Sermon on the Mound') and series of speeches (such as those made to the annual conference of Scottish Conservatives in Perth), where there is a delineation of political theory, analysis of political situations, and proposed political actions. We then treat those letters, minutes and speeches as integrated bodies of work, and criticise them in the way we might do, and have done with published books by other theorists and practitioners.

Speeches, even collections of speeches, are, of course, not books. The thesis, for example, is necessarily dissipated into a different form of presentation. Can the two be set side by side? In the case of speeches by Margaret Thatcher as Prime Minister, this difficulty suffers of great magnification. For as noted above, so much of the presentation of the analysis and the proposed action depends on the delivery in terms of physical timing and tone of voice. Her ultimate methods of exploiting those factors, we also noted, did not come naturally to her – so can it even be said that it is really *she*, Margaret Thatcher, who is delivering the speech? Or if she has been merely programmed to deliver, then on whose behalf, or to whose agenda was she programmed?

But let's look even deeper, to the actual writing of the speeches. There we find that the question is more complicated still. On the eve of her first speech to conference as leader of the party in 1975, Thatcher was still experimenting with her voice and enunciation, but another worry arose – that of the writing of the speech. It was, she says,

> 'clear to me that none of those working away in my suite was what in the jargon is known as 'wordsmith'. We had the structure, ideas and even the foundations for some good jokes, but we needed someone with a feel for the words *themselves* who would make the whole text flow along.'

But this is not the royal 'we'. At least not yet. It is clear to us now, in fact, that her speeches were a joint effort by, amongst others, the Tory Party Research Department, and the journalist, and former Labour MP, Woodrow Wyatt. But still Mrs Thatcher wasn't happy, until that is, they managed to bring Ronnie Millar, a playwright, on board to give the finishing touches to the speech. In the final event Millar added to the speech some lines that have been attributed to Abraham Lincoln, but which are in fact an excerpt from writings of the twentieth century pamphleteer, Rev. William J.H. Boetcker. There appears to be nonetheless, a sure tone of at least Thatcherite authenticity in that bold misappropriation:

> You cannot strengthen the weak by weakening the strong
> You cannot bring about prosperity by discouraging thrift
> You cannot help the wage-earner by pulling down the wage-payer

Epigrammatic and sententious – typically Thatcher we might say. Or else, typically Mary Poppins. But in reality, typically provided by Ronnie Millar. At any rate Millar stayed with Thatcher throughout her period as leader of the Tories and subsequently Prime Minister, and no major speech was said to be finished until it had been 'Ronnified'. We think we know Thatcher when we hear her, yet many of her best lines came direct from Millar. It's a bit of a turn-up for the books – or speeches rather. This man Millar turns up, and yes, it was he who gave us her best line, 'the lady is not for turning'.

Nonetheless we are dealing here with political ideas which are by their nature discovered in discussion, and observation, in interaction. There probably never was such a thing as an absolutely original political idea – unless you go back to Plato. And even then that's only because of a lack of written evidence from Socrates, and Pythagoras.

So yes, it is disappointing to realise that Mary Poppins is ultimately derivative, but that's only as far as political theory goes. For when it comes to human spirit, let's make no mistake, Mary Poppins was the real thing, and Mrs Thatcher on the other hand. . .

In her celluloid world Poppins actually humanises a blank-faced, grim, money-grubbing capitalist system. She inspires the kids through sympathy for a bag-woman street seller to precipitate a run on a bank, and actually causes the banker (he of 'sound money') to laugh (God forbid!). Thatcher on the other hand, was an entirely other sort of bossy-boots, who inspired one of her government ministers to famously say of bag women and other such unfortunates down on their luck and down on the street that 'the homeless are those people you step over when you leave the opera'.

Thatcher herself may have stepped out with the apparently humourless façade of the Poppins type ('a practically perfect person cannot afford to be emotional') but unlike the Popp, there's nothing wry or ironic in it at all for the Thatch. There's no suspicion of anything other beneath the mask as it were; she doesn't bring any human content of her own to the role. And when in 2000 at a Plymouth party rally she told the audience that her arrival wasn't unannounced because she'd seen a local cinema billboard flashing 'The Mummy Returns', she didn't even realise that the joke was on her. A wizened, lifeless relic wrapped in other folks' bloody bandages then – but was that line, we wonder, an expression of Millar's revengeful conscience? In the light of this revealing episode it's hardly surprising that Norman

St John Stevas, 'wet' cabinet member in the early Thatcher government, had dubbed his boss 'The Immaculate Misconception'.

Given its extraordinary influence on our politics, our institutions and our expectations, it is somewhat shocking to conclude that Thatcher is indeed a reanimated puppet, no twinkle-toed Julie Andrews but a creepy, blank-eyed Harryhausen ghoul. Even her celebrated, long romance with that other Ronnie, Reagan, seems to have been precipitated by her husband Denis, who, her volume of memoirs tells us, heard him speak at a function and saw in him a natural ally. Not only did Denis communicate his approval of Reagan's ideology, he actually got a copy of the text of the speech for Margaret to look at that same evening. This does not sound like the act of the cheerfully canned-up 'Dear Bill' buffoon along for the ride of popular imagination.

So were the formative years of two thirds of the authorial team based on the manoeuvres of a monetarist shill? Looking beyond the various Ronnifications (or indeed Reaganifications), we come to the inescapable conclusion that Thatcher was merely an apparatus around which a radical anti-establishment, monetarist yet centralist agenda was constructed. As mentioned above, Mrs Thatcher's writings and statements give us plenty of what, a lot of spit-spot, and almost nothing of *who* she is (as the real Poppins might say, were she to give up nannying for political commentary). She is by and large, all business, ergo all bluster, all effect and ergo all evasion. Those who have tried to penetrate through to the 'real' Thatcher, have never succeeded (and we are no different). The extent of such failure can be spectacular, not to mention perverse; Nick Broomfield spent the entirety of his film *Chasing Maggie* doing so (in the least sincere fashion) all the way to her hairdresser; while Christopher Hitchens appears on the same documentary to confess that her mystique led him to fantasise about her sexually. But he at least is in touch with his perversions – many others of that generation were flirting with Thatcher in a dangerously kinky, yet platonic fashion they would later regret. To recapture it, we have specially re-written one of *Mary Poppins'* best tunes (cue dancing Penguins):

'When Magg-eeee 'olds your 'and you feel so grand
Your 'eart starts beatin' like a big brass band

Oh it's a jolly 'oliday with Magg-eee
No wonder that it's Magg-eee that we love. . . '

Who could seriously contemplate Thatcher's sensual side and not wake screaming and bloodied in the dark watches of the night? Luckily, for most us Thatcher was padded with a steely bouffant and surrounded by penguin-suited handlers who ensured the public appearances were rigorously rehearsed, practically perfect performances that let nary a sign of ordinary human functions come into view. Maggie remained feminine, but sexless as the Virgin Queen whose adamantine cult of personality she so frequently invoked. There were of course those matronly tears shed leaving number 10 but she clambered briskly into the car and sped off, leaving us wondering whether this was not a mere theatrical gesture. As is evident from this sampling, 'her' writings retain the occasionally weird enunciation, brisk formality and precise cultivation of image, and serve, just as effectively as the speeches, to keep us at arm's length. There is it seems, only a surface. But that might be the best way to sum up the whole of her legacy, as the tea party scene in *Mary Poppins* shows us:

Maggie Poppins:
Now then what'd be nice
We'll start with raspberry ice
And then some cakes and tea

Talking Penguin:
Order what you will
There'll be no bill
It's complimentary

Alas, we do/did not live in chalk-picture England – and many of us not even in actual-England either. In chalk-picture England wily Irish cartoon foxes dodged bloodthirsty Tally-Ho Toffs; in the United Kingdom dogged, gung-ho security forces faced determined, murderous paramilitaries and both sides were as ruthless and as stone-hearted in pursuit of their aims. It was a land where no one shot to wound, where supercalifragilisticexpialidociousness gave way to blank, chilling brands and abbreviations – IRA, SAS, UDF, TRIDENT, POLARIS, NATO, SDI – and instead of quaintly barmy Admirals firing cannons into the sky, terrifyingly barmy cold warriors tested nukes and fired giant ray-guns into orbit. It was, to those who remember it, a fearful time marked by callousness and sociopathic values.

And those raspberry ices did appear on a bill, not so much some-where, as somewhen. As the banks melted over 2008/09 (not into liquidity so much as the runs), anger at the then-incumbent politicians must surely be tempered given where the now discredited (ho-ho) era of tally-ho finance originated. Or indeed, the dully superficial, imitative Thatcherism that spread beyond just politics, into the infrastructure of public and civic life.

Take for example, the realignment of public services according to the Thatcherite notion of the 'internal market'. This is most prevalent among the semi-autonomous public agencies, many of which have inserted a new breed of 'Business Managers' into the middle tier of their hierarchy whose titles that suggest a business-like, monetarist approach. But these are surely rhetorical sinecures that *sound* as if they are dependent on the successful accumulation of profit and the creation of wealth. The capital is tax-raised, or grant-funded or paid by other tax-funded public institutions in return for their services – in short, moving public funding from one part of the system to another. In terms of governance there is mimicry of business but only in the most shallow terms; there are boards of directors, but no shareholders inspect their financial returns. 'Business' is thus, a desired *impression*, a trick of language.

The idea given out is that the 'business' supports and secures the work of the agency and makes it less dependent on the taxpayer; but this notion of business is skewed, based not on efficiency but, in classic civil service fashion, building budgets and departments and creating activity only to justify continued funding. When the first devolved government proclaimed the advent of the 'knowledge economy' and a 'smart, successful Scotland' the country's hugely important public sector, lynchpin of the economy and the biggest single employer could be shored up under the guise of encouraging entrepreneurialism. Government agencies and ex-quangos spoke of branding and 'off-the-shelf' portability, and research and development teams were renamed as 'market intelligence'. The overall effect was to redraw the language of public life into a cartoon of monetarist ideology.

But to get back to this small matter of economic disaster and crunching credit, it is something the late but guilt-ridden Sir Keith Joseph, may one day, take the blame for; whether he *should* is for the delicacies of the historian's craft. Whatever prong of the political horseshoe you cling to, it is easily understood that the dramaturgy of politics distorts, devalues or even ignores the words; Joseph's critique of Keynesianism was not so radically different from that of the later twentieth century Marxists, the difference being that they identified points of attack whereas he identified priorities for repair. To Joseph, the task for a post-Callaghan government was to ensure stable money supply. This required, in ways Joseph did not always specify, considerable changes to Britain's economic and social structure; unions had to be declawed and the general public educated in the necessities of monetarism. These simple directives would be exploited for authoritarian purposes and later, and successively, misinterpreted by economic stewards who, contrary to Joseph's own rules, artificially boosted the money supply through credit. People were encouraged to borrow, to buy their homes, becoming, in cruel mockery of the liberated Mary Poppins's Banks family, clones of the Robertses (Margaret Thatcher being née Roberts). It was surely for Joseph, a cruel irony, for in his seminal lecture on monetarism (see below) he had attacked consensus economists as 'pseudo-Keynesians' yet he would be succeeded by scores of pseudo-Josephians who called themselves Thatcherites.

Around the same time as Gordon Brown was attempting to synthesise the various strands of the Scottish left, Thatcher and her shadow cabinet were participating in a range of discussions around the implications of Joseph's ideas for dismantling the post-war consensus, records of which show just how radical these departures were to many in the Tory establishment. A handwritten minute entered into Lord Hailsham's diary in 11th April, 1975, records one such confab. Hailsham's pencil records a discussion on the very meaning of Toryism that reads, on occasion, like a political science symposium accidentally booked into Smoke Filled Room #101. The reactions of the shadow cabinet are, we must assume, assiduously captured, the minute taker having an excellent ear for dialogue and the individual styles of each of the participants. These scrawls show something of the vulnerabilities and uncertainties felt among the fragmented Tory mainstream, and also offer vital clues as to why Thatcher's synthesis of monetarism and centralism would be so immediately successful, whereas Brown's agenda was one for the long haul.

Even so, it was no cakewalk for the Thatcher group. The minutes open with an angry Ian Gilmour, who is affronted. Consensus, he says, was a Conservative idea, not a Labour one. Howe takes the path of most passive resistance and claims the 1970 Tory manifesto had already departed from Consensus and that therefore, there was nothing new in Joseph's proposals. And then comes the first of Thatcher's many interjections, all of them recorded with an ear for her style of oratory – and how striking that she should maintain it, even in a private meeting!:

Thatcher: Ian, you <u>do</u> believe in capitalism?

The 'do' is deliberately underlined in Hailsham's notes. Reading this the former Thatcher subject instantly recalls that husky voice, its unique emphasis and the agenda of commonsensical, sententious persuasion. Of course this wasn't really a private meeting; surrounded as she was by individuals who represented mainstream Conservatism and by nature hostile to the Lincolnshire shopgirl and her Jewish Svengali, Thatcher was still very much in public. To get some sense of how far we still are from an immediate wedding of Conservatism with monetarism, it is notable that in Poppins-ing her questions to the group, Thatcher does not for a moment talk of 'conservatism' but expressly and precisely of *capitalism*. Gilmour replies:

Gilmour: That is almost blasphemy. I don't believe in Socialism.

And then again, comes another perfectly practical Thatcher epigram, followed up by Joseph's rebuttal of Howe, echoing arguments made in *Monetarism is not Enough* (1975):

Thatcher: To ensure a <u>free society</u> you must have a mixed economy.

Joseph: The hundred years of relative decline (since the Great

Exhibition) is objectively demonstrable. There was NOT a Conservative consensus before 1970.

Thatcher underlines, Joseph capitalises, the nanny and the chimney-sweep stepping perfectly in time. Reading this, there is a sense of histories separating and a new narrative being imposed, not on Britain in this instance, but on its Conservative movement (and what force could possibly be more radical than that?). There were still plenty in this shadow cabinet – before Thatcher was powerful enough to purge them – who believed, in the words of Ian Gilmour that Conservatives needed to 'command consensus' to take power.

> Raison: Too much misery in Keith's paper. There are matters on which we have got to operate a consensus – e.g we must try and persuade Healey to produce a sensible budget.
>
> Francis Maude: That is not on. The Right of the Labour Party will always let us down.
>
> Pym: Society is moving more left. There must be continuity – the Keith paper is a recipe for disaster.

It is Maude's statement that is most striking – he does not rule out the idea of consensus as a Conservative ideal – because it was – but is clearly fed-up of cross-bench alliances foundering as Labour acceded to the demands of the unions, their main interest group. Even Pym says that the Labour right are 'men of straw and will always let us down'. And so the seeds are planted. We can understand here how an energised and determined vanguard, selling the idea of Tories putting *their* interest groups first could have broken down resistance, enough to overcome the Raisons and Pyms. And amidst all this sharpening of the long knives, whither – or indeed wither – Scotland? Gentleman George Younger gives Thatcher some fateful advice on its 'Conservative defectors' – those who should vote Tory, but somehow do not:

> George Younger: The majority of Scots do not wish to break up Britain. Conservative defectors in Scotland had a more attractive haven to go to than in England. They defect for the same reason.

What Younger seems to be trying to say here is that the disaffected swing voter in Scotland is not expressing disquiet over the union, but the state of conservatism – and, that the SNP or even the Labour right in Scotland is a much easier shift, and one not even available to Tories in England. The right wings of other parties are thus something of an obsession for this group. Later on in the meeting, Sally Oppenheim beats the war drum even harder:

> Oppenheim: We must smash the Labour right. They constitute our worst danger.

This refers to England, but we can also understand it in context with Younger's statement on the defectors. 'There was hardly a dull moment' seems an apt conclusion to these minutes, underlined, three times, portents the minute taker could then have barely grasped.

In the first edition of *The Drouth* we analysed the hidden social and political conservatism within the Scottish Labour establishment, and have picked at it ever since. It is surely notable that in 1975 we have the Labour *right* identified as the enemy of conservatism, a political force clearly seen as powerful enough to threaten their traditional powerbase – possibly the 'alternative' noted by Younger. The Labour right would be temporarily trounced in England in 1975, but never defeated at the ballot box in Scotland. What seems to have happened here was that the Labour right regrouped almost as solidly in opposition to the model Thatcher and Joseph were proposing. They emphasised the community bonds and industrial traditions Thatcherism set out to attack. And is it not striking how much of that resurgent Labour right wing was recruited wholesale, in answer to the Anglocentric Thatcher-cabal, from the intact apparatuses of the 'fringe nations' (not fringe at all, in Labour terms) from Kinnock's Wales and the then still entrenched 'shadow government' of Scottish Labour? ◻

THE AUTHORITY OF GOVERNMENT GROUP REPORT THE RT. HON. GEORGE YOUNGER ET AL (1975) & MONETARISM IS NOT ENOUGH SIR KEITH JOSEPH (1976)

Viewed in hindsight these two slim but significant volumes are essential to understanding where the Thatcher project came from. Firstly, they sketch the essential architectural features of its early days, confirming that the great dramatic events of her eleven years in power were long in the planning. *The Authority of Government Group* report was headed by George Younger and published in 1975 and sets the moral framework for the dismantling of union power in the aftermath of the miners' strike. Keith Joseph's *Monetarism is Not Enough* was published in 1976 by the same think tank that powered the Thatcher cabal to power.

Thatcherism is not considered, even by its supporters as an especially cerebral calling. It speaks of motives visceral rather than intellectual; of greedy-guts and hearts swollen under a tightly wrapped union flag grimed with the mud of Tumbledown. The Thatcher appeal, as represented in her odd cadences and general pugnacity was unapologetically (in)sensual. But in her foreword to *Monetarism* her emotive rhetoric is tamed and reined in, providing a layman's summary of Joseph's high-end economic theorising; essentially, the rhetorical pattern of her entire career.

Sir Keith Joseph was just the sort of well-connected, nonconformist outsider that forms a familiar pattern within the Thatcherite circle, the relative outsider who like Grammar-School-Roberts, held a vested interest in dismantling the powerbase of the aristocratic Tory grandees. He was nevertheless, a second-generation vizier, the son of a Jewish merchant, pioneer of financial services and heir of the family firm Bovis. Joseph senior was a Baronet who earned his title by playing the kingmaker in inter-war Tory politics. Joseph Junior was also a baronet and continued to run the family firm, but was also possessed of considerable intellectual prowess, excelling in academia, the bar and the boardroom.

Monetarism was the Stockton Lecture for 1976, built around a re-reading of Keynes arguing not, as was conventional, that he was an anti-monetarist, but that as an economist, all his theories are underpinned by monetarist principles. Playing a gambit similar to that of those leftists (Noam Chomsky among them) who reclaim Adam Smith from the libertarians, Joseph inverts their assertion that Smith was not a laissez-faire capitalist by showing that Keynes was not a socialist. Joseph argues that Keynes' criticisms of economic processes have ossified into the dogma of the pseudo-Keynesians (as ignorant of his true meaning as the Adam Smith Institute is of Smithian sympathy). Whatever the ironies of these repeating dialectical tropes, there are certainly echoes of the Smithian in Joseph's summary of true monetarism;

> . . . monetary stability provides a framework within which the individual can best serve his own – and therefore, if the laws and taxes are appropriately designed, the nation's – interests.

That is Joseph at his simplest – Thatcher would have come up with something more resonant, Churchillian and visceral, but there is an admirable clarity to how he deals with often highly technical arguments. But scholarly he is, and the academic particulars that shape this pamphlet explain something of why, in an eerie parallel of Brown on his off-days, Joseph's forays into 'front stage' politics would be so disastrous. For Joseph, monetarism rested on a 'just right' approach to the flow of money supply, neither too low – the 70s, or too high (today?). Even so, this was only a 'pre-essential' – Joseph cites the actions of the West Germans in floating the mark to ensure the money supply did not grow too large, and rejects creating demand as a 'wonder drug' short cut to growth. If only they'd listened. . .

Joseph frames the history of the years since the economically ruinous World War I as an ongoing denial of prevailing realities; that industrial hegemony was decaying and that the 'cartels' of workers and oligarchs built a protectionist system, rationalised through 'heroic socialist phraseology'. This may seem mild today, but it is hard to imagine Joseph's criticisms voiced by any other Tory grandee of the time.

Which brings us to his background. Keith Joseph's Jewishness has been somewhat over-analysed, but is there not something of the diasporid, who owes nothing to the traditional establishment in his guiltless analysis of consensus rhetoric? He is shrewd in teasing out the *Ancien Regime* paternalism inherent in the traditional Tory classes, too timid to challenge the Keynesian consensus:

> There was guilt. We (the Tories) came increasingly to be thought of as the party of the well-off, though millions who were not well-off preferred to vote for us rather than for Labour. We found it hard to avoid the feeling that the lean and tight-lipped mufflered men in the 1930s dole queue were at least partly our fault. And so paradoxically we were inhibited from questioning the misleading unemployment statistics of our own times since the last war which exaggerate the numbers of those who were unemployed – in the sense that an expansion of economic activity would permanently absorb them into productive employment – and understate the numbers of vacancies. It was as though we were trying to make amends to the unemployed of a generation back by exaggerating unemployment in our own time.

It is less than two years until the famous 'Labour isn't working' posters.

Joseph continues by diagnosing several other ills – the 'not enough' part of the argument, founded on 'Detaxing and the restoration of bold incentives and encouragements to business and industry'. Joseph builds his case historically. Britain's grim record of high inflation and minimal growth could be linked to its diminished 'zest for enterprise' coupled to increasing capital taxation on the 'makers of wealth'

Ever careful to show his own true-Keynesian piety, Joseph reminds us that that the old master had stressed the importance of the 'animal spirits' of businessmen such as his own father, but this was all but withered among the existing managerial classes, schooled in collectivism and cartels. Unions are marked down as contributing to the flight of wealth-creators, and manufacturing is blamed for skewing the economy disproportionately in favour of high-risk measures to create false demand, with ever-diminishing rewards (and thus, the enemies of the Thatcher-Joseph axis are marked).

The problem with the public sector was not, according to Joseph, in the philosophy of publicly maintaining certain services, but that it is so large – and being large, yet insensitive to the economy, it leaves the entire system dangerously imbalanced. This fundamental criticism was applicable to the Scottish economy right up to recent times (often applied by Royal Bank of Scotland economists) and continues to underpin the current thinking of the business-friendly, entrepreneur-obsessed Scottish government (headed by an ex-RBS economist) that must contend with the huge risks of dismantling the largest single employer in the country. In Scotland at least, the perceived crises of the late 1970s are still being played out.

Of course, in the same fashion as the dogmas of Joseph's misguided pseudo-Keynesians had led to stagflation, pseudo-Josephists (Thatcherites) mistook their master's criticisms as instructions. Joseph was probably right in saying that the British private sector was remade in the image of the public, but is it not the case that so many of his current day public-service disciples try, disastrously, to return the favour?

Throughout, *Monetarism* repeats the refrain of fatally bone-headed trade unionism and Walter Mitty Socialists wearing their Y-fronts the wrong way. But how would a delicate, essentially gentle intellectual who believed in capitalism but abhorred capital punishment and much of the general viciousness that spiced the Thatcher project, enforce this? For that Thatcher had already turned to a grandee from another covenanted virtual nation, George Kenneth Hotson Younger, 4th Viscount of Leckie, Beer magnate, grandson of the Tory who overthrew Lloyd George in 1922, future Chair of the Royal Bank of Scotland, head of the *Authority of Government Group* which drafted the 1975 report of the same name. Written in blank, functional language it is no great contribution to literature, but in many respects greatly more significant than the *Red Paper on Scotland* published by the future Labour Prime Minister the same year. Like the *Red Paper* it responded to the chaos of 1973-74 as incited by 'organised groups of workers'. Its concerns are much less high minded than the *Red Paper*, centred on possible challenges of credibility to a new conservative government. It begins;

> We have interpreted our remit as calling on us to submit suggestions on two related questions –
>
> 1. How can a government avoid getting us into a situation in which its authority, even when backed by Parliament, is put at risk?

2. If it cannot or does not succeed in avoiding such a situation, how can it deal with such a crisis of authority?

From Smith and Keynes to Hobbes. The assertion of central authority was a crucial plank of the Thatcherite project, and as this report shows interlocks with Joseph's plans to remove obstacles to wealth creation. The scaremongering language only confirms that Hobbes is more a 1970s guy than Locke (or Friedman, or Marx or Keynes). The report recommends a constitutional review to bolster government authority and the establishment of a new unit. . . to take steps to reduce the risk of a crisis before any crisis occurs. The unit would be built from the Ministerial Committee on Emergencies and the Civil Contingencies Unit. Top among the 'vulnerabilities' is the risk of industrial action, and among the more distinctive recommendations made by Younger's group was the physical modification of premises owned by then-nationalised industries to prevent strike action, making it difficult for pickets to form thus ensuring the 'security of supply' – prophecies of the grim compounds of Rupert Murdoch's Wapping. The report also mentions that distinctions must be made between strikes that are economically damaging, and those damaging to government authority. But in calling for a distinction, the report equally leaves open the possibility of its being blurred, from which point proceedings become increasingly sinister.

> Opinions are divided about the scope for the use of volunteers and troops. The main requirement is the creation of a climate of opinion when their use is unlikely to lead to escalation of the conflict.

The report also mentioned the prospect of calling a referendum to support strike-breaking and validate slipping off the tassled loafer to replace it with the Hobbes-nailed boot. And thus the history of the Miner's Strike (1984-85) and even shoot to kill in Ulster, is drawn in blueprint.

While Trade Unions (and Northern Ireland) are firmly in their sights, the paper also mentions:

> Groups of protestors at planning enquiries (the leadership of which has been by no means solely working class) and if collective action by tax-payers or rate-payers were ever to achieve the degree of solidarity associated with official industrial action, the orderly collection of public revenue would become impossible.

So there we have it, the script notes for the entire Thatcherite drama as essayed by the odd pairing of Scot and Jew, Lord and Lawyer, Banker and Builder, Beer-magnate and Construction captain, Hobbes and Smith, pinstriped thug and high-minded bean counter. As the inheritor of beer (the real opium of the masses) Younger knew the most effective pragmatism is conscience-free. Joseph's notion of an essentially inclusive monetarism clearly spoke to Maggie Roberts's Grocer-Shop personal mythology, but she needed the flinty pragmatism of Younger to actualise it. Between the two, we find all the key scenes of the Thatcherite era fore-shadowed, although we might lament that it was the Scot whose influence was most deeply felt.

Speeches to the annual Scottish Conservative Party Conferences in Perth as Prime Minister 1979-1990

If Thatcherism was a mood settling itself down blanket across the country – a national character topos gone total – then the speeches Thatcher made as PM to the annual Scottish Conservative Party conference in Perth help us gauge the dominant tones and tendencies in that mood. The fact that this 'national character' is recognisably middle class English in its ideal of prim reservedness and New Jerusalem solipsism, as opposed to Scottish or working class makes the ragged edges of that blanket all the more apparent here.

Thatcher herself was evidently very moody. Although this specific audience of party faithful hung on her every word, she was clearly conscious in the speeches that she spoke in and to Scotland at large, and over the years 1979-90 her disappointment and impatience with the junior nation's failure to shape up and take the cure becomes palpable. The 'Mary Poppins' act may have soothed enough English hearts long enough to make the headcount, but her attempts to incorporate Scots into the model seem more exasperated and desperate as the years pass. In 1988 after a disastrous electoral showing the previous year in Scotland she insists tetchily that the 'Scots invented Thatcherism'. It would take a while to unravel all the manic psychological truths implicit in the making of such a statement before such an audience, but a very brief resort to

psephological truths would speak immediate volumes about its real effect.

Yet it would be a mistake to think that things necessarily always looked so unlikely for Thatcher in Scotland. We ought not to give too much weight to the idea of essential national differences and the mythology of such: as though the reality can be fabled as Mary Poppins turning up out of nowhere onto the close landing and announcing to the extended yet close-knit family of the Broons that they're all individually going to have to pay their way for the use of Glebe St. facilities, that the 'poll tax' is necessary, as Thatcher said in Perth in 1988, because 'local services are used by people not houses'.

For the truth is that in 1979 Scotland seemed to be prepared as much as any other part of Britain for a sharp right turn in political direction. Only one week or so after winning the election Thatcher speaks at Perth, and full of delight and a perhaps naive optimism she announces the figures that dispel those essentialist myths of non-Scottishness: the Tory vote was up one quarter of a million in Scotland and their party gained six more MPs in that election. Here was the Conservative Party, it might have seemed, with gained political territory, on the threshold of refinding those glory days of the 1950s when they commanded overall majorities of the Scottish electorate.

Yet this is where Thatcher gives the game away and fails to popularise her party in Scotland. At the beginning of that speech in 1979 she speaks of the 'bitter blow' of losing Teddy Taylor as sitting MP for Cathcart. 'We lost our standard bearer at the hour of victory' was the typical bellicose metaphor employed, but it is true that Taylor was a powerful and effective symbol of popular Toryism in Scotland –homophobe, witchhunter, and (less predictably, but even more shrewdly) teetotaller. What is significant is that in his place as figurehead of Thatcherism, she relies instead on George Younger, a Viscount and super rich (if recent) aristocrat. Not only is he somewhat blasé and remote from the daily life and concerns of the average Scot, but he is, as pointed out above, one architect of the aggressive anti-working class policies which we now know under the collective term of Thatcherism. So Scotland was, right from the beginning, denied a popular or classless front man or woman, recognisably 'one of us' – like say Thatcher herself or Norman Tebbit was for so many English voters – and an obvious autocrat, with dual membership of the *ancient regimes* of aristocracy and banking was appointed to front the 'revolution'.

Yet Younger clearly represents no casual expediency as a replacement by Thatcher for the unavailable Taylor. For in line with Younger's own recommendations in *The Authority of Government Group,* in this first Scottish Conference speech as PM, Thatcher announces the immediate award of pay rises for both the armed forces and the police. Could these two moves – boosting the security and policing capabilities of the regime, and taking a

literally 'cavalier' approach to the social and political make-up of Scotland – really have been independent and inadvertent? The absence of representation of social super-elites in the Thatcher cabal running England is, by contrast, very noticeable.

If there was then, in Scotland, *never* any attempt to make Thatcherism popular there was nonetheless a distinct enthusiasm to Thatcher's unleashing of the project in that first speech. In her epigrammatic excitement she occasionally tips over into a fevered version of that solipsism mentioned above – 'It was because we were a free people that we built an Empire and gave that Empire its freedom.'. But by the second conference in 1980, much of the naive enthusiasm had been dropped, and Thatcher's mood is definitely more mean. 'Realism can be painful now' she says, and everything seems closed already in the hectoring, superior and smug formulae of definitions and dismissals which are so easily recognisable.

Is there a delight or an enthusiasm in her voice when she announces that Sir Keith Joseph will 'have a go' at the post and telephone services? To the reader now it is certainly chilling to see these aggressive 'have a go' policies – privatisation, monetarism and so on – gradually racked up alongside council house sales and the push to a 'property-owning democracy', and to watch as she turns the screw from last year's announcement of army and police pay rises to this year's union reform, ballots and a banning of secondary picketing.

After the first speech of 1979 in fact, she never returns to that original style of thanksgiving, sharing hopes and aims,

87

persuasion and argument. (Although in 1982 Thatcher does assert by way of thanks and, it has to be said, in a manner reminiscent of the Third Reich leader, that 'though the office Secretary of State exists for another thousand years, there will never be a better Secretary of State than George Younger'). For a couple of years as unemployment rises steeply she turns to the blame game, and heaps opprobrium on Labour, or just simply, 'the socialists'. But that's not to say that she can't dish the opposition occasionally with a degree of panache: for in 1981 she sees off Labour leader Michael Foot's extra-parliamentarian exertions with,

> The leader of the opposition apparently thinks we shall get more mileage out of marching. Not for him the microchip. Not even the wheel. He offers us the pedestrian revolution. Left Foot forward.

Implicit was the Poppinsesque doctrine that all good people only travelled by air. And again in her last speech of 90, she says of Neil Kinnock's manifesto,

> It's what you might call Labour's Medium Term Gastronomic Strategy. I dread to think what's on the menu. A few red herrings, perhaps? Or some Welsh tripe?
> And after landing us all in the soup, a hearty helping of humble pie.

Some attacks were evidently more successful than others, and no doubt a number of the some were penned by the 'wordsmith' himself, Ronnie Millar. But the stench of the corner grocer may be authentic.

By the time she had come to the speeches delivered in 1982 and 1983, Thatcher

had the ongoing and then victorious Falklands War to preach about, and the revival of patriotism on her side. At any rate her repeated prognoses of great prosperity pulling us out of mass unemployment and poverty had begun to wear thin by then, viz.

> 1980: 'Already there are signs that the policies are beginning to work.'

> 1981: 'Unless stock markets are wrong we are in for a dramatic recovery.'

> 1982: 'There are signs of an "economic spring".'

So Thatcher would be glad to be able to change her tune, and get the whole country singing from the same patriotic Falklands hymnsheet. But she was not to be blown off her course by a nation of wets and whingers. By 1983 into 1984 she is talking – apparently without irony—about the 'battle' against Violent Crime, and then other 'battles' (besides Falklands) at the election, and in 1984 against the miners. And despite the level of personal and political unpopularity she faced in Scotland the policies just kept getting racked up. In the 1981 speech for example, there had been a first mention of a need to reorganise Local Government Finance. In 1984 Rate Capping is introduced because 'local businesses need defending' against high spending Labour councils. In 1985 we have 'reached the stage where no amount of patching up the existing system can overcome its inherent unfairness' and Thatcher promises to publish proposals. In 1986 the Scots are assured of special treatment re the Poll Tax, 'because of the urgency, domestic rates will be abolished ahead of England and Wales.' And how (g)rateful must have been the nation when in 1987 'it was in response to your needs in Scotland that we finally decided on the introduction of the community charge (poll tax).'

It was all downhill from 1987 on for Thatcher after major losses of MPs in the elections in Scotland, but nonetheless she seemed to gloat over the unwilling body politic as she stuck the pins and barbs of her epigrammatic wisdom in deeper. In 1985 she had claimed 'Scotland ought to be natural Tory territory' evoking a pawky, penny-pinching Lauderesque stereotype (or the origin may have been Donald McGill postcards sold in the corner shop). She seemed gleefully unaware (but is it possible?) that on the one hand many of the natives regarded that stereotype as slanderous, while on the other, those who actually believed they could occupy said territory living proudly on such Lauderesque precepts had been put off the Tories by her own autocratic disdain as seen in the Younger appointment. In the same speech she even went as far as to say, 'I didn't expect to find so much pure Toryism in Burns'.

Were there no bounds to this prime ministerial literary and political criticism? – from Lauder to Burns, from the Bible to Jeffrey Lord Archer. It's definitely post-modern in its range, pastiche in its presentation and appreciation, so there's no doubting she was a woman of her 1980s time with her 1950s royal blue suits, but we are afeared to ask what unexpected political insight she was afforded from that last writer's weighty texts. Unabashed, she soon ropes the entire Scottish Enlightenment canon into her literary orbit too (1989), but all the rhetorical chumminess and faux admiration of the Scottish territory becomes more strained and ropey as the years go on.

The 1989 speech is otherwise largely taken up with self-congratulation on the Tory 'achievements' of the decade, and in 1990 despite the poll tax riots in the streets and one million non-payers of the tax in Scotland she is claiming that 'for years Labour have taken Scotland for granted'. There is of course an element of truth in that, but perhaps some politicians just care too much. . .

Assorted Letters 1949-91

Thatcher's letters range from missives to potential constituents in her pre-parliamentary days, to letters of state exchanged with Premiers and Presidents. Plenty of scope, one would think, to glean some psychological insight, to establish how interpersonal transactions moulded Thatcher's politics. Perhaps there are letters to Mark, or Denis or even, miracle of miracles, poor old Carol that could tell us more? In that respect, the Thatcher letters are disappointing, lacking colour or spontaneity, but there are some tiny glimpses of what was moving beneath the surface. Carol Thatcher interviewed her mother on the eve of the 1983 election – and even she couldn't extract an entirely human response, but Thatcher's replies are somewhat self-aware – and yes, as Poppins as Poppins can be.

> Carol: What, as Britain's first woman Prime Minister, have you brought to the job?
> Margaret Thatcher: I'm not the person to answer that question.
> Carol: O.K. How's it changed you?
> Margaret Thatcher: I'm not the person to answer that question either. But as I've got to know the job, I have become more and more a square peg in a square hole. As far as I'm concerned, it seems to me that the job and me fit together rather well.

Beyond this, there are precious few missives from Mummy to Carol. What chance then, of seeing anything more personal this side of a state funeral (and what risk of turning this sober Poppinsing of the Thatcher edifice into a tacky rifle through her celeb trash can)? Still, a tea-stained missive telling Mark where to dump the warheads – or another, asking Denis what he thought of the Eurozone, would be precious indeed, not least to the forces of International Law.

The first piece of correspondence to surface on the foundation website is an early letter, dated 1949, to a potential constituent. Thatcher is, as you might expect, all business, focused solely on the query. She responds with facts and figures, on coal, on imports, on exports and other bread and butter aspects of economic policy. Much later, we have letters between Thatcher and Reagan, signed to 'Ron' or to 'Margaret'. The language remains stiff, precise and formal, but there are touches that testify to the closeness between the two leaders, Thatcher choosing to add scrawled addenda to typewritten notes as a measure of her ardour, while Reagan is personable even in type. The written correspondence between her and Reagan was in every sense mundanely special; no other World Leader (in the history thus far approved by the Thatcher Foundation) appears in her in-tray with such frequency or regularity. No Europeans, nor indeed the other prominent female premier, Indira Gandhi, for whom Thatcher felt a degree of sympathy but no great ideological or personal warmth. In a letter from 1981

Reagan, the chatty one in their relationship, mentions conversations about Gandhi that show a relationship evolving into something not unlike a transatlantic cabinet

> I thought your comments about Mrs Gandhi to be most illuminating, and I agree she is not a Marxist. Although she has instigated a rather lengthy correspondence with me which I find encouraging, I still remain unclear as to what it is she really is prepared to do to strengthen relationships between India and the United States. I, too, have the impression that Mrs Gandhi has an exaggerated fear of Pakistan.

But Thatcher and Reagan would remain enamoured, and 'Ron' would be Thatcher's notion of, in her own words 'a true gentleman'. Their general agreement on economic and social matters make the bulk of their correspondence boring reading, as so much is already mutually understood as common articles of faith – in a sense, the letters of St Paul with all the heat, fury and self-examination edited out.

To redux to our small province, where articles of common faith could not be so readily assumed, home of Gentleman George (of whom yet more in a minute), do we find that the correspondence between prime Minister and Scottish Secretary offer us much more? It does not. No letters of note for instance, and perhaps tellingly, between Thatcher and Rifkind. Although he was her early brief on devolution (and perhaps, through his consensual approach to the issue, allowing some concessions, marked for life as a result) there is no body of correspondence, nor surprisingly, any

apparent lines of contact between her and Michael Forsyth, for so long the Thatcherite béte noir of the Scottish left. This does not mean of course, they do not exist, but he merits no mention on The Thatcher Foundation thus far.

Other Scots do, often of the most buffoonish sort. There is a 'yours ever' scrawled to Nicky Fairbairn on receipt of his resignation letter, dated January 1982, over 'the Glasgow rape case'. He begins in the original letter:

> I have been considering my position following the apology which preceded the Statement I made to the House this afternoon about the Glasgow rape case. . . I have decided that I ought no longer to remain in office as Solicitor General for Scotland.

But for evidence of how Thatcher's associates began to mouth along to the words, Fairbairn offers us a wonderful example of Thatcher's portentious Churchillian lyric:

> I would like to thank you most sincerely for having given me the honour of serving as a Scottish Law Officer during past two and a half years – but much more of having had the privilege of serving in your Government which is *devoted to our national survival*. (our emphasis)

> I will do all in my power to support you and your Administration in the House and in the country in your unflinching *dedication to the salvation of our country*.

Thatcher then, shows us not her characteristics, but her gradual personal abstraction into an ongoing crusade for life and death, something Fairbairn, sozzled as he frequently was, seems on a deep level to understand. Thatcher replies:

> It is characteristic of you that you should have written as you did. I believe that you have come to a responsible decision which accords with the highest traditions of office.

And in this remark 'I am glad to know that we shall continue to have your loyal support' we note just how far we have come since the liveliness and individualism of those early shadow cabinet meetings, as Consensus has been replaced by – another Consensus. 'We' is not royal. There is nothing monarchical about Thatcher, her collective strength being much more reminiscent of the politburo than the Privy Council.

George Younger, her longest serving Scottish Secretary does of course feature in her letters. In a letter from early 1975, apparently so pivotal a year for both right and left, she solicits for advice but makes clear what sort is wanted, imposing the Thatcherite narrative of national decline firmly on the agenda and forcing Younger to comply or react:

> I shall need a lot of advice on Scotland but am ready and willing to take it. I believe the problem is the same as further south – people lost faith in us and our job is to restore it.

Even in private correspondence, the infinitely complex is reduced to the simplest equation – the consistency is in many respects remarkable, striking, to paraphrase the American Senator Charles Sumner, no pose in private she would not strike in public. But then, for the mask, there is no performance; no corresponding process of introspection and self exploration. You can only be what you already are, a visage, with no individual capacity to speak, or answer.

THE SERMON ON THE MOUND, 1988

It may offer no novel refinement of her definition to say that Margaret Thatcher was both formed and deformed by non-conformity. But there is a nice paradoxical and nonsensical ring to the statement. And not much 'nice' is said about the Iron Lady, who really ought to ring when you hit her properly.

But perhaps there is a lack of the 'nice' commentary because she made *us* pay so long and hard for *her* awkward political constitution: raised in the Methodist church; schooled as an elitist 'snobby' Roberts; underclassed at top-notch forties Oxford; kept out of political debate in the men-only Union; apprenticed in politics as a dirty-working snatcher of milk from the mouths of babes as Education Secretary; and finally excelling as the lonely, only ever female ruler at no.10, surrounded by a crowd of naughty clubbable cabinet men. You cannot say that such and such was her element – eg. iron – for Thatcher had no element – nothing was ever so consensual – she only ever had a mode of operation.

Is it not indeed plausible that the monetarist policies from which she did not turn even as millions were turned out onto the dole queue, were in fact a dissenting personal, rather than a politico-economic, expediency? That may be to go too far, but one gets the suspicion at times that had monetarism been the 'convention' by the late 1970s rather than an 'outmoded currency crankery' (seeTom Nairn below), then the Lady would not have turned that particular financial screw so tightly (or so gleefully).

It is in this non-conformist light that we must read the so-called 'Sermon on the Mound', a speech which she was invited to deliver to the General Assembly of the Church of Scotland in May 1988. It was a critical period in modern Scottish politics: two months later the Scottish Constitutional Convention (containing representatives from this church) was to publish *A Claim of Right*, including a demand for Scottish Home Rule. But on the face of it, and for any reader not steeped in the bitter waters of 1980s Britain class crises, the lecture seems a harmless reiteration of some Christian home truths: the saving of individual souls, the position of the Established Church, and so on.

So was the reaction to her speech a measured one? Why in the popular imagination was it accorded the importance of an honorary and resonant title, and why indeed has it resounded as such down the decades, and enjoyed a notorious reputation as the stroke of an uncompromising iron that broke the allegedly moderate and compassionate back of middle Scotland?

Before the Church that has not only historically played such an important part in the nation's welfare – in health, education, poor relief, housing etc – but which made, as Owen Dudley Edwards, editor of *A Claim of Right*, puts it here (see Tom Nairn), 'a vital contribution to winning Scotland's Parliament', Thatcher first threw down her gauntlet in the form of an unattributed quotation. 'Christianity,' she said, not half a page into her speech, 'is about spiritual redemption not social reform.' That's not exactly John Knox's vision of the division of labour in the godly commonwealth, but it's only her opening gambit.

She goes on. But only after first giving a hint of her annoyance that 'independence of mind' (think the church and home rule) has been one of the 'powerful characteristics of the Scottish people'. She then throws a few more gauntlets down – she evidently had a whole handbag full of them – before declaring more or less that she doesn't care whether they pick them up or not. 'Democracy,' she has to tell them, is a word 'mentioned . . . nowhere in the Bible.' It's a provocative thing to say before this gathering – and it's a pity there is no soundtrack to go with the script for there may – nay, there ought to – have been an audible gasp.

Mrs Thatcher is a very clever woman: the research, that is to say, has been done. At the beginning of her speech she shows herself also very knowledgeable regarding the position of the Church of Scotland and the constitution, and the Sovereign. Later she asks rhetorically how it is possible to understand Walter Scott and the constitutional conflicts of seventeenth century Scotland without 'adequate instruction' in the 'Judaic-Christian tradition'? Can it be however, that despite these demonstrations of subtle and

sensitive empathy and understanding, she did not know what it means to be 'Presbyterian'? Perhaps the assembled divines felt this particular gauntlet – an English leader of London government coming to Edinburgh to lecture the Kirk on the place of 'democracy' in Christianity – was aimed at their collective cheek rather than at the floor. They weren't minded to turn the other one.

This gathering of ministers, each voted to their pulpits by the elders and parishioners of their Kirk Sessions are then told, direct from London, that 'when Christians meet, as Christians, to take counsel together, their purpose is not (or should not be) to ascertain what is the mind of the majority, but what is the mind of the Holy Spirit.'

But Mrs Thatcher is, she quickly adds, 'nevertheless . . . an enthusiast for democracy.' Only she is apparently so not at the behest of biblical commandment, not because she has been told to be so, nor because she cares for the 'mind of the majority', but simply as some sort of 'Holy' mission. Would this type of democracy be called a non-conformist consensus?

Mrs Thatcher is jealous of her democratic position here, effectively denying it as a possibility for the assembled divines. But this is not just a chance disagreement, the constitutional historian might say, for such a confrontation of world views follows a political pedigree running from Cromwell, through the Killing Times, to the Disruption and beyond. What is most striking however, is how the Scots are stirred from their political slumbers by this iron-stroke and forced to review their shibboleths of democracy and egalitarianism. Is, or was there ever, any substance to the belief that Scottish civil society has historically been always more egalitarian than neighbouring societies, and in particular the English? (Mary was Queen of *Scots*, Elizabeth was Queen of Eng*land*) The notion of a native egalitarianism had surely over the centuries become completely depoliticised, and in effect it was manifest now only in a fossilised ecclesiastical government of much diminished national importance, and a folk myth of dubious provenance and effect. It is arguable however, that Thatcher's imposition of a reformed concept of democracy set the agenda for the re-examination of this question, and that as a direct consequence of, and a reaction against her policies the question of democracy has now the chance to become truly politicised in the workings of the Scottish Parliament.

Alex Salmond famously said that the Scots didn't mind Mrs Thatcher's 'economic side' so much as her 'social side'. It's impossible to quantify that alleged preference, but is not the truth about Scots egalitarianism and democracy, whatever they may be, just that in the history of Scottish moral and political thought, (*pace* Mrs Thatcher and her compartmentalisation of redemption and reform) the social and the economic have always been inseparable?

FROM DENIS AND MARGARET THATCHER

10 Downing Street
S.W.1. 94 FLOOD STREET
LONDON SW3

Dear Bill,   May 18

So sorry I couldn't make it on Tuesday. Monty rang me last night to report, and obviously I missed a jolly good day. I haven't played down at Sandwich since '68, when poor old Archie Bracketts dropped down dead at the fourteenth. I remember we drove over to the Dolphin afterwards and had a slap-up meal, which I am sure is what Archie would have wanted had he been alive.

Anyway, as you may have seen in the Telegraph, all hell has broken loose around here since we were last able to have a chat over lunch that day at the Army & Navy. M. has become Prime Minitser, and it's caused no end of a flap. Telephone never stops ringing. All my daffs got trampled by a lot of bloody pressmen on election day. I actually spotted some photographer-johnny from the Sun nipping up the fire-escape trying to catch Carol starkers in the bath, dirty bugger.

To cap it all, we've now had to ship the whole shooting match over to Number Ten, and I don't know yet whether I'm coming or going. The bloody fools from Pickfords seem to have lost that set of Ping Irons Burmah gave me when I handed in my cards. What with decorators, policemen and politicos running about all over the place, Number Ten is the worst shambles I've seen since the Dieppe show in '42. What's more there doesn't seem to be a decent local, and they've even got some Ministry of Works chappie called Boris to take care of the garden, so any hope I had of taking off a peaceful hour or two in the greenhouse is out of the window.

Anyway, back to Tuesday. Why I couldn't make it was that M. insisted I turn up for some kind of State Opening of Parliament or other. I had assumed now the election was over I would be excused this kind of thing, but oh no. I had just carried my spare clubs out to the jalopy, when heigh ho! Up goes a window, and M. is giving me my marching orders. It's off to Moss Bros. for the full kit, and at that moment, I don't mind telling you, I couldn't help thinking pretty enviously of you, Monty and the Major enjoying a few pre-match snifters at the 19th without a care in the world.

It took ages to get kitted out. The staff at Moss Bros. all seem to be gyppos these days, and there was a bit of a communications problem. But eventually I managed to get a cab back to the House of Commons, only to find that I'd left my Invite back at Downing Street. I told the chap on the door that I was Mr Thatcher, and he said, "That's what they all say." After about 20 minutes they agreed to go and get M. out to vouch for my bona fides and, as you can imagine, I wasn't top of the popularity stakes at that particular juncture! !!

Dear Bill Courtesy: *Private Eye*   [SEE page 98]

II.

THE MALE OF THE SPECIES

I MUST come to terms with a person whom even in days of power in the UK, I knew to be ruthless, brutal, selfish, class-protective, cynical, manipulative, and of cunning almost unmatched in the surrounding world. Yet from start to finish I had a sneaking admiration, indeed frequently an outspoken generous acknowledgment of my enemy, the enemy of so much that I held and hold dear. Time has done nothing to unravel my perennial bouquet for Denis Thatcher.

Now that he is gone, and his puppet whose clownmaster he was for so long has subsequently subsided in her sawdust, surely we can unite in honouring the political giant whose strings pulled a Judy show for eleven years, not to speak of the faultless preliminary auditions.

History searches itself in vain to produce his like. Certainly, one can think of Richelieu as the most obvious precursor. The achievement was comparable. The iron hand jerked the wretched Louis XIII into all the postures of kingship, statesmanship, leadership. But where was Richelieu's sense of humour by comparison with Denis Thatcher's? Where was the ability to keep pursuit perpetually at bay by kicking

M. then had to go off to do her stuff, so I just
mooched around for a while, looking for a watering hole.
What a place, Bill! If you ask me, it's just an antiquated
rabbit warren - miles and miles of corridors, with chaps
in evening dress wandering about like a lot of super-
annuated penguins. Luckily I eventually bumped into a
familiar face, in the shape of George Brown. He seemed to
know his way about, and we ended up in a nice little bar over-
looking the river, with an awfully jolly crowd of chaps who
were watching the show on the TV.

It all seemed to go quite smoothly, but I was a bit miffed
to see M. fussing over that fellow Stevas, and taking the fluff
off his collar. To tell you the truth, I don't like the cut of
that chap's jib. If you ask me, he's not absolutely 100%,
and when I said as much a lot of the chaps at the bar agreed.

On a more serious note, do tell Monty and the Major that
I am definitely on for the 24th. I've checked with M.'s
secretary, and there's absolutely nothing in the book. So I'll
get the usual 11.08 from Charing Cross, and if Monty could
pick me up at Tonbridge, we'll meet you in Ye Olde Shippe In
Ye Bottle at 12.00 sharp. (I wonder if they've still got any of
that Glen Keswick we had the night poor old Tuppy bought it?)
Must close as M. has got some Hun coming to dinner and I've
g ot to do my stuff again. I sometimes wonder who won the
bloody war!

Yours Aye !
Denis

away the sublime and wallowing in the ridiculous? Where was the disdain for vanity? Richelieu, for all his cunning and wisdom, could not forbear posturing as playwright, and signing his name to the work of the grand Corneille. Denis Thatcher ensured his name would be used in a childish and obviously artificial series of letters which therefore nobody believed he could have written.

Richelieu would have revered Denis Thatcher's grasp of the nettle of alcoholism. Many great men in time past have allowed themselves to be dismissed as alcoholics only for their enemies bitterly to regret the dismissal; Alcibiades, for instance, or Mark Antony. But while drink may never have become their master, it proved ultimately a servant too powerful to discharge. Denis Thatcher played the same trick, but gave alcohol no concessions apart from assuring the world he was its slave. He needed a very close eye on it. He must have realised very early on that one member of the Thatcher household was at risk from alcohol, and he was not that member. He may even have fashioned his puppet's ultimate political elevation to keep her away from the bottle. Certainly, when that career was over, the bottle came into its own. As it did its work in the family circle, and in saturated speechifications to wealthy American Rightists, we must assume Denis Thatcher was left to carry out what little damage limitation was still in his power, shrugging his shoulders with the feeling that at least he had deferred the ultimate capitulation for twenty years.

Denis Thatcher seems to have been a supremely observant man, and having lived through Winston Churchill's last years in office, coinciding with the first years of Denis Thatcher's last marriage he would have picked up the revelations emerging so soon after Churchill's death: that from 1953 to 1954 the Prime Minister was kept in office as therapy demanded by his medical advisors to shore up what parts of his mind had not already disintegrated. That from the point of view of Queen and country a Prime Minister in full possession of his faculties was required, clearly never stood in Churchill's family's way. Denis Thatcher learned the lesson. Churchill had no doubt passed the limit of fitness to govern because of his alcoholism; Margaret Thatcher would be kept in power to prevent hers. The game would ultimately be up for both of them. But so long as appearances could be kept up, no consideration of sane government should be allowed to stand in their way. It must have amused Denis Thatcher to hear the vulgarity with which his spouse would refer to her illustrious predecessor as 'Winston', as though she had been one of his dearest intimates. A common disease no doubt gave them a relationship of some specialty.

It was true that Winston Churchill was the saviour of his country, and quite possibly of the entire world. And Margaret Thatcher neither then nor later had such claim on the goodwill of the UK electorate. One might argue from an ethical standpoint that while the UK had certainly not owed Churchill a term of office in 1945 since he would not give the country the welfare state it needed, it could be said to owe him a continuation when actually in office for a term for which he had been elected. But Denis Thatcher's steely resolution, which had already won him great financial success, was no more likely to worry about the ethics of a job for his girl than he was about those of his investments in South Africa.

Failure is one of the greatest of all motives for ruthless action in the future, and Denis Thatcher had failed in one particular. His marriage to the first Mrs Margaret Thatcher had collapsed. The fact that he had the genius to see himself portrayed from end to end of the UK as a gin-soaked moron to be a perfect camouflage for his second wife's predilections and his own control of her, is the proof of his readiness to face his own tragedy. He could not control the first Mrs Margaret Thatcher; he was not going to lose control of the second. He kept the press and the public convulsed with laughter at his expense, and thus none of them questioned the fiction that he was terrified of his second wife.

As a result, there was far too much Denis Thatcher gossip for the press to think about the real story; what had happened to the first Mrs Thatcher? It is probable that Denis Thatcher's razor-keen mind found his second wife and her political associates rather stupid people, and the press gave little reason to think any better of them. It was easy to see greed as their basic motivation and philosophy. Denis Thatcher had no objection to greed himself, but he was no more ready to make it his master than alcohol. Certainly steps had to be taken so that the press, drunk or sober, would not fall over the first Mrs Thatcher, but that was easily managed with the characteristic ingenuity that stamped

Denis Thatcher's work. The first Mrs Thatcher's husband was made a lord.

One does not know how wide Denis Thatcher's literary interest may have been, but we may toy with the thought that he had read G.K. Chesterton's Father Brown story, 'The mistake of the machine'. Its location is Chicago, and it turns on an escaped criminal being suspected of having murdered a missing lord, and of having many years beforehand swindled prostitutes, and it turns out that it is the lord who has been arrested, and that it was he who so long ago had swindled the prostitutes. Father Brown mocks the US authorities:

> I think you Americans are too modest. I think you idealise the English aristocracy – even in assuming it to be so aristocratic. You see a good-looking Englishman in evening dress; you know he's in the House of Lords; and you fancy he has a father. You don't allow for our national buoyancy and uplift. Many of our most influential noblemen have not only risen recently but . . .'

Even the famous British political soap acknowledged the House of Lords as a haven for concealed parts in its first instalment of *Yes, Prime Minister*, when the Home Secretary is arrested for driving while intoxicated, and Sir Humphrey remarks that since he was drunk as a lord, after a decent interval 'they' would probably make him one.

It is a pleasure to contrast Denis Thatcher with Henry VIII when it comes to disposal of former wives. It was the perfect disguise. Some utterly unknown person whose wife only receives mention as Mrs John Doe is handed a Barony with nobody the wiser. The delicacy of the thing placed it beyond the imagination of the Murdochs and their minions.

But Denis Thatcher had not wanted to dispose of that wife, until it became irrevocably certain that she had disposed of him. It was kept secret even from his children (he had none by his first wife). Eventually Carol Thatcher, researching a book about her father when her mother was out of the office, found the lady and informed her father who asked was she still the incomparably beautiful creature that she always was? It is our only knowledge of the depth of that wound. It was evidently deeper than any shame his second wife could inflict on him, but he clearly intended to leave no means by which she might be the cause of shame.

In 1951, when they were married, he was 36, she was 25. He naturally assumed that as a Tory from non-landowning origins, she would have been educated by Oxford at least in knowing how to disappear those origins, and when to revive them. Her parents dimmed in memory and acquaintance until dead, after which their devoted memories could be summoned when electorally convenient, such as her father in the Grantham corner grocery could see fashions on their way for certain goods, and know when to discard and when to reinvent before popularity raised the priced. Denis Thatcher had not expected to dance much attendance on his second wife's father – groceries and lay Methodist ministry are unlikely to possess many charms for a businessman whose chief business was to become a millionaire by 50 – but even he seems to have been startled by the infrequency with which his second wife returned to her family ties. It might have startled her peers at Kesteven and Grantham Girls'School somewhat less; she had earned the name 'snobby Roberts' and earned it diligently. He would already have deduced the fluctuations of accent which graduated her progress in Grantham, and the superior finish which marks the true Oxonian. Grantham had left its own deposits. Denis Thatcher's combination of steel and diplomacy would by example and perhaps by precept restrain her natural proficiency as playground bully, and her upward mobility in Tory ranks would require her judicious rations of respect to better-connected if less ruthless superiors. It was only in 10 Downing Street that the Gloriana of Kesteven and Grantham Girls' could come into her own, adding to the refinements of Oxonian and Dionysian education the aroma of a lynch-mob leader haggling in a bankruptcy auction.

The shaping of Margaret Thatcher's career can hardly have been achieved without initial restraints on her habitual indifference to the views of others, at least in the extent that for the time being her husband must have successfully directed her to look as though she was listening. Once she was in power he seems to have made no noteworthy efforts, and she simply bellowed her monologues until the survivors found their lifebuoys. There was, of course, nothing unusual in some of the graces she developed or resumed; yelling in English at the top of a

Tory voice had long been accepted in the brasher circles as a superior alternative to proficiency in European languages.

On the other hand, neither the grocery store nor her husband cared for exhibitions of snobbery when benign plutocracy beckoned, and Margaret Roberts herself had been far too thrilled by Hollywood heroes to share the crustier Conservative disdain for the usurper in world power. Her swooning snoggery in the arms of Hollywood in apotheosis, President Ronald Reagan, turned the largely mythical US-UK special relationship into a Mills & Boon romance. It was graceless, but Denis Thatcher's priorities included no stupid male chauvinist vanities. As a sugar daddy he kept an indulgent Christmas-tree, and Reagan was merely the most exotic present under its branches. As for Nancy Reagan, she had long known how to keep her marital leash extended loose but firm. She was a marital diplomat of Denis Thatcher's kind, and she intended to be President de facto before she was finished. And she was. Sex-crazed fans had to be accommodated as part of the Hollywood to White House progress.

Denis Thatcher must have undertaken some highly skilful mental anatomisation not only of the official Tories, but also of the natural Tories, many of whom might never acknowledge a Tory vote, and yet whose instinctive Tory loyalties could be pressed into secret service. Margaret Thatcher herself was an old fashioned authoritarian. She had no interest in females, competitors at best, potentially questioners of her male chauvinist values in any case, and they seem to have reciprocated her distrust, give or take a few fox hunting dykes. Males, when not objects of transatlantic cultural diplomacy, were called to heel by her in what seems a psychological recognition that the Tory mind at its most basic yearns for the fabled nurse, hard handed if benign to favourites. No doubt scrutiny of her maternal performance would have shown the strength of this, and so too, did the intrusion of key words – we might term them recognition-words – notably 'nanny' and 'nanny state'. 'Nanny state' was supposedly bad, but even the dumbest Tory could read that riddle; nanny state was bad until Nanny ran it. Denis Thatcher was in the best position to diagnose this potential winner, and to groom his Frankenstein nanny appropriately. As fulfilment of sexual fantasy it seems to meet desires of straight and gay Tories alike.

But for all this traditionalism, this ultimately Victorian appeal (the nineteenth century hairbrush was unrivalled for its hard back) coincided with what might seem its converse; Thatcher was a delicious symbol of Tory rebellion. She may never have realised it – she really was not very bright in any intellectually interesting way – but her husband certainly did. The Tory rebel of modern times begins, of course, with Disraeli, and continues with Lord Randolph Churchill, his son Winston, F.E. Smith, the short story-writer H.H. Munro ('Saki'), Evelyn Waugh, and the leading outlet for Waugh's son Auberon, *Private Eye*. Officially, these people might seem anti-Tory, or at least more anti-establishment than Tory, and they might sweep into their immediate circles genuine leftists. Paul Foot was the house leftist in *Private Eye*'s case. But one only has to look at the nauseating snobbery with which *Private Eye* lampooned the unfortunate wife of Harold Wilson, to see the public school brat baring its fangs at the lower-class occupants of centres of power from which civilisation should exclude them. And it worked. They subverted respect for Wilson (aided by his own solipsism) and kept their mushrooming readers in sniggers at the supposed genteelisms of his wife. The readers felt the better at knowing their own cultural superiority to the lady of 10 Downing Street despite their sniggers showing they were cads cheering on bounders. Mary Wilson herself showed matchless dignity and patience throughout. But what would the brat-pack do for a successor?

They detested Edward Heath, whose accent they painstakingly exhibited as contrived and pretentious. They resented his flaunted cultural interests such as music, and his hearty sportsmanship notably sailing. Since their humour consisted chiefly in eternally repeating the same supposed witticisms, Heath's boat became Morning Cleoud. They told themselves that Heath was the poor booby whom Waugh's Basil Seal or Saki's Clovis would perpetually puncture; more secretly, they told themselves Heath deserved it, being a scholarship boy. It may have been that they suspected him of homosexuality. In order to prove it was run by adults, *Private Eye* distinguished itself by its homophobia, thus cutting loose from the dear old schooldays.

To the shrewd businessman, *Private Eye* could have its uses, but to enlist such a wayward beast, good bait might be necessary. The bait Denis Thatcher offered was himself. The means would have to be carefully chosen. The obvious channel was someone in the political higher echelons, but not a power-wielder, if occasionally a power broker. It would need to be someone who knew journalism, and who had won respect in the past as a secret informant.

How much of Margaret Thatcher's career would have happened if Denis Thatcher had not known Bill Deedes? Not very much, it may be. Deedes had precisely what she would never have: a sense of humour, sometimes wickedly irresponsible; a comfortable awareness of his own good taste, without wasting its time on deployment when it would mean nothing; a pleasure in being able to run his hands over the instruments of government without the slightest necessity to do more than advise on the bases of their capability; an enjoyment of young company when its flattery was not too crass; a certain charm in deflating politicians with relatively little concern about their principles, if any; a genuine interest in news. It had made him an ideal Minister without portfolio to Macmillan, unlike most of the Cabinet at one time or another (Thorneycroft, Sandys, Heathcoat Amory, Julian Amery, Hailsham, Heath, Selwyn Lloyd, Lennox-Boyd, Madling, Brooke, MacLeod, Christopher Soames, Butler, Hill, Home) mentioned by nobody as a possible successor, especially not mentioned by himself. Macmillan probably trusted him far enough without going overboard. He was witty enough to make others feel how they shone in his company.

How Denis Thatcher and he might come to like one another is easy; how they came to trust one another will probably never be known. And he probably had several good reasons, aesthetic, personal, or even possibly political, to see a number of promising figures of the next generation go under the hooves of the rising Margaret Thatcher. He was by now faintly editing the *Daily Telegraph*, an institution of far more lighthearted frivolity in those days than its largely humourless readership would have imagined. (At one point its leading intellectual Right-wing theoretician, the brilliant, blind, T.E. (Peter) Utley handed over his column to a dissident Irish Trotskyite whose place in his underground publication he took for a month, nobody apparently noticing any conscious ideological change.) Deedes fitted in admirably with the real concern of the paper, which was hard news if it could get it, with enough Right-wing lunacy to give customers their fix. And

Deedes naturally stayed on excellent if covert terms with the wicked revolutionaries of *Private Eye*. He may even have contributed a few anonymous rude remarks on himself to its pages – such things would have given *Private Eye* a feeling of integrity.

Did Deedes godfather the 'Dear Bill' letters signed 'Denis' which so enlivened the Thatcher administration and raised *Private Eye* from its usual condition of infant *Punch* and recycled underground America? Or did Denis Thatcher himself face its icons and morons in one unmentionable interview? Certainly they must have had iron guarantees that what they were getting would never be double-crossed into a ruinous libel action, for the depiction of Denis Thatcher himself seemed merciless in its ridicule. The treatment of Mary Wilson was chivalrous in comparison. There was nothing particularly libellous about their treatment of Margaret Thatcher, merely the reiteration of her bullying, Nannying, insensitive, inconsiderate, ignorant, ham-handed, Xenophobic brutality, the very qualities for which she wished to be known and on which her reputation for statesmanship depended.

Moreover practising politicians get little latitude from the courts in claims of libel. But a blameless consort pointedly outside politics was another matter, and the damages awarded for the perpetual implication of Denis Thatcher's hopeless alcoholism did not bear contemplation. The cheap nastiness about Mary Wilson had been despicable but not actionable; this lay naked to its enemies, had Denis Thatcher ever chosen to recoup. But *Private Eye* kept the series on an escalator of outrageousness with evident conviction of invulnerability. The thing even made a bad West End farce, *Anyone for Denis?* But the Thatchers preserved miens of utter indifference. Margaret Thatcher even managed to deliver lines in character such as hymning the glens of Scotland on an unwanted visit, adding that Denis would particularly enjoy Glen Grant, Glen Morangie and Glenfiddich. She had learned her lesson, knew when to deliver it, and when to keep silent. As a disciplinarian Denis Thatcher was effective without the slightest desire for ostentation; she could not rule without whip-cracking and ultimately paid the penalty.

So far as we can gather, Denis Thatcher attached little importance to government, provided it followed his own small agenda. On South Africa, he expected his wife to support the existing regime as long as it did not prove electoral suicide and she would repeat the lessons he had taught her with the scornful complacency of recent learning. Told that support for the Zulus and their supposed pretensions was a good means of delaying general reform, she would say 'Chief Bu-ta-la-zay' with all the smugness of a successful raider on the answers at the back of the book. Why the Chief should be a devastating answer to her opponents she probably never knew; beyond the usual logic of the corner grocery store; one customer had liked the product under adverse criticism and therefore it must be maintained so long as it was economically rewarding to her shop. She had the wit to recognise that this made her allies among those favouring apartheid, mostly secretly, and she was given credit for courageous rearguard action when she was simply doing what her husband told her.

On the other hand, he would never have encouraged her in too close a cultivation of archaic activists. In general, he let her drift with her animal reactions. On Ireland, for instance, she seems to have been governed entirely by irritation at Garret Fitzgerald's hopeless attempts to teach her economics. Denis Thatcher's care in limiting instruction to the specific necessities fostered her impatience against any surplus intake of knowledge, and Fitzgerald's vocational desire to relieve her appalling ignorance simply won her detestation. She repudiated an agreed statement on the talks they had just been having within the time it took to walk from talking room to briefing-space, and substituted (for their carefully worded statement) common ground yells of 'OUT! OUT! OUT!', tying them into proposals never made to her. She enjoyed that.

Demonstrators yelling it at her made her ache to follow back with louder yells, as she had learned in the Grantham playground, and it was even more satisfactory to scream it at an unpopular teacher. She probably never encountered a politician who was so obviously a teacher as she met in Fitzgerald, and the chance of repudiating and humiliating him would not be missed. That it would throw Irish political success nearer to Haughey and his Anglophobic harps never troubled her for an instant. She knew no doubt that Haughey saw his political future resting on his Anglophobia, but that kind of perpetual ill-feeling was the natural Anglo-Irish relationship to her, and if one had to have Irish it was better for them to be obvious crooks.

The Irish, with their unscrupulous diplomacy, were formidable enemies to make. Margaret Thatcher may never have grasped how the disgust with which her bellowings were received by the European powers would make fortunes for Ireland. She isolated her country apart from the Hollywood hero, and even he would not maintain her in her imperial whackery-to-Paddy which she tarted up as a bogus heirloom. The shock must have been a nasty one, for she could normally rely on Reagan to grant her co-dominion of an Axis of Ignorance, being as limited in intelligence and information as she was herself. But Reagan, however ignorant, was a professional; and as acting was the profession in question, he knew all about taking advice from all the appropriate parties before the next coupling of the stars, viz. Himself and the American people. Irish-Catholic American in paternity, he also knew that his psychologically self-absorbed but politically self-advantageous ethnic group had many like himself, climbing into Republicanism as symbol of greater socio-economic success and potentially elite status. Unfortunately not all of them could put the seal on their new Republicanism by becoming Governor of California and President of the United States, and anything that looked like Republican contempt for Irish-Catholic identity would be punished, signally and rapidly. Reagan had no intention of putting that vote at risk, and saw Fitzgerald making ecumenical gestures suitable and sincere (whatever the last word meant for Reagan – it's a consolation prize for actors).

Denis Thatcher would have known better; in becoming a millionaire it is advantageous to keep in with the Murphys and O'Reillys nowadays, especially the O'Reillys. But he seems to have restricted his interventions in her policies to his own interests, particularly South Africa. Otherwise her career was the equivalent of serial Presidency of the local Women's Institute. As a wise husband, Denis Thatcher turned up where he was supposed to turn up, smiled when he was supposed to smile, applauded where he was supposed to applaud, drank tea when required, and gave himself the slightest touch of amiable foolishness to illustrate the *Private Eye* version of the public mind. If anyone got in his way, they felt a paralysing grip of their muscles, a quick shift of their persons, and still smiling, Denis Thatcher strode forward two purposeful footsteps behind his lady.

If she basked in her favourite film's star's beams, that suited Denis. If her favourite film-star made her reverse her 'OUT! OUT! OUT!' to Garret Fitzgerald and back the Anglo-Irish Agreement, that was too bad, but Denis Thatcher did not make his money by quarrelling with bigger money and thought his wife was wise to be foolish about Reagan. The fact that she aspired to Tory apotheosis by mouthing rhetoric of pre-1914 vintage unfortunately impressed Ulster Unionists with her sincerity, thus making the bitterness of their exclusion from the Anglo-Irish Agreement all the greater, but however archaic and aspirant her political vocabulary, Margaret Thatcher had risen to power over the corpses of older Toryisms. As it happened, both forms of Ulster Unionism would survive her as an effective political force.

Presumably Denis Thatcher found his wife's supercession of her original accent no more alarming than her rejuvenescence of face, hair, etc. She was the crudest premier of the twentieth century, but she was also the most cosmetic. The desired effect was certainly intended to make her look 10 to 20 years younger, and thus put her husband in the category of a father, but Ronald Reagan (whose raven locks were four years older than Denis Thatcher) could embrace his special relationship with all the vigour required in a substitute John Wayne. Nancy Reagan was only two years older than Margaret Thatcher, and she didn't look 60-ish either. Tories use clichés as oxygen, but in these days one heard few references to mutton sold as lamb, and fewer to spring chickens. One of the key points of *Private Eye*'s attack on Michael Foot was that he was prepared to look the age he was.

Yet Margaret Thatcher had a modicum of sincerity. Her's was a gospel of greed, and she never disguised it. She began her notoriety by snatching free milk from schoolchildren, an activity for which her Grantham days had no doubt qualified her; the corner shop gave no freebies, the school bully snatches where she could get away with it, 'Snobby Roberts' had no use for those she ranked as her inferiors. Her patriotism was a noisy creed demanding defence of all the loot accumulated by 'us' to date. She prided herself on her Oxford degree in Chemistry with an air of demanding the delivery of her Nobel Prize, but intellectually she can hardly rank above Addington, stopgap Prime Minister from 1801 to 1804, when Pitt was out of office on a point of principle (Catholic Emancipation). The jingle of the day ran:

Pitt is to Addington
As London is to Paddington.

And she would not have resigned office on a point of principle, but she would have been good for Addington's later achievements as Home Secretary, like the Peterloo massacre.

She may cause a problem to the Heavenly powers in due course. She explained that she thought of Heaven as a place where one would hold a few shares in British Telecom. It looks as if Heaven may be unfit for Thatcherian use. On the other hand, theology like that might qualify her for the special charity reserved for the village idiot. Those who choose to be governed by the village idiot may require even greater charity, but that never included a majority of the voters in the UK. As for Denis Thatcher, we may indict him for ruthless self-protection at the public's expense, but at least we owe it to him that his encouragement of his own self-mockery made it easier to endure what he had saddled and bridled us with.   ❐

TOM NAIRN

I. THE ENCHANTED NAT

GARLIC, VINEGAR AND THE TASTE OF TOM NAIRN

> I for one am enough of a nationalist, and have enough faith in the students and young workers of Glasgow and Edinburgh, to believe that these forces are also present in them. I will not admit that the great dreams of May 1968 are foreign to us, that the great words on the Sorbonne walls would not be at home on the walls of Aberdeen or St Andrews, or that Linwood and Dundee could not be Flins and Nantes. Nor will I admit that, faced with a choice between the Mouvement du 22 mars and Mrs Ewing, we owe it to 'Scotland' to choose the latter.
>
> Tom Nairn, *Three Dreams of Scottish Nationalism*, 1968

WHETHER to believe that whole '68 thang to be a sideshow or a landmark is entirely optional but the reader must have spotted the merchandising. It is interesting how the glamorous student protests in London and Paris take centre stage, the confrontations of Chicago and Berlin become text book fodder, and the desperate struggles of Prague and Belfast barely feature. The Glasgow celebrations of the fortieth anniversary of the fabled 1968 protests and the emergence of a 'new left' included the Glasgow Film Theatre's '*Mai '68*' season, a special Radical Independent Book Fair in Govan, and a stop-off on a special international speaking tour by various celebrity '68ers. Elsewhere *Prospect* and the *New Statesman* released '68 themed issues commemorating 'the year that changed the world'. '68er Action Figures, a Board Game and 'Placard', a third person shoot-em-up for the Playstation 3 would not have seemed too extreme.

Is this response by the market an acknowledgement of the significance of the event, or is it tied into the relative stature of those identified as the '68ers' such as Tariq Ali or Christopher Hitchens? Little was said of arch-militants such as Guy Debord, author of *Society of the Spectacle*, or (to be less elitist and more focused on what really mattered), the countless demonstrators and ordinary workers who put life and livelihood on the line. These celeb boffins mostly indulged in nostalgic anecdotes over how 'the band' got together. But there was another, important sort of nostalgia at work here too, one embraced by younger, post-68 generations who have read the books and rediscovered the music, identifying it with a time when revolutionary change was breaking free of the big ideological frameworks and could actually be believed in.

Ultimately, the repacked '68 legacy amounted to a social spectacle of its own, where the feted ringleaders of the popular imagination, pin-ups of a massive civil disturbance became the stuff of souvenir supplements, of 'our' 'radical heritage' or, as in the case of Ali, authors of rock-star-style reminisces in the *Sydney Morning Herald* (replete with photograph of the young, black-mouser'd firebrand locking elbows with the young, willowy Vanessa Redgrave). Debord would surely have abhorred.

Scotland had a long 1968 that arguably culminated in the nationalist victories of the 1974 election and was felt in aftershock right up to the 1979 referendum. The part played by Tom Nairn in this ferment is (in hindsight) surprising. He co-authored an account of the '68 events with Angelo Quatrocchi and in that same year, published a hostile analysis of the SNP's first flush of election victory in 'The Three Dreams of Scottish Nationalism', initially in The *New Left Review*. Madame Ecosse (a.k.a. Winnie Ewing) failed to impress him at the time, but in due course his mind changed in parallel with the thesis of British decline he developed with Perry Anderson. From this he would emerge as on the one hand, the scourge of pseudo tradition and 'heritage' as outlined in *The Enchanted Glass* (something all the left could cheer about) and on the other a fierce and withering critic of old style socialist internationalism as shown in *The Left in Europe* and *Faces of Nationalism* (cue sectarian fragmentation . . .). Mixing these two *formulae* presented a seemingly straightforward solution, one he has spent the best part of his career presenting to anyone who would listen; independence for Scotland, leading ultimately, to the dismantling of the British state and rescuing the left from the 'big gun' school of history.

As such hard and unpopular paths have been Nairn's by choice, moving along them at a skip rather than a trudge, you might expect this 68er would disdain the 'Mick n' Keef' anecdotes, jab furiously at the misty eye rather than wipe it. But Nairn has become somewhat respectable, having made his own progress into elder-statesmanship within Scottish nationalist circles, and it is this trajectory we have documented here. This litany of notes, memoirs and confessions date from before he received such devolved state sanction, but in many respects explain why he should have become so integral.

They include *The Left and Europe* (1973), *The Break up of Britain* (1979), *The Enchanted Glass* (1988), *The Modern Janus* (1990), *After Britain* (2000) and *Pariah* (2002), followed by an essay from Owen Dudley Edwards, an oft-time collaborator and at times, fellow accused (see the *MacDunciad*). Edwards gives a thoughtful and substantial account of Nairn's evolution in print and person, reflecting on Nairn's most recent essay, published by the Institute of Welsh Affairs in *Gordon Brown – Bard of Britishness* (ed by Tom Nairn, 2006). Short but timely, it is an interesting reiteration of Nairn's views which are then interrogated by those of a different Parish, guest contributors culled from (Welsh) politics, English universities and old acquaintances from the Scottish intelligentsia (David Gow of the *Red Paper* and Neal Ascherson each make an appearance). These contributors pay their respects to the preacher, but it is hard to miss the occasional scrape of knives over whetstones. Labour's Leighton Andrews fair waggles the chib:

> Reading Nairn today is like eating lettuce doused in vinegar: void of nutritional value, and indigestible, at the end all that remains is the acid.

With the amiable, entertaining malice at which Tories excel (to the envy of their left-wing adversaries) David Melding declines to comment on the 'personal antipathy Professor Nairn feels towards Mr Brown', leaving the room as the fists start to fly. Melding also enjoys 'the rich, garlicky vituperation with which . . . [Nairn] . . . dresses his prose' and with an additional rabbit-food punch, wonders if Nairn is a Burke parodist:

> . . . like Burke [Nairn] makes some prescient observations, even though he fails to convert them to sound judgements.

Leave it, in these topsy-turvy times, to a Tory to accuse a Marxist theorist of being a closet reactionary – and an impotent one at that. But what should most interest the serious Nairnologist picking up this book is the drafting in of multiculturalism to replace internationalism as the default objection to Scottish or Welsh independence. Nairn had oft-noted that internationalism was the last refuge of the eternally disappointed leftist, some distant wider revolution being logically, the only reservoir of hope and ideological purity. This view was resurrected somewhat anachronistically in the second *Red Paper on Scotland* (ed. Vince Mills, 2005).

But in the IWA book there are signs of arguments evolving. Now that the notion of 'the workers' has changed its meaning and inter-community harmony and minority rights have superseded for many at least, the redistribution of wealth as the quantum of social justice, multiculturalism has created a new form of unionist argument along the principles of some kind of convergent evolution, here espoused by Andrews and in the following example, sociologist Charlotte Williams:

> His construction of Welshness/Scottishness implicitly relies on a retreat at least to the organising principle of a cultural homogeneity, albeit in a new configuration.

And:

> If renationalisation – Welsh or Scottish-Style – is Nairn's answer then it is an inadequate one in the face of contemporary realities. This is not a radical agenda at all. It is not for example an appeal to the broad-based equality strategy of socialism or feminism. It is not a call to revolution or a call for a sophisticated anti-race philosophy but to a reawakening of the clans . . . White Welshness and white Scottishness, for want of better terms, with all its ethnically exclusive

referents all too readily form a powerful allegiance with all things British when it comes to managing the alien wedge . . .

. . . Breaking Britain up into its constituent pieces may do no more than replicate the problem [of excluding or ignoring certain identities] as we spin off in search of an all-embracing Welshness or Scottishness without considering the new and novel ways in which identities converge, coalesce and emerge.

The notion of Britain is thus protected by a degree of cynicism over the ability of corporate identities such as the Scots, Welsh or English to deal with their own internal complexity, which may be fudged by Edinburgh as easily as in London . . . so best stick with being Brits.

Indeed a revealing and exemplary insight into the real blood and guts grounding of these defenders of the union faith was gained later, from one of the gang, Vernon Bogdanor, when in a 2009 BBC TV programme discussing Scottish Independence the Oxford academic declared that 'we fought for 35 years to say the Irish didn't mean it when they said they wanted independence', and 'it was a tragedy for Ireland she could no longer send MP's to Westminster'.

Williams surely ignores (as does Bogdanor) Scotland's long tradition as a *civic* identity and furthermore, makes no comment on whether 'managing the alien wedge' is somehow better and more sensitive within a British context, or if a Welsh or Scottish context would be somehow worse, especially if the latter were using Britishness as a prop for their chauvinism. What is important here is to understand how Nairn's opponents can change their shape, face and language at will, while he must remain adamantly, stubbornly, sometimes maddeningly fixed on his great theme.

That being the case is there any other Scottish theorist who could attract such strong reactions, even if these sum up his contribution as so much bad breath and heartburn? But so it goes with Nairn – as Owen Dudley Edwards's epilude to this section shows, he has survived far worse maulings. For this is a writer who does not just play in the domestic leagues; international recognition was just one of many distinctions that marked Gramsci's interpreter out from the influential group of Scottish public intellectuals who laid the groundwork for home rule in the 80s and 90s. David McCrone, Alice Brown, Arthur Midwinter, Henry Drucker, Lindsay Paterson and James Kellas were social scientists, organisers and analysts of data, who marshalled facts and labelled trends to prove that something called Scotland existed, and that this existence somehow mattered beyond the wish-fulfilment of a few Tartan chauvinists. Nairn was on the other hand, a polyglot philosopher who formulated the Nairn-Anderson thesis and argued for Scotland's relevance as a rational reversal of uneven socio-economic development. Bolstered by what Bogdanor in *Bard of Britishness* describes as a faith that 'the people are Ironsides but their leaders are flunkeys'. Scotland mattered because it was one of the best examples of where we were headed; that the United Kingdom was a 'pseudo-synthesis' that throttled democratic progress and confronting this truth with rational mind made the case all the stronger. His gift for phrasing, shibboleths and scornful semi-satirical conceptualisations (Ukania being the most memorable) also set him in a different literary class, an academic whose truths were based as much on his Burkean under-standing and manipulation of language as they were on the accumulation of knowledge.

Nairn's first forays into his great theme, *The Left and Europe* and *The Break up of Britain*, enraged radicals and conservatives of every political stripe. They still do. Bad enough that they pricked many cherished bubbles of self-delusion and mythology, the author's (garlicky) humour and intellectual agility having established him as a distinctive prose stylist. He also, through his appreciation of Gramsci and the notion of 'hegemony', injected a powerful dose of continental thinking into the bread and butter, empirical tradition of British political thought. And it may have been this, as much as his desire to dismantle the central state (a logical conclusion of his analysis of British hegemony) that was so shocking. As Melding puts it (cheerfully stealing from elsewhere, while wearing his own assumptions proudly on his sleeve): 'We Brits don't like to see clever ideas wandering around unchaperoned by experience.'

Bogdanor likewise notes that: 'Nairn is not very interested in empirical explanations – for they would endanger the sweep of his rhetoric.' He further notes:

In the old days of the New Left, many of its adherents used to dismiss a respect for the empirical as 'positivism', mere fact grubbing, unworthy of attention from serious thinkers. This made it easier for them to present their own fantasies as securely grounded. It was a form of wish fulfilment that could not survive cold contact with reality. Sadly Tom Nairn stands four square in this tradition.

And he also has the bad taste to wield theories in open debate and suggest some of them might actually be applied to do more than line stomachs and protect house prices (as he remarks in the *Bard of Britishness* essay, 'those things deemed "the real stuff" of politics'). The Gramscian strain is what allows him to make a convincing case in books such as *The Enchanted Glass* that constitutions and 'traditions' have their own ideological content – and thus, agenda. Without so much as a by-your-leave Nairn has (to an extent) mainstreamed a 'European' current into political thought on the archipelago. If you doubt it, then simply pick up *Bard of Britishness* and count how many of the fellow contributors-cum-disputants use the word 'hegemony' to contradict him.

His subsequent books accordingly won Nairn widespread recognition, even grudging admiration as one of the four leading experts on nationalism alongside Benedict Anderson, Anthony Smith and Nairn's de facto mentor Ernst Gellner. His status as a 'professional outsider' and outspoken critic of the political mainstream was assured and gave him a strange security from which he could launch successive strikes against the British establishment and the Scottish politicians who supported it. Contrast this with the fortunes of Gordon Brown, embossed within the British Labour establishment (whatever that is) and you will struggle to find, at this present time, any starker. The grinding power struggle over Number 10 seemed to leave the flamboyant student rector broken and bewildered, while as First Minister, Alex Salmond gleefully tugged at every rein (or reign . . .) he could grasp. The sense that the intensive debate over Scotland's future initiated by the original *Red Paper* has reached a climactic point is hard to avoid. If this sense can be trusted, then the ramifications extend far beyond Sark and Tweed.

In the first instance, there is the potential of break-up, initiated not by disgruntled Scots but black-affronted English. Watching the

'Broonites' at work in London, all cliquish and clannish and ultra-defensive, it was tempting to compare them to Jamie Saxt's gang of Scottish Lords who followed their king over the border in 1603, to grab as much graft as could be grabbed. Once enthroned the wise fool and his favourites ran England with the same hunch-shouldered cunning and jealousy they had exercised in Scotland – to devastating effect. But England was different; their failure to take account of this nearly derailed the impending shotgun wedding, yet once enforced, began the slow push towards closer union. Will the Broonite covenant now have the *opposite* effect and lay the ground for divorce?

Such ahistorical speculation is fun, but limiting. What can be said is that while Scots tend to blame England for its insensitivity to Scottish sensibilities, traditions and lifeways, the prevailing assumption that a Scottish carrot, stick and cabal methodology suited England just as well is one of the most pernicious and dangerous myths underpinning Unionist ideology, and is also an equally dangerous and pernicious practice deployed by those keen to keep the family together. Nevertheless, Brown appointed from beyond his natural clique – Alistair Darling, far from being a traditional Broonite, was of a very different cut (grandson of a Tory MP for Edinburgh South), while Douglas Alexander was still in short trousers when Brown forged his most significant political alliances in the Scottish Labour Party. But to an English audience – and an English establishment – it *seemed* like an enclave, a cabal of graspin' Jocks as characterised in *Private Eye's Broons* parody – and the British system of government and politics is heavily reliant on 'seeming'. In practice the Brown sulk, casting a pall then expecting the minnows to come a-swimming – clearly didn't work in English waters.

It pays to bear such matters in mind when considering Nairn's central thesis; that Scotland can and should act as a laboratory for a new, forward-facing nationalism that will dismantle the phoneyness of Britain's arrested revolution and presumably, provide a model for other polities similarly hobbled by crafty elites. Is it not also interesting to note the extent to which this '68er has taken on a talismanic significance for a currently ascendant political faction (though not, mercifully, the neo-con hawks perched on Thatcher-fantasist Hitchen's shoulders)? In March 2008 First Minister Alex Salmond bounced onto a podium in Edinburgh's Surgeons' Hall to introduce Nairn as the final speaker in the Lothian Lecture Series. Leader of what Edwards has called an established anti-establishment, Salmond milked the symbolism and kudos by association, stating that if he wasn't allowed to give the lecture himself, then the professional outsider would be the next best thing. A joke, but it masked a deeper solemnity in that moment; nothing less than the anointment of Nairn as the Pythagoras of Scottish Nationalism, the man who described it, measured it, then found cosmic significance in the numbers.

Take the politics of one moment as exemplary: There was a week in May 2008 when the Establishment – or should we say, the Established Establishment – seemed to be breaking up quicker than Brown in his wildest post-*Politics of Nationalism and Devolution* nightmares could ever imagine. Brown was PM, his lieutenantess Wendy Alexander was leader of Labour in Holyrood, and the question was whether Scotland should have a referendum on independence. Irn Broon gave a public no, nay no never to such a referendum: Alexander popped up to say perkily, 'bring it on', let's have it now, and she added, bafflingly, that she had Brown's backing. Meanwhile Salmond, as sly fat fox and First Minister, said 'aye, we'll have a referendum, but in a wee while, and when I'm feeling ready.' With Brown and Wendy Alexander's respective TV appearances and at questions in Westminster and Holyrood that week the Establishment was disintegrating before our very eyes – although not perhaps as quickly as Nairn would wish.

Doubtless by the time you read this the constitutional question will already have shifted again quite some. But at that moment what we had – not to put a fine point on it at all – was the unedifying spectacle of an Establishment which couldn't find North-South consensus on whether to force now a *Wendyrendum* (if it sounded speedy, bouncy and bendy, it's because it was), and an anti-establishment flying by the leisurely seat of its pants and insisting on the slow-working bacterium of a *Salmondendum*.

The point being that referenda themselves were unthinkable in the United Kingdom of forty years ago, and unconstitutional from the point of Parliamentary Sovereignty. They were even declared undemocratic by Keith Joseph when Labour announced their EEC (and Britain's first) referendum in 1975. (Such democrats of the parliamentary dictatorship feather like Joseph always have, of course, the alibi of the 'hanging' question ready to frighten the liberal horses from galloping too readily out into the country.) But now we bandy referenda with the dogs in the street, we needn't even stretch our tongues to articulation of the full name, we whistle on a plebiscite, we call it by its pet, its diminutive, its nickname: referendums, that is to say, are become the meat and drink of quotidian plebs' politics. And no-one is more vindicated in this crucial turn of the political screw than Tribune Thomas himself. We can hardly assert that he actually led the liberal horse to a public watering, but the fact is that the only topics on which Her Majesty's Government have ever taken such a thoroughly public sounding are Europe and the nations' fates. And are these not the two very badly tied-up ends from which, as Nairn has always said since the beginning with *Left Against Europe* and *Break-Up of Britain*, the ragged Constitution of the late seventeenth and early eighteenth centuries would unravel? ❑

THE LEFT AGAINST EUROPE
TOM NAIRN (1973)

Nairn's first full-length publication was an analysis of the failure of the left in the UK to 'win' the debate about Britain's entry to the then EEC (or, Common Market) in 1971. The book was published in 1973 as a Pelican but the text had first appeared as an extended article in *New Left Review* in 1972. As such the analysis had the benefit of hindsight and came out only once the debate appeared to have already finished, and the early 1970s broad left – who had more or less weighed in unanimously behind the Labour Party (and CPGB) against membership – had already 'lost' as Britain had been taken into the EEC by Edward Heath's Tory Party.

Nonetheless when in 1975 the Labour Party back in power got to stoke up the debate again and run a referendum over Britain's membership, Nairn's book may have been one of the most important influences in softening the left's antipathy to all things European. For those of us who were either not born or were too young to remember the issues at stake, Nairn's deft separating out of the sheep from the goats of pre-Thatcher British leftist politics answers a lot of questions for our understanding of just where we are at today, and how we got here.

Nairn adequately details how not only were the left in his opinion, on the 'wrong' side of the debate, but the 'debate' itself never really happened. He outlines the parameters of the lack of real debate. In the first place any questioning

of the 'no' campaign was perceived as threatening the 'unity at all costs' of the left front, and as being 'uncomradely' (and it is surely the cosy, folksy ring to us of this last word, shorn now of all its frightful Stalinist connotations, that shows us just how much British politics have changed in four decades). Nairn goes further then, and asks whether any real national 'debate' can ever truly be staged through party political channels alone? He points to the pre-1914 crisis in British imperialism for example, and reminds us that the 'debate' then was carried on by strikes, mobs, suffragettes, artists and music hall songs, as well as by editorialists and parliamentarians:

> They propelled society forward willy-nilly, and forced people to think new thoughts and act originally.

Finally, one other major structural factor that prejudiced against the possibility of honest, full and open debate, was Marxism's complex relationship to, and indeed, its 'blind spot' of, nationalism. The role of nationalism in Nairn's discussion here is not unrelated to the concerns of his later books cited below, but is more understated. Nationalism here, that is to say, is not so much the cure, but part of the problem, or at any rate, one of the keys to understanding the problem. In this sense, for Nairn, the important power blocks in the European 'debate' can be deconstructed in terms of the way in which they represent respectively 'nation' and 'class'.

The Left against Europe • Tom Nairn

The main promoters of EEC entry, the London 'City', the most successful financial sector in global capitalism, had according to Nairn, been effectively the 'chief broker' to the most successful capitalist economy, the USA, since the British Empire had started to crumble. The City, offshore wheelers and dealers, clearly do not act on behalf of the nation, but of capital and the class that owns it. And as the USA by the early 70s had long been entangled in Vietnam, the City needed new expanding markets (eg. EEC) freed up for its operations.

The Tory Party, while claiming at large to operate on behalf of the whole nation – one nation Toryism, and all that – in fact, according to Nairn, really only represents the interests of the capital-owning classes, and thus at this stage were largely pro-EEC (apart from a Powellite fringe). This analysis of the Tories' real interests may have had some revelatory power for the politically slow in the early 70s, but since the Thatcher years surely only the extremely complacent and the insane could still be in any doubt over it.

Nairn's dissection of the Labour Party's respective relationships to nation and class is the real object of this study, and as such they will not suffer summation in such a small review. Nonetheless, there are certain features whose importance ought not to go unstressed. At the most basic level, Labour, even by its very name, represents itself as operating in the interests of class. In effect however, through the various periods of Labour governments, and also in this phoney EEC debate, it is demonstrated that the Labour Party has to lean heavily on its resources as a national voice in order to establish some sort of wider credibility in its relationship with the state:

> Labour is, to employ one of its own historic programme-words in a different sense, the *nationalisation* of class.

The left's evidently incoherent attack on Europe thus seemed at once to be based on the notion of protecting 'national sovereignty', and a vague preference to operate 'internationally' rather than as a member of a closed economic gentlemen's club; and bizarrely, on the idea that the continental countries were both more nationalistic and capitalist than Great Britain (although as Nairn points out, no such charge was made against the internationalist USA).

The arguments in this book lay out a British political landscape which from the twenty first century vantage point we can't help but feel is separated from us by a Hadrian's Wall (or Offa's Dyke) of Thatcherism. Events have outmanoeuvred much of the debate. That's not to say however that it is in any way irrelevant; and oddly, there turn out to be very few clangers amongst Nairn's bold assertions and predictions from yesteryear – although writing 'the now-outmoded currency-crankery of Milton Friedman's Chicago School' in 1972 does seem a bit previous – not to say, hubristic – now. Ultimately this work also allows us to understand much about the background to the post-1997 governments – how Tony Blair became leader, how he managed to drop Clause IV, and how the 'betrayal' of class by Labour leaders is 'a structural fact and not a moral problem'. It's a text that is of vital importance to political historians, and gives insight into a way of life that, for Nairn, just keeps on collapsing . . .

The Left against Europe • Tom Nairn

The Break-Up of Britain
Tom Nairn (1981)

Until the mid 1990s it was still possible in schools to study Scottish politics and government as part of Certificate of Sixth Year Studies Modern Studies, so it was strangely appropriate that CSYS was a victim of the British establishment. The qualification allowed Scottish sixth year pupils to study a single area in considerable depth at university level, and was superior to A-Level and more advanced than Higher. Nevertheless, English universities refused to recognise it. Scottish institutions refused to see beyond the shorthand formula that was 4+ Highers and followed suit. It's algebra out of whack, the qualification failed to gain any credibility.

The existence of a different way of doing things in Scotland (such as CSYS) and the inability of the British establishment to recognise these heterodoxies were an abiding theme of the many studies that began to appear in the late 1970s and throughout the Thatcher and Major eras. Henry Drucker, Lindsay Paterson, Christopher Harvie, James Kellas, David McCrone, Arthur Midwinter and Alice Brown all appeared in the CSYS Modern Studies syllabus, trailblazing academics whose chosen theme made them maverick, and whose scrupulous study effectively wrote a devolved Scotland into existence. They did so by turning the national question on its head to suggest home rule was merely bringing a 'phantom' polity within the unitary British system into the light of day. Influenced by the Prague school of social scientists under Ernst Gellner, they conceived of nationalism in very different terms to the traditional 'big guns' school of social studies as typified by A.J.P. Taylor.

The infusion of the Prague school may have had a lot to do with the frequently émigré Nairn, the Pythagoras whose algebra was just as out of whack as CSYS. Whereas the likes of Kellas were solid empirical technicians able to parse the mechanics of non-statehood, Tom Nairn was soaked in European thought (his first published work was a study of '1968') and engaged with the issue through theory, consciousness and existential satisfaction. *The Break-Up of Britain* is his seminal work and is as much a hex as a title, maybe even an order or a signal to some hidden demolitionist. It is also, ironically, the bridge between Nairn's summation of socialist thought on and in relation to the continent, and his emergence as the most internationally recognised of Scotland's nationalist, devolutionist or post-nationalist academics.

At the risk of being reductionist, there are three essential chapters in this book. The first, entitled 'The Twilight of the British State' persuades us that the British political system is in state of terminal decline due to profound inconsistencies, structural weaknesses and the vested interests of its gentry-bourgeoisie. There then follows a series of case studies of nationalisms within the constituents of the United Kingdom before the crucial theoretical meat of 'The Modern Janus', and a Postscript added in 1981. A sort of reversed – or exploded – sandwich, if you will.

Nairn wrote about break-up in the late 1970s, when nationalism was for many equated with atavism and irrationality, and the majority of Nairn's Marxist colleagues believed it to be at best, an irrelevance. Nairn turns this around to argue that nationalism has been a widespread response to modern development with as rational a basis as any other social and political movement. Furthermore, there is a common underlying pattern to any nationalism you care to study, namely the uneven development of capitalism and industrialisation since the eighteenth century. Development was not easily exportable; it tended to be clustered in particular countries that had the civil, political and social mechanisms to sustain it and spread the benefits – what monetarists describe as trickle down.

But in transposing this model elsewhere, to countries within the great colonial empire or the less developed European nations created and nurtured nationalism, Nairn identifies, but avoids the problem of mistranslation that stymied Turnbull and Beveridge in *The Eclipse of Scottish Culture* (see next section). What Nairn describes as 'peripheric elites' (a term that can include Scotland or Catalonia, in a way 'postcolonial' cannot) could be co-opted into the imperial capitalist system, but were, as time wore on, faced with large sections of their own population

who saw such a system as a hog roast to which they are not invited – and which, in any case, carved up too rich a meat for local palates. The solution Nairn posits, was to seek out a political ideology that could appeal across class divides and reassure local interests. This can be understood in two ways – as *national*ism – that part of the ideology based on the particularities of a country, a culture, a region – and national*ism*, a widespread phenomenon manifest in many different sites and situations linked by these commonly identified features – all of which Nairn finds in distorted form, within the apparatus of the British state.

It is, by Nairn's own admission, a commonsensical analysis that seems perfectly rational within the neo-Marxist framework he constructs (although if you scratch the surface of his British empiricism, you see a lot of Gramsci marbled through the mix), and importantly, posits that nationalism is not necessarily an evil, or a relic, or a reaction against progress. In Nairn's analysis, the 'Modern Janus' is as necessary a mitigant to the development of capital as the organisation of labour. Like Janus, it is two-faced and two-sided, potentially chaotic and destructive, but possibly more harmonious with contingent realities. Indeed, while his call for a British break-up may seem premature, his analysis of *nationalism* as an active force has been borne out by the post-Soviet experience and is also reflected in theories of globalism, specifically, Amy Chua's *World on Fire*, which argues that the current development of global markets exacerbates ethnic tensions because the control of capital is unevenly distributed between ethnic groups. In such a reading reasoned nationalism becomes a more attractive option in that it at least provides structure and civic discipline to what are potentially, savage responses to an arbitrary and vampiric international system.

At the time (and to an extent, to this day), such a thesis went against the grain of British Marxists – their 'blind spot' – and constitutional analysts – who simply could not take the notion of constitutional change seriously. As we now know it provided a weighty intellectual basis upon which nationalists could carve out a space where they could also be socialists or social democrats without becoming paradoxical. The opinions voiced in Gordon Brown's *Red Paper on Scotland* raise a useful yardstick to where Nairn's writings led the debate; in 1975 widely influential socialist authors such as John McGrath were convinced that socialists could not by definition, be Scottish nationalists – even though there were many writing in that very same book who clearly were. This myth – that all left-leaning nationalists must be hiding a deep, dark secret – persists today and is retold at every opportunity by the ailing Scottish Labour establishment as a popular bogey story.

Scotland is Nairn's prime example of where uneven development leads, and he is eloquent in expressing England's sense of confusion over its own identity. But there are other constituent nations of the UK; it is a little surprising that Northern Ireland should deserve only one chapter and Wales should fail to really crystalise beyond a personal account of his experiences there. Both Scotland and England are essayed in two, which raises the question as to whether Nairn is deliberately, and perhaps dishonestly, recasting the union as a straight opposition between Scotland-and-Englandshire. But his assessment of the British state as a sick, stumbling morass holding back social progress and incapable of reform is rather persuasive, frequently devastating, and while it may not have changed unionists into separatists and only galvanised those who were already nationalists, it demonstrated very clearly why at least devolution should be included on the progressive agenda. By tying nationalist concerns to the pressing social and economic problems current in Britain at the time, rather than the nostalgic rumblings of the Northern Brits, a conceptual space opens up where nationalism can secure its own legitimacy.

It is in fact, the ultimate pole reversal, wherein a supposedly solid British State is held up as muddy, occluded and superficial while nationalism glides with its solid, crystalline point to puncture the layers of façade, all the way through to the Enchanted Glass . . .

THE ENCHANTED GLASS
TOM NAIRN (1988)

Nairn's 1988 publication *The Enchanted Glass: Britain and its Monarchy* remains perhaps his most important and influential book and established his reputation as not just a political writer but a constitutionalist of insight and understanding. In many ways the British constitutionalist – writing in a long tradition including Hobbes, Burke, Bagehot, Orwell *and* Mackintosh and Kellas – has to be a deeper and broader thinker than his/her colleagues elsewhere in the world simply because the multi-national British state is founded on the rocky enigma of no written constitution. Hence we find the writers in this tradition are much influenced in their judgements by their own personal background, education, temperament and outlook.

Nairn, the lowland Scot, and dominie's son, thus plays it to form as he marks the ongoings in the English metropolis, and, as his blurb says, 'refuses to treat the Royal Family as a jokey leftover from feudalism or a mere tourist attraction.' Instead he is able to show how Monarchy had a vital role in maintaining the post-1688 settlement in 'United Kingdom' politics. Basically the Nairn view seems to be that with the Glorious Revolution and the coronation of William and Mary, and the 1707 Union following close behind it, an early modern constitution regarding relationships between territories, classes and power structures was established. The new 'constitutional' monarchy was the figurehead of this new politics, and the power was basically held and wielded by an alliance of new-money merchant capitalists and older order landed aristocrats, all centred on London. The monarchy thus acting at the alliance's, or city's, behest, is on the one hand very different from other *ancien régime* monarchies, but on the other hand, is used as a bulwark to defend this early modern oligarchy against further modernisation and democratisation as threatened by the revolutions of 1776, 1789, 1848, and so on. This is one of the reasons why the constitution for this arrangement was never, and never could be, written. (The view has much in common with that in G.K. Chesterton's *A Short History of England* (1917) although not with the panegyric for the UK cause in World War I with which it concludes.)

The monarchy instead provides this protection against democratisation for the ruling classes by creating a mystical symbol of an ancient, traditional, goodly, organic and natural order for the whole 'nation' to cohere around. Needless to say the actual royal families (those imported from Holland and Hannover, etc.) have nothing to do with feudalism, or ancient tradition, and as Nairn says, 'still less to do with folk or ethnic tradition.' To illustrate this point, Nairn describes, for example, the 'Prince of Wales Investiture' as a 'pantomime drag' wholly invented in the early twentieth century by Lloyd George and others for whatever cymric expediencies. The ceremony was even decried by the then Duke of Windsor, its first victim, as a 'preposterous rig'.

But nor is Windsor-bashing just a simple matter of trashing the neo-traditional fetishes (the gold coaches, the corgis, the kilts, the polo ponies, etc.), for the point about English/Britishness is that the monarchy is at the mystical heart of it; it embodies its very ineffable nature. There is no material heart to stab here. And in fact there is no small irony in the fact that for this country with no written constitution, the task of defending the mystical wonders of this unwritten constitution has fallen to writers. From Edmund Burke to George Orwell, ruling class writers have extolled the natural unwritten 'traditions' (invented since 1688) of this country's political habits, and inveighed against those philistine wreckers, the modernisers and democratisers. But if all this homespun British or Irish common sense – and the principles which Nairn borrows from Musil's depiction of the decaying Hapsburg Empire to describe it, 'muddling through', 'not too much', and 'decent chaps in control' – appeals precisely to the anti-intellectualism of middle England, then again the irony is that as a tradition it is a truly intellectualised one. For Leavis and other 'connoisseurs of bread and butter' had long been working up an anglo-redemption from vulgar '-isms' and '-ologues', by way of a tradition of *literature*: that is to say with etiquette, manners and good writing style – a more gentle and imaginative British moral culture (so God Bless Jane and save her from Hegel's sentences!).

The book shows its age since the death of Diana and the certain decline of the royal family's fortunes throughout the 1990s. But one of the most delightful aspects of the text resides in the terse dismissals the personal Nairn dishes out to all those he clearly considers as establishment lackeys. Beside Burke, Orwell and Leavis, he rudely sees off Roy Jenkins, Roger Scruton, T.S. Eliot and Peregrine Worsthorne. And Nairn doesn't let his internationalism get in the way of a lowland Scot's justified criticism, as all the foreigners sucked up by the toffs – Wittgenstein, Popper, Berlin, Gombrich and Eysenck, are also subject to his intemperately scratchy pen.

Some people might want to protest that it's just not cricket, Tom. But in this just-non-cricketing-country of ours we all happen to be enjoying Nairn's constitutional game massively – until that is, we start to wonder if all this *schadenfreude* is not just feeding the giant scotch chip on the shooder.

But then, of course it is! And so what? Tom's refusing to give it manners and good style in the gentle British imaginative moral way. But that much is only customary for the Scots with their long tradition of literary flyting, and with MacDiarmid famously asserting that invective is a valid part of the dialectic. – Hegel with hot sauce, you might say. So when T.S. Eliot, self-confessedly 'royalist in politics, anglo-catholic in religion', declared that the Scots tradition is an alien one, it might not just be for obsessions like the Kraut, but for the way they cook him too.

The Modern Janus:
Nationalism in the Modern World
Tom Nairn (1990-1999)

Janus, as any fule no, was the Roman God of gates, doors, ends and beginnings, much war and little peace. He, as a figure, or perhaps an *alter ego*, is also central to the evolution of Nairn's increasingly layered and metaphorical vocabulary. Judging by the range and scope of the targets in this series of thematic essays and impressions the 'Modern Janus' of the title is a double-head spinning right and left, gobbing corrosive spitballs at nationalists, centrists and historians of the grand battalion school, none of whom can keep hold of his spinning top tendencies. While the right wing is not ignored in this gobfest, it is Nairn's colleagues on the left, including many connected to the *New Left Review*, who are most thoroughly gunged. Freed from the empirical constraints of mapping the British political system – already done, thoroughly in the foregoing – *Faces of Nationalism* allows Nairn to dismantle what he sees as errors in progressive thought and refine his unified theory of nationalism.

In *The Enchanted Glass* Nairn had already established an idea of the British state system as a perverse, protectionist racket (UKania) or 'pseudo-transcendence' run by an ulterior colonial elite and their 'symbol operators'. The role of this servitor tier in the system is of particular interest to Nairn who is himself one of the more sophisticated symbol operators. While he still makes his points through facts – many impressively erudite and occasionally esoteric – and analysis (especially fine on his mentor Gellner), he is also one of the few writers in this particular field – one which necessarily contends with myth and metaphor as used by state interests – comfortable in expressing, as well as explaining his thought. Two-faced, in the best, hearth-God sense of the word.

Nairn's expression often goes beyond analogy into the realm of symbolist poetry, where 'the Janus' of nationalism glowers with double brow at 'The Owl of Minerva', a chapter title which gives an excellent flavour of Nairn's Carlyle-like language, and the equally Carlyle-like *modus operandi* of deploying such powerful language to *will* his rhetorical enemies (as in, the faux-generosity of internationalism) into oblivion:

> Who does not know the internationalist sectarian, sternly weighing distant triumphs of the Movement against the humiliations at home? His national proletariat is a permanent disappointment and reproach. Unable to dismiss it, he is compelled none the less to make the situation more palatable by an exaggeration of the distant view. The revolution is always better from somewhere else.

The 'old Janus' of internationalism is simultaneously nihilistic and romantic – at home the proles zone out to primetime telly and fill their bellies, whereas in Chiapas/Venezuala/Burma/anywhere conveniently distant they are lean, committed and heroic.

Read the above, then read the so-called *Red Paper on Scotland*, an entirely new publication of 2005, which resurrected an age-old conceit of the Scottish left – its sacred duty to bolster the cause of English socialism. Cut ties with the union and so the logic goes, you cut ties with the fragile progressive cause south of the Tweed – and so Scottish sovereignty is a necessary sacrifice (an argument has been recently reconfigured, at least in its basic structures, along multicultural lines). In Nairn's book this flagellant tendency explains why so many on the left are hostile to his understanding of nationalism – but beyond that it is surely prophetic, diagnosing the structural weaknesses that saw the left buckle in the face of growing conservatism and market fundamentalism.

Of course, leftists who use internationalism as an excuse to hate the homeland present an easy target. Nairn takes on some that are more surprising, even sacrosanct to the emerging consensus over Scotland's social and political existence. Take for example, his scathing analysis of the notion of 'civil society' and its Orwellian emphasis on 'decency':

> . . . a basically resentful dependence of collective impotence, and the turgid misery of bureaucracy or low politics. On its own, cut off by these strange conditions from normal or

high politics, civil society itself can amount to a kind of ailment, a practically pathological condition of claustrophobia, cringing parochialism and dismal self-absorption.

Jings! Given that the existence of a demonstrably separate Scottish civil society powered many of the arguments for home rule, the Scottish reader must wonder at a deeper meaning behind this. Janus necessarily turns his face home; the 'low politics' of the first batch of MSPs (the very first to be declared in 1999 was Tom McCabe, a Labour councillor also responsible for administering the count). High politics may well mean control over social security policy, or perhaps the ability to opt in or out of potentially destructive wars. Written in 1997 on the eve of the British General Election, this passage seems to pre-empt the sense of anti-climax over devolution's freshman year even as it dares to be hopeful of what the election might bring.

Being a sage is never easy, and Nairn over-extends the neck on occasion as events, inevitably, overtake him – where for example, would he place Islamic internationalism and pan-Arab idealism in his analysis of a future where:

> the contestant worlds and the end of prehistory seem to be those of ethnic nationality politics and a civic or identity politics more worthy of modernity's garden . . . [?]

But, says Nairn, what about home? Progress's journey must begin there, hence the end section which deals exclusively with Scotland. This might be attributed to an authorial peccadillo, but Scotland also appears as a comparator in chapters on Andorra, Palestine and Micro-nations – returning to the community of nations through intellectual scrutiny, if not political constitution. Surely then, Nairn as symbol operator has supplanted the imperialist notion of Scotland the Brave with 'Scotland the Lab'? Once, the Enlightenment era white-hot centre of proto-Ukania and an Internationalism purged of its Scotticisms, now the post-electronic, post-genetic mould and test-site for a necessary alchemic fusion of 'primordialism' and 'modernism'. Whether it convinces is up to the reader, but it is impossible not to admire Nairn's truly Machiavellian ability to turn the backward glance into a Parthian shot.

After Britain: New Labour and the Return of Scotland Tom Nairn (2000)

Having established his credentials as British socialism's Evel Knievel, a sort of neck-always-at-least-on-the-line sage, Nairn seems, by now, unable to do without a daredevil prediction or two. Not that he's ever wrong . . . but he has to keep proving to himself that the old magic is still there. That, at any rate, is the feel of the book

After Britain: New Labour and the Return of Scotland written around the turn of the century when Britain's traditional set of constitutional settlements and agreements (ie. London knows best) appeared to be in short circuit. This book, not really a book at all, but a collection of essays of varying length and relevance (one originally a speech given to the 70th anniversary bash of the Scottish National Party, and another a paper of 'Evidence Given to the House of Commons Select Committee on Scottish Affairs') claims in some way to be an update of *The Break-up of Britain*.

What Nairn really does with this rushed and mixed cauldron of letters is wag a cassandric finger and shake the hoary wizard's locks at us in warning. For the radical reforms that we thought to see unfolding before our millennial eyes with New Labour were, in fact, no such thing: this was not at all Nairn's long-predicted 'Break-up', but a dastardly spell and a trick, a final last desperate set of phoney radical measures designed to shore up power in London.

This may all seem obvious to us now, but Nairn was quick and eager to seize on the clues even back then. England's establishment, for its own reasons, has preferred to pretend on the one hand that Scotland's restlessness is a symptom of an endlessly weak and failing, ethnic and national liberation struggle; and on the other that Scotland's position is somehow similar to autonomous regions in truly *modern* democracies (principally Germany and Spain) across Europe (just waiting, that is, for a hand up from daddy). The problem with these simultaneously held yet mutually exclusive views are that they ignore, and are uncomfortable with, the reality of Scotland's status as an imperfectly absorbed state in the process of reconstituting itself (according to Nairn). Thus Nairn can talk about an 'underground topography' of remnants and effects of former Scottish statehood which have refused to wither away; and with this sense of crippled and crippling continuity, he can speak in the same breath as it were, of Lockhart and Fletcher, and of O'Hagan and Dunn, as if all those writers were sitting together counselling one another on the pathological effects of this underground disfigurement.

This has also meant that London has been able to ignore the work of Scottish thinkers, writers, social scientists and politicians (typically those examined here in *Tartan Pimps*, who worked in the 1970s and 80s to establish that sovereignty was located in the will of the Scottish people) and to claim in effect, that it *gave* devolution to Scotland.

As Nairn says:

Revolutions from above can happen; but feigned or non-revolutions from above have been more common.

So when Blair made the slip with that remark about the 'Parish Council', and then when all his talk about a 'Council of the Isles' giving everybody their word was quietly dropped altogether, we should, like Nairn, have seen Blair immediately for what he was. Namely, the radical preserver of 'the heartland's continuity . . . undiminished at the centre stage of the world'. It's a great tradition, after all, following that tried and tested maxim of British constitutionalism, the one uttered by the Great Cham himself, which tells us that 'the man who is tired of London is tired of life'.

There is lots of related stuff here which is interesting in an anecdotal sense – on the West Lothian Question (or, how England always deserves the best); on the endless Local Government rejigging to avoid facing up to real constitutional problems until the poll tax fiasco stuffed that game; on the spectre of Thatcher; and the prospect of English indifference turning to blame and panic (as it did with the Irish). It's all good but there's not much new now, and that's the problem with this sort of literary cobbling. (But were not the shoemakers always amongst the most prominent revolutionaries?)

After Britain: New Labour and the Return of Scotland • Tom Nairn

PARIAH
TOM NAIRN (2002)

Tom Nairn is, unquestionably, dogged in pursuit. With *Pariah*, his quest to kill off phoney internationalism, cod traditions and sham democracy and replace it with a self-aware, mature form of nationalism finds yet another channel. It is a reprise, an instalment, another chapter in the perpetual drafting of Nairn's book of Scotland. This consistency has made it impossible for him to critique the feigned revolutions of the Blair government without, inexorably, returning to the position of Scotland within the union. *Pariah* presents us with the problem of the 'parody Britain' created by the New Labour project – elitist, facile, seemingly social democratic yet riddled with contradictions – and, in a remarkably short space of 162 pages the solution any assiduous Nairn reader has come to expect.

There is an honour in pursuing a theme, in rigorously engaging with a subject over the fullness of time, in recapitulating and re-assessing ideas in the light of emerging evidence. Unfortunately *Pariah* gives the impression that Nairn's attitudes already hardened a long time ago and that this is a serving of that very Blairite confection, policy-based evidence. Like much of the later Nairn, *Pariah* is not a book but an essay double-spaced and large-typed, and all of the facts available on Blair's brand of modernisation are strained through the tight holes of Nairn's prejudgements as to the moribundity of the union. What we are left with is seemingly assembled according to the sticky-backed plastic recycling ethos of that junior bastion of bourgeois Britain *Blue Peter* – 'one I made earlier'.

In its favour, it reads well, replete with the expressive, explosive, 'garlicky' and goading language Nairn has made his own. It works rather well as a brainy, slightly hallucinogenic satire on 'Redemption Britain'– a post-Imperial Britain 'refreshed' and 'absolved' by adding the prefixes 'new' and 'modern' wherever the English language will permit (and frequently where it will not . . .). Nairn's analysis is perceptive and occasionally lacerating but relies for all its punch-lines on sharing Nairn's givens – which are here left unsubstantiated, so that only the patient work of years re-treading the back catalogue will flesh the bones. Nothing wrong with that, but in the confines of such a short book the anger and hate condenses and overspills. The jokes – especially the construct of a 'music hall Britain' – rapidly outstay their welcome and smack of the very elitism Nairn eschews, so that the overall result resembles some sort of erudite voodoo curse. Or, to find an analogy closer to home, the po-mo equivalent to that celebrated vindiction of Scot against Scot:

> I curse their head and all the hairs of their head; I curse their face, their

brain (innermost thoughts), their mouth, their nose, their tongue, their teeth, their forehead, their shoulders, their breast, their heart, their stomach, their back, their womb . . .

This grandiose and elaborate curse is emblazoned across Carlisle's 'Cursing Stone', a modern sculpture that commemorates Bishop Dunbar's famed invective against his fellow Scots – reivers who switched sides between Edinburgh and London as it suited them, blackmailing the national interest. As to the identity of their modern equivalent – with whom Nairn truly has the biggest beef – then the reader need only move on to the subsequent *Gordon Brown Bard of Britishness* to learn whose briskets he'd dearly love to baste.

The 'Reiver gambit' should be familiar to anyone who has followed the ins and outs of the Scottish Labour Party; but Nairn's persistent hexing of the new 'synthetic' establishment created by the Blair government suffers in comparison to the establishment it assails, for said establishment can afford to sit tight, stay complacent. Nairn appears angry, sour, messianic yet vitriolic. One senses a shift here from analyst to magus, from science to spell-casting, hubble, bubble and all

that. It is dangerously close to enchantment – a very Nairnian evil – but is at least far, as yet, from becoming 'sound and fury'. There are some very astute satirical moments in *Pariah*, and the best use for this book is as an often hugely funny *Devil's Dictionary* of British politics.

It is also worth remembering that, almost without meaning to, Nairn and his contemporaries created a new 'republic of letters' where they wrote Scotland back into being. The book continues to be written as it must be, but Nairn's chapters seem increasingly repetitious. Is *Pariah* all Scotland's foremost public intellectual has to contribute to debates over politics and power in the early century; of the decline in parliamentary (Embra, London or elsewhere?) scrutiny; of global terrorism and its structures or of the role of the corporation and its relationship to polity, individuals and development? Surely not? Somewhere along the way we have fallen through the wardrobe from languid Ukania to frosty Nairnia, where theory becomes theology, invective incantation and Nairn rules his See as a speilcasting bishop, custodian of a prayer-book now wearing a little thin. Still, a prayer-book worn thin indicates extremely active use.

The Troika

...And pat upon their Q they come,
Q's own troika, Stephen, Owen, Tom,
A Right and Left and somewhere in the rear,
Snapping at trifles, comes, as charioteer,
Hibernian Philistine, a poor man's Thenites
- A petty waspishness in all he say
No Irish rhetoric, lacking Cambrian hwyl
Despite his name, name-dropping with a will,
Dredging the past to make a reference fit,
Biting a back-and passing it as wit,
A surface erudition, substitute for thought,
Pleasing the Rose Street - or the College -lot.
Happy with sycophantic sneers, or undergrad
response,
A dilettante? More an intellectual ponce
Soliciting approval, Surveying local scenes,
And thinking he has found there all that
Scotland means.
Uses, instead of axe - the edge too keen-
An over fastidious, slightly withered, spleen,
Producing not bile, for him the substitution
Somewhat less nasty, a verbal convolution,
So that when mighty issues come upon the
scene,
Demanding at the least all say just what they
mean,
His columned filigrees for Q each second
week
Stand like stout Cortes (or Balbao) silent-
upon a pique,
Happy to gain, th'award of every hack,
Applause from all that claustrophobic claque.
But back to the troika-you thought I had
forgot
The charioteer is O.K. for the trot,
But for the charge you need a stronger metal,
Hooves flying, eyes a-gleam
to show its fettle,
A leftward dash, a philosophic
bound
To traverse all that wild
uncharted ground
Who better than our Tom?
For he's no fake,
Intelligent, deep, indeed at
times opaque.
For years he'd laboured in
the New Left stable,
A veritable Houyhnhnm, a
Marx, a Hegel,
Imparting wisdom and,
eschewing brevity,

Skewering British politics for its levity,
Its lack of theory, its Philistine approach,..
Making respectable the nouveau gauche,
Saving us quarterly in New Left Review.
How can he-what does he-in this strange
milieu?
Dunedin's petty bourgeoisie? Oh, spare the
thought,
No longer neo-Marxist? Fanon? Pablo? Trot?
Exile can play strange tricks on many folk,
- Returning, stranger. Tom accepts the
voluntary yoke,
Sheds fast the dusty years and has a beano;
Turns frisky, ears pricked like a Palamino
He hears the call from Ayr, he grasps the
tiller's
Weightier end - and forthwith joins Jim
Spillers.

I've changed the metaphor. But that's no
crime.
Byron would change his mistress for a rhyme;
The fate of nations is no lesser matter.
If Tom can change, who, at the latter,
Savaged the Left for chauvinistic error
Over the Market, then I need have no terror
In changing a metaphor. He stressed the
rationale
Of carrying the battle on each multi-national
To wider (Peter) Shores than Britain's.
Now he has changed his largesse to a
pittance,
Like Hamlet in a nut-shell, glad to be,
Or not to be, a member of the S.L.P.
And now, in Q. where he is much in fashion,
Releases, for a coterie, his passion.
But Tom, it really isn't very fair
Simply to tear round
Charlotte, or St. Andrew's
Square,
And, what is worse, and to be
more particular,
Your route is getting more
than somewhat circular.
Bring back your leftward
charge, forward the flying
mane,
Return to us your Wisdom
once again!

The MacDunciad Norman Buchan

II. THE PROPHET NAIRN

I.

O whustle, and I'll come tae ye, my lad,
O whustle, and I'll come tae ye, my lad:
Tho' feyther and mither and a' should gae mad,
O whustle, and I'll come tae ye, my lad!

Robert Burns

'Antidisestablishmentarianistically' may be your most obvious adverb with which to indict my present proceedings, but I would argue nonetheless that whoever the present UK Establishment may be ('UK' to me, 'Ukania' to Tom Nairn, always a tad more formal), Brown as Prime Minister lay outside it. Stick a Thistle up the rump in any Establishment dump and when the screamer descends s/he will curse Brown from both beam-ends. The Establishment may be a dead duck, but it never knows it, which is why it survives. Brown as PM was as much the outcast of the Establishment in spite of his official status second only to Elizabeth II & I as he was when as Lord Rector of the University of Edinburgh he nominally and (to the rage of its Establishment) actually presided over its government second only to the University's Chancellor then and now Edinburgh's Duke. He was of course anxious to win, which is why he loses: Establishments do not seek to win, they have won.

I was no member of any Establishment then or later, I was not even speaking antidisestablishmentarianistically, I was merely opining in 1974 that Scotland would ultimately (and perhaps sooner) establish its independence. For which the Lord Rector looked upon me with the sad though kindly eyes of a John the Baptist reprimanding a Pharisee friend (with whom he paid due allegiance to virtuous publicans). And he said, in the shining gladness of a forerunner without a spark of jealousy for his Messiah, that I would soon discover how wrong I was, because TOM NAIRN was coming back to Scotland and had agreed to write the major essay to the *Red Paper on Scotland* (which Gordon Brown was editing and to which I was heretically contributing). Gordon's enthusiasm was pretty, and quite difficult to resist, all the more because his gentle, affectionate, forgiving manner was far less easily answered than the usual student bullying of tutors. And I knew the works if not the man under advisement. I suppose I said how.

I had subscribed to *New Left Review* since I returned to our archipelago from the USA in 1965. I even did some writing for it, having the honour to author a piece which was in type when bumped to make way for an unexpected contribution from Che Guevara 'somewhere in the world'. Nairn won my supreme gratitude for his ability to write English, an accomplishment indifferently held by many of the *NLR* earnest brethren. God knows Karl Marx had known how to write, vide *The Eighteenth Brumaire of Louis Bonaparte*: why did so many of his otherwise slavish disciples hold themselves superior to lucidity – unless it was that clarity would fail to cover the multitude of their sins? Anyhow, Nairn could write, and on return to Scotland would write, and if SNP household gods were to be blasphemed, they would at least know its meaning.

They had to wait for fifteen years to get a real Nairn sockdolager, which would be in a volume to be edited by myself, and myself rapturous with delight when I received his copy. The SNP had pulled out of the Constitutional Convention conjured into being by the Church of Scotland, and vitriol would have been a milk-shake to what Nairn poured over them and I printed, in the Polygon edition of *A Claim of Right of Scotland* (1990). Last year, Tom Nairn's 75th birthday inspired Anthony Barnett's recollection that in 1992 Barnett had set up *Charter 88 Sovereignty Lectures*, inaugurated by Gordon Brown in the Logan Hall (in London, I presume), and at the end facing the vast, applauding audience, the lecturer asked Barnett: 'Is Tom Nairn here?' At a later lecture (Shirley Williams) with Tony Blair as 'discussant', Blair's enquiry was 'where did all the people come from?' gazing over a far smaller body than the rapturous ranks whom Brown had counted as less than one Tom Nairn.

And on this, if on nothing else, the Prime Minister's priorities were correct. But later, as with so much else, it was Alex Salmond who chose Tom Nairn as the Master Lothian Lecturer in 2008, second to none save himself, and Gordon Brown as PM lay ensnared in the toils of an imaginary nationalism dreaming of a vision called ' Britain' six Northern Irish counties short of a Ukania and maybe a Scotland short of it as well, a Peter Pan whose medicine was poisoned even by Wendy.

II.

And what should they know of England who only England know?
Rudyard Kipling, 'The English Flag'

The prophet Nairn, being also the Prof. Nairn, is by now so far Establishment as to inhabit *Who's Who*, holding the chair of Nationalism and Global Diversity in Royal Melbourne Institute of Technology since 2002. He was born in Freuchie, in Fife, educated at Dunfermline High School (its denizens blissfully unaware who would represent them in Parliament fifty years thence) and graduated from the University of Edinburgh M.A. in Philosophy in 1956, presumably under the great left-wing Professor John MacMurray who would retire in 1957. Nairn later studied in Pisa and in Dijon. In 1962-64 he was Lecturer in Social Philosophy at the University of Birmingham. He had by this stage been on the editorial board of the *New Left Review* for some time. I have never discussed any of this with Nairn, although the effect of his return to Scotland for me was that he became and remained a very dear friend, who drove myself and my noisy infant family to Wales, stayed with me in a monastery, travelled long distances with me, saw Hogmanay in my house undisturbed by a drunken Tory friend bitterly complaining that Nairn didn't wear a kilt, and played intellectual hop-scotch with me in various literary enterprises including our being jointly libelled in verse by Norman Buchan, MP. One of the first things I discovered about him was his sense of humour expressing itself in the delight a child shows for something funny. Despite knowing big words, he is a man for all ages. I am therefore biased.

I never discovered whether his Marxism at some point entailed a sojourn in the Communist party, and/or some Trotskyite coven, but if either it made little psychological mark. He always was very much his own man, although a phenomenally generous collaborator and his receptivity and interest in the ideas of others are personal and not – as was usual with Stalin/Trotsky votaries – tactical or commercial. On the other hand he has been the victim of Marxist bullying, and clearly disliked it, although adept in replying to it. His major literary beginnings appeared in the *New Left Review* in the early 1960s, and reading or re-reading them now makes me modify one ancient thesis of mine. Having been a graduate student and raw lecturer in the USA during Martin Luther King's Revolution and the revolt against the war in Vietnam, I found Britain's belief that its 1960s were comparable to be an egocentric self delusion. The Aldermaston marches were great, but 1950s Scotland may have had its 1960s but it had them in the 1970s. Yet now, I would admit Britain made at least one contribution to the 1960s, viz. Tom Nairn.

The Hungarian Rising of 1956, coinciding with the Suez adventure and the US Presidential election, was a traumatic and bitterly disillusioning experience for any honest Communist, imperialist or Americanophile, and the asylum-seekers from the Communist Party of Great Britain may have been the most honourable of the three categories: Suez meant that the British free hand in peace and war was ended, and the unanswered USSR repression in Hungary belied all the promises which the USA had unofficially made the insurgents through Radio Free Europe, but few Tories or Republicans denounced the dishonour. Yet however high the glory of the British ex-Communists of 1956, it followed years of dishonourable silence regarding other crimes, sometimes offset by readiness to bully more independent dissenters in the party. It also meant that as advance agents for progress under the USSR, British party members took their own utterances with appalling seriousness, as though nothing more momentous could be happening in the realm of intellectual discourse. Edward Thompson proved himself one of the greatest English historians of all time when he produced *The Making of the English Working Class* in 1963, but while liberating so much of the unrecorded past he was less ready to give others greater liberation than himself.

The ex-Communist academics compensated for Hungary by bringing out the *New Reasoner*, having been forbidden by the party (while in the party) to continue with its predecessor *The Reasoner*. The titles themselves were characteristically stuffy, and even more characteristically arrogant: nobody else, it would appear, was to be given credit for any reasoning whatsoever. The same went for an allied product, *The Universities and Left Review*, which implied more disparity in its clientele than was intended. They were married in the *New Left Review* whose *pronunciamenti* rivalled the Vatican in speaking to city and to world, and clearly assumed city and world would attend with high fidelity. The cardinals of this *magisterium* were not, perhaps, as suited for capitalist activities like magazine publishing as they had fondly assumed. Younger activists were required, and then took control of their own work.

It may not have been coincidence that the founders, Thompson, John Savile, and Ralph Milliband (father of Brown's cabinet Millibands), resented most among those who had displaced them, the Scot Nairn and the half-Irish Perry Anderson. Tom Nairn's early articles in *NLR* were instant targets for Thompson counter-attack, in the *Socialist Register* founded by Savile in 1965. (It was an annual, and thus easier to manage: the title again was a little unfortunate, at least for Dublin readers, accustomed to describe scab workers as 'registhered bowsies'.) Nairn's 'The English Working Class' *NLR* no. 24 (March-April 1964) declared:

> British socialists are fortunate indeed to possess the great account of the origins of the English working class which has recently appeared, Edward Thompson's *The Making of the English Working Class*. Above all, because it concentrates attention upon what must be our primary concern, the role of the working class as maker of history. Engaged in constant polemic against vulgar determinism, Thompson insists that: 'The working class made itself as much as it was made' . . . The

working class was not merely the product of economic forces, but also realised itself 'in a social and cultural formation' partly directed against the operation of these very forces. Thompson's book is essentially the history of this revolt.

The review-essay ran for over twelve packed pages, but Thompson was unforgiving, partly because Nairn did not defer to him at all points. They agreed in holding people morally accountable, instead of opting for the Marxist alibi of blaming heartless, irresistible economic forces (against which determinism Marx himself constantly rebelled). They both had fathers in the working class and hence were sure-footed where their colleagues were treading, perhaps, on clouds of glory. The international Left was always good for nauseating apotheosis of the working class, pursued by anarcho-Troskyites into individual isolated icons. Norman Buchan's *MacDunciad* in 1977 denounced Nairn, Neal Ascherson, Bob Tait and others for supporting Jim Sillars's break with the Labour Party before he entered the SNP:

> 'He is so quaint!'
> 'He has a worker's voice.'
> 'He actually is fluent!'
> They rejoice at having found one worker with a brain,
> – Which means they treat all others with disdain,
> And, if he knew it, so they do with him.
> – Their statutory worker is our Jim.

It was a little difficult to sense who 'they' was: it was an embodiment of Edinburgh (Buchan always pronounced 'Embro' as having four letters) and he had in any case retreated so far into analogy that his Aunt Sallies in this passage were otherwise unidentified Madames de Stael and Recamier, apparently in Corstorphine (where in fact Scottish nationalism ran thin and dry). But Nairn, Ascherson and Tait were the clearest named recipients, and nothing less like them could be imagined. For myself, I really liked Norman Buchan, although I had never met him when he wrote the *MacDunciad*, and wondered how he had managed to caricature me so accurately, but Tom Nairn was understandably disgusted, disdaining the obvious reply that Buchan's lines satirised what their author had known much better than the New Left, viz. the Old Communist Party, Kelvinside Branch.

From his first major essays in the *New Left Review*, Nairn blazed his loathing against falsely sentimentalising the working class, in the abstract or in the trades unions, thereby further alienating the ex-Communist class of 1956 whose Stalinist superstitions were too deeply ingrained to be eradicated by an upstart usurper. Had Goliath survived, he would probably have felt the same about David ('A sling. *A Sling*! It's an insult to the honest decent sword!')

Nairn seemed to have been inspired by Macaulay's triumphant finale to the first volumes of his *History of England*, published in 1848, that the reason 'England' had escaped Europe's radical revolution in 1848 was because it had a conservative revolution in 1688. (Macaulay later admitted it was less conservative in Scotland.) Nairn reworked this to argue that 1688-9 had been a bourgeois revolution compromised with an aristocratic revolution, new money allying with older land, and the working class (as Marx and Engels had posited) supporting the revolution only to be put back to servility. Nairn in fact saw the working class in England as immunised against revolt by judicious rations of upper-class culture, and likewise saw literature in England as fundamentally reactionary, always critical of the new wealth and the apparent new power.

The thesis makes sense to any who pondered why long after agrarian capitalism had passed a sell-by date, it continued to dominate high politics (consider Gladstone after the most democratic election campaign Britain had ever seen – Midlothian 1879-80, stuffing his next cabinet with aristocrats in half its jobs). It was also supported by aristocratic manners aped by the bourgeoisie and carefully rationed among workers anxious to qualify for bourgeois status. Nairn assumed that Thompson, perhaps unconsciously, had recorded that working-class capitulation: the revolutionary atmosphere of 1832 petered out largely to aristocratic advantage with the bourgeoisie sated by a few token victories and the workers in the 1840s settling for docility.

Thompson assumed that Nairn's analysis was hostile to him: what in fact Nairn opposed in Thompson was what neither of them would have termed Thompson's English nationalism, Thompson's reverence for the working class forming itself around the only working class he really knew, the English workers. Thompson in part defended himself by accusing Nairn of preferring abstract theory to empiricism. Nairn had actually been building up his knowledge of English history by assimilating conventional but reliable histories of English landed society. Thompson's suspicion of Nairn's theorising derived partly from the Communist party's hostility to any theorising not marked A1 in the Kremlin, and partly because revolt from the Kremlin meant Thompson's return to the simple honesty of the English worker unfettered by any further foreign fatuities. Thompson evidently had to wait until far enough away from intellectual subjection to Moscow before he could proclaim the making of the English working class.

Nairn did not say so, but he evidently found the new, untheoretical discovery of salvation in England to be no more satisfactory than the preceding theoretical conviction of salvation in the USSR. Nor did he add that Thompson's English empiricism was simply a refusal to recognise his own lovable but unrevolutionary patriotism, much as a Tory would take Englishness as the universally appropriate standard:

> The Americans live in America;
> The Romans live in Rome;
> The Turkeys live in Turkey:
> But the English live
> At Home.
> (Quoted – and quite possibly invented – in the Dutch historian
> G.J. Renier's *The English: Are They Human?*)

Nairn was never going to play the returned traveller, either in Odyssean story or in Herodotean history: If he pushed over the Leaning Tower of Pisa, we must go elsewhere to learn of it, ditto whether he had cut the mustard in Dijon to make Burgundy bow down. But its obvious effect was to leave him angry, impatient and bored with London parochialism. A parish convinced of its internationalism by devotion to the USSR was as bad or worse.

My own reading of that would be that the heroic British of 1940, standing against all Europe (hostile or dubiously neutral), saved the continent but remained permanently suspicious of return to it. Nairn apparently agreed with this as far as permanent suspicion of nostalgic relaunches of British time machines to 1940. I remember once quoting J.B. Priestley on the brave private craft at Dunkirk; I wanted to immunise a Scottish nationalist audience against Anglophobia, or something: Nairn agreed with the motive, but found the quotation by now mythologically pestiferous. It was all very well for me, a foreigner, to admire it; as homebrew, it was opium for Socialist masses, who throughout the 1960s and early 1970s ran up Union Jacks in their cul-de-sacs and called them Red Flags. By 1999 he was prepared to give it brief but fair acknowledgment, remembering as he drove from a dying friend's bedside, through his boyhood's West Fife on Referendum voting day, suddenly shot back 59 years:

> In those days the wireless was life itself, everyone listened to the news over and over again for fear of missing something, and never forgot the Prime Minister. He said: 'Our British life and the long continuity of our institutions and our empire' were at stake in the battle now upon us, if it all lasted for a thousand years, men would still be saying 'This was their finest hour.' One lifetime later something of that hour remains, he was not wrong; but almost everything else has gone. . . Of course, what I could actually recall were very small things: the look of the radio, the warm smell of gas, my mother's tears at abandoning the seacoast for somewhere far inland – and above all, the excitement of being so close to a favourite fishing pool among the rocks. The long continuity of our institutions meant extremely little then. And yet, this does not imply it was all really 'over our heads'; on the contrary, I see now *that* was how it got into our blood, without missing a single beat over the generation which ensued. The minnows which any individual can recall are like pilot fish, beneath them swim far greater ones, at different and unsounded depths. Often these are sustaining and deadly together; and difficult to get rid of.
>
> (*After Britain* [2000], 'Epilogue', 284-85)

The lyricism (and the instant social history) of this brings us to a new understanding of Nairn. If he was rigorous in his 1972-73 assault on the anti-European Left, it was because he knew its wellsprings. Equally, if in retrospect he was brutally critical of the Labour Party in the 1940s ('The Nature of the Labour Party' in *NLR* 27-28 (Sept-ember-October, November-December 1964)) it was because his memory possessed enough of the potential revolutionary moment which Labour let slip. (He was writing in hopes that Wilsonism would make the most of its own moment, and his adult life would be fuelled by the white-heat of its opportunistic self-destruction.) His passionate European sense had nothing in common with that of the genial, bibulous Roy Jenkins, apart from respect for civil liberties. The Europe he knew erupted in 1968, and declared its independence of the Left Bank Hemingway nostalgists:

An American in Paris means an army deserter
hurling a *pave* at a policeman.

But he saw internationalism all right in the causes of French student revolt such as:

the enduring bourgeois prejudice (common to East and West) that education is a 'privilege' of some kind, to be paid for. If not with money, then with misery. Or, more accurately, with a gaily endured insufficiency of means. It was well known, until the month of May, that students (like the early factory workers and the plantation slaves of the old South) are happy with little, having each other, and their natural *joie de vivre*. Also that one is happier without 'responsibilities', however poor. Then again, why should not one 'pay' for one's future as a trade-marked and guaranteed exploiter with a bit of hardship?

This would give him a credential in the eyes of the student Rector Gordon Brown, whose government forty years on busily percolated the *mentalité* against which the French students revolted. Maybe that is internationalism, of a kind. Of course some things have changed. 'Professors are God-like creatures, hopelessly deformed by the process in most cases', continued Nairn (in *The Beginning of the End: France, May 1968*, coauthored with Angelo Quatrocchi [1968]). True, no doubt, in many cases still, but they have been satisfactorily undeified by the new administrators who see the slightest practical expression of intellect as a professional solecism.

'We shall need years and years to really understand what has happened,' said Edgar Morin. 'So we shall, in one sense,' answered Nairn. 'But we do not have years and years.' But their enemies – did, especially those evolving from their own ranks. Nairn was to see British academic authority's confrontation of students himself when as a Lecturer in General Studies in Hornsey College of Art he was dismissed for supporting a student protest (1969). He returned to the continent, as a Fellow in the Transnational Institute of Amsterdam between 1972 and 1975 where he took sardonic pleasure in noting the reversal of:

Popular lore . . . that the Right is pessimistic – about human nature, social reforms, the discontents of civilisation – while the Left is optimistic.

But in fact Right-wing colloquia in 1975 found that, upon reflection, things were not that bad. It would (they concluded) take more than a recession, the oil sheikhs, or Western Europe's vague fumblings towards independence to disturb US hegemony seriously: the globe was safe for capitalism for a good while yet, provided that the latter's statesmen exercised a modicum of rationality. On the other hand, where a left-wing conclave might have been expected to find some reason for hope in the great post-Vietnam crisis of imperialism, (that whose afterward he was writing) found none at all.

> Tom Nairn ed. *Atlantic Europe? the radical view* [1976]

Nairn concluded that 'Afterword':

> The problem of Europe in any . . . 'new economic order' . . .
> is a different one. Europe is in the middle. Its role is the most
> indeterminate, the hardest to decipher, potentially the most
> dangerous. . . the European states have tried, and failed, to
> construct a new multi-national reality, losing some of their
> legitimacy in doing so.

This was written well before the breakup of Yugoslavia, or of that of Czechoslovakia, failures of multi-national reality still hidden from most foreign commentators.

What happens to faltering or collapsing 'national realities' in the still mercantile world? There were few answers to the underlying questions in our meetings; but at least the questions themselves were posed forcefully, without complacency or indulgence in falsely optimistic solutions.

Nairn's claim would hold good for most other colloquia of which he formed part. His rigour, his humour, his range, his wisdom and his receptivity made him one of the most influential figures encountered by his various audiences. But what would he make of the homeland to which Gordon Brown had so optimistically called him?

III.

'Tis ever sweet to lie
On the dry carpet of the needles brown
And though the fanciful green lizard stir
And windy odours light as thistledown
Breathe from the lavdanon and lavender,
Half to forget the wandering and pain,
Half to remember days that have gone by,
And dream and dream that I am home again!

James Elroy Flecker, 'Brumana'

Probably Gordon Brown's interest in the Edinburgh Festival was relatively small, bar Fringe theatre involving friends, but Tom Nairn's first Scotskill (why did John Buchan never invent that neologism?) was 'Festival of the Dead' (*New Statesman*, 1 September 1967), a pseudo-obituary which galvanised revolt against Festival atrophy, more particularly giving rise to *Infringe*, the nearest Fringe revolt got to a *journal de combat* until supplanted by its offspring the *Festival Times*, both of them products of Edinburgh Student Publications Board, inherited by Gordon from his brother John. Gordon Brown was more benign patron than parent to these things – the Board's manager, John Forsyth, was close to father, godfather or stepfather as occasion required – but Gordon Brown's educational infancy in 1967 made Tom Nairn's reputation all the more godlike. Edinburgh was Tory Town in those years and the Festival begun as brave postwar refertilization of cultural scorched earth was now high Establishment, or, as Nairn saw:

> . . . it was Culture, it has become Scotland. It has not merely succeeded; it has turned fatally and permanently into another Scottish Thing, another structural element in the tiresome fantasy life the Scots have been doping themselves with for the past three centuries to avoid their real problem. . .

> . . . Some societies could perhaps survive the loss of statehood, the political means to construct their own destiny. The precarious and bloody earlier history of Scotland made it absolutely vital to preserve these means. Hence, the loss of them was an insufferable void, and Scottish cultural history is the dismal record of the attempts to escape from this void – either by literal escape to the south, or by fantasy-escape, a peopling of the emptiness with romantic shadows.

Gordon Brown, as a devoted son to a Church of Scotland minister father, may have found Nairn's pivot painful.

The soil Scotland offers to this fragile festive culture is mildewed religiosity a mile deep, and what could thrive in this? Edinburgh soul's is bible-black, pickled in boredom by centuries of sermons, swaddled in the shabby gentility of the Kirk – what difference could 21 years of Festival make to this? In Edinburgh the iron age of Calvinism has long since turned into rust, and it is this rust which chokes and corrodes the eye and ear.

But the lesson to be drawn was in its way comforting for Brown, especially when re-read in the atmosphere of SNP victories in 1974 (the University Library, with a run of the *New Statesman* on its open shelves, was diagonally across Buccleuch Place from Publications Board):

> . . . political nationalism in Scotland is a contradiction in terms, everyone feels this, and hence the subject is a joke. . . Society is language: Scotland is silence. . . Scotland has no voice, and no present. . . For Scotland, reality and speech obviously lie somewhere on the other side of rejection.

This was a clarion-call for would-be makers of a new Scotland. It was less obvious that Nairn was not so much repudiating Scottish nationalism as demanding replacement of existing varieties by something of greater durability and integrity. And even if a faint aroma of that began to filter through, Nairn's next trumpet-blast was reassuring. 'Three Dreams of Scottish Nationalism', in Karl Miller's collection *Memoirs of a Modern Scotland* (1970) after preliminary runs in *NLR* grasped the nettle of new nationalism's superficial attractions:

> Like the companion nationalism of the Welsh, it brings an element of novelty into the hopelessness and corruption of the post-imperial political scene.

But its value as shake up for Wilsonian compromise and complacency brought no real threat:

> The now dominant dream of Scotland reborn should perhaps be seen as the third phase in the dreampsychology (which has very often been a dreampathology) of Scottish history. It is deeply marked by both the great dreams that preceded it. Like them, its most important trait is a vast, impossible dissociation from the realities of history. The best short definition of Scottish history may be this: Scotland is the land where ideal has never, even for an instant, coincided with fact. Most nations have had moments of truth, at least. Scotland, never.

The previous two dreams of Scottish nationalism a little too conveniently thesis and antithesis, were: at bottom there is the bedrock of Calvinism, the iron, abstract moralism of a people that distrusts the world and itself; then, overlaying this, the sentimental shadow-appropriation of this world and itself through romantic fantasy. Nairn was allowing for the modicum of national consciousness in Socialism which the recently rediscovered Marxism of Antonio Gramsci allowed for, and which Brown would acknowledge in the *Red Paper on Scotland*, but Nairn was quick to pre-empt the use of Gramsci:

> The only solution is by fiat, from above, by an Authority that selects the Elect from the ranks of the damned. Hence, a kind of masochism, a craving for discipline, in fact, accompanies [the] Scottish sense of equality. Gramsci has pointed out the analogy between Calvinist and vulgar-Marxist determinism. In fact, there is no Stalinist like a Scottish Stalinist, a truth which must have impressed itself on many students of modern British politics.

Nairn's sense of humour was back in action here: the obvious allusion was to West Fife's MP 1935-50, Willie Gallacher, of the Communist Party, but many other examples would naturally occur to readers' minds, ironically (though probably not intentionally including Nairn's own future versificator-libeller Norman Buchan). But Gallacher, who certainly was intended, might have invited a moment's thought. Gallacher was not Calvinist by origin: his antecedents were Irish Roman Catholic, as indeed were those of many Scottish Communists, notably Mick McGahey.

Nairn had in fact denounced the Kirk while falling prey to the Kirk's own fantasy – that Scots were Calvinist, and that any other mass religion was an aberration soon to be disspelled. But Irish Roman Catholicism, although down to a trickle since 1923, had sent its Burkes and Hares, its Conan Doyles and James Connollys, in their thousands and their tens of thousands throughout the preceding century. As Nairn wrote the Papists were giving rapid chase in total numbers to the Church of Scotland. And if the argument be made that Scots Calvinism was too deep-seated to be adulterated by alien Christianities, then the thousand years of medieval Scottish Catholicism was deeper. Scottish nationalism certainly produced its anti-Catholics, but they were much less visible in Scottish nationalist literary circles than the Catholic Compton Mackenzies and Fionn MacCollas; and if their day was past, the eleven SNP MPs elected in October 1974 included Iain MacCormick, a Catholic convert, and George Thompson, a former Catholic clerical student and future priest. Nairn acknowledged an Irish relevance, but purely in its dismissal:

> It may not come amiss either to indicate the ludicrous phoneyness of the comparison of themselves with the Irish that the Scots are fond of in this context. The Irish rose up and wrenched their independence from imperialism when the latter was at the apex of its power. With sleekit Presbyterian moderation the Scots have restrained themselves until it is abundantly plain that the English would be incapable of stopping an insurrection in the Isle of Wight. The Irish had to fight the Black-and-Tans.

This was codswallop, though commonplace codswallop at the time: I am uneasily aware of having made my own contribution to it. The Irish (that is to say a couple of hundreds of them, many unaware that their manoeuvres on that day would involve fighting) had their Easter Rising in 1916 (headed by Tom Clarke, a native of the Isle of Wight) when the UK was in a World War and almost bankrupt: it was the result of clever German intrigue to trap the British in overkill and hence gain a much-needed propaganda victory. The later rising-up was, like its predecessor, a resort to killing unwanted by the overwhelming majority of the Irish people, and ultimately inducing terrorism on both sides, Black, Tan, and Green (many of the soldiers on both sides having served in UK ranks in the recent world war).

Nairn was of course quite right in seeing no comparison between twentieth century Irish and Scots nationalism, and it was entirely to the credit of the Scots, who kept far from the poison cup of violence whose ultimate result would be the thirty years' war in Northern Ireland. Nairn did rightly condemn them for use of 'an image further blackened by a sickening militarism, the relic of Scotland's special role in the building up of British imperialism' – the SNP's Bannockburn rallies necessarily drew from the fount of the same cult – but failed to recognise that all militarism is sickening. And the Irish 'wrench' of independence was in fact the work of the most effective propaganda machine against which the UK government has ever had to contend, all the more because its leaders, Desmond Fitzgerald and Erskine Childers, were English.

Nairn repudiated most of the essay long ago, but at no point more than the finale which embodied his most famous aphorism (borrowed and adapted from Diderot), and while Brown repeated it with glee its parental connotation must have induced a slight twinge:

> I see that Scottish Nationalism now has the benediction of our annual General Assembly of crows. It must already be dreaming of the Inaugural Procession of the new regime to St Giles, where the All Mighty will smile on it too. As far as I'm concerned Scotland will be reborn the day the last minister is strangled with the last copy of the *Sunday Post*. I hope I'm not alone.

My belief in the sense of humour of the Almighty is strengthened by the sequel. Probably Nairn would not withdraw his maledictions on the *Sunday Post* – although he might agree that it is at least preferable to the miserable parody of it in *Private Eye* – but he certainly now prohibits its lethal use, especially on Kirk ministers, since the Church of Scotland at last showed itself representative of all the Scots when it opened the doors of its Assembly Hall to a Constitutional Convention in defiance of the then Prime Minister, Margaret Thatcher, and her Secretary of State for Scotland. Nairn has publicly saluted its leading commentator on Scottish nationalism, the Revd Professor Will Storrar, as one of the greatest Scots of our day. (What 'Three Dreams' was talking about concerning Assembly proceedings in 1970 is hard to remember, but in any case it would seem to be exaggerated.)

Yet even there Brown could have taken warning in 1970-74. However ludicrous the homicidal uses of the *Sunday Post*, it did imply that Nairn was prophesying – and, under certain circumstances, welcoming – a rebirth of Scotland. A little before it was the demand for Scotland to take its place in the new world emerging from the 1960s:

> In the same year which nationalism again became a force in Scotland, the western world was shaken by the first tremors of a social revolution, from San Francisco to Prague. I for one am enough of a nationalist, and have enough faith in the students and young workers of Glasgow and Edinburgh, to believe that these forces are also present in them.

But suppose on his return Nairn were to find the internationalism lacking in England, and to discover that Scottish students could share the dreams of Prague and San Francisco while giving it a Scottish nationalist meaning? Suppose he was to find that Scottish nationalism was no longer an alcoholic Anglophobia, or what he had predicted as a 'junta of corporal-punishers and kirk-going cheeseparers', and indeed that the Kirk was beginning to complain about cheeseparing at the expense of the poor and the students?

And he did. Gordon Brown could have told him about the Kirk. But Gordon Brown was more likely to want to show that he qualified for San Francisco status, if not exactly for Prague. If he did, the *Red Paper* was the limit of his political rebellion. It was only the next stage of Nairn's.

IV.

'It rests with you, Mr Mulliner, to save England.'
'Great Britain,' corrected Clarence. He was half Scotch on his mother's side.

P.G. Wodehouse
'The Romance of a Bulb Squeezer' *Meet Mr Mulliner*

It is depressing to flog dead horses, especially when their owner has buried them and any exhumation critique may stink as badly as explanations from Messrs Bush and Blair. Tom Nairn educated himself and the rest of us in the ensuing years. But for all his wish to unsay his invective against Scottish nationalism, so representative a work as Andrew Marr's *The Battle for Scotland* (1992) quotes him thrice, every time anti-Kirk or anti-SNP. Yet Nairn, if not converted to the SNP fifteen years before Marr's book, was certainly half-way to it by then. Marr, fascinating in detail, never seemed to grasp the vital contribution of the Kirk to winning Scotland's Parliament. Alex Salmond would joyously remind Nairn in 2008 when thanking him for his Lothian Lecture that on being elected to Westminster in 1987 his comic use of Nairn's strangled minister as a notice-board joke resulted in Salmond's defamation by local Tories as a self-proclaimed prospective Kirkocide, or pastoricide (Salmond won the ensuing legal case).

Nairn was but one of a number of Scottish literati, not to say 'glitterati' (as Norman Buchan certainly would have said, could he have found a rhyme for it) who migrated homeward permanently or intermittently in the 1970s, though he was probably the only *NLR* staff person to do so. Many were vigorously hostile to the SNP in print, or had been; many more had at best been ominously silent. All ended up either in the party, or warmly sympathetic to it. Some were academics, again permanently or intermittently, but few were in the Scottish universities, where a rare few staff were lifelong SNP. Being from Ireland via the USA I don't count in this. Nationalism was a natural condition to me, made repulsive by violence and its cult; the SNP's hatred of violence, Bannockburn apart, made them seem lovingly prelapsarian Eden-dwellers. World War II had left many British intellectuals convinced that nationalism begat Hitlers and Mussolinis, or at best Francos. Probably none of them thought their Odysseys through from repulsion to acceptance with Nairn's depth, subtlety and learning, but their paths would have been comparable, not necessarily from his influence. Nor were all stations manned by friends or foes of nationalism. Norman Buchan did me too much credit in lampooning me as the charioteer steering *Q* – *Question* magazine, or at least steering its leading intellectuals Tom Nairn and Stephen Maxwell. If there was a charioteer it was Sandy MacCall-Smith, not yet the dazzling novelist of international fame: he was the dynamic assistant editor, and he was, and remained a Liberal. *Q* itself was owned and edited by much more unobtrusive SNP men. I was the resident clown, would-be Scottish Mencken: Buchan's acidities on Maxwell unintentionally amounted to an almost accurate compliment:

> Poor Stephen! Seeing himself Philosopher
> But valued by them only as Press Officer!

He was in fact deeply valued by many of the SNP leaders and members, and was the most extraordinary Press Officer I have ever seen. A tutor in Politics at Edinburgh University, he instinctively treated the reporters like bright students, encouraging them to ask well informed questions, raise issues of substance, by all means to be critical but to be intelligently critical, drove them to read useful treatises, and all but marked them on quality. There has been nothing like him since Gladstone reading the hostile *London Standard* and regretting that its normal editorial diatribe against him had fallen from its own standards ('Mr Mudford must be having his holiday'). The *troika* only existed in my liking Maxwell and Nairn very much, and disagreeing from time to time with each.

Norman Buchan's portrait of Nairn was part failure. But he resembled Maxwell himself, and Gladstone, in his acknowledgment of the adversarial intellect. I mattered no more than a particularly annoying and apparently unswattable gadfly. Stephen Maxwell was more formidable, but however Buchan might admire him in open secrecy, he was clearly an irredeemable Scottish nationalist, seen as Robespierrean in his dedication. But Tom Nairn was of the Marxist Left Norman Buchan knew, thus finding his deepening acknowledgement of nationalism as crucial to Scotland's future not ordinarily wrong, but cosmically wrong. It also let in a most unwanted spectre to haunt Buchan. I had flicked pollen from Buchan flowers while gadflying hither and thither, and found phenomena of Scots cultural nationalism in his wireless programmes on folksong and in his essay in Duncan Glen's *Whither Scotland?* (1971) whose essays by Michael Grieve and Anthony Ross would also inspire later generations. (The Catholic priest Ross's essay, 'Resurrection' became the Church of Scotland professor Willie Storrar's favourite political text). So when Buchan published his *MacDunciad* I was asked to reply in verse for a TV programme, and my effort, to him, concluded:

> So keep it up, kick hard against the goad:
> Have a nice journey down Damascus road!

But if I did the diagnosis, Nairn's was the infection. Some part of Norman Buchan wanted, not to join the SNP but to produce a better SNP, whence he became the more acid as in 1976 Jim Sillars invented a Scottish Labour Party which drew in Nairn, Neal Ascherson, etc, and then purged itself to death. Buchan mocked the outcome, and may well have voted against devolution in 1979 (it was almost impossible to work out what side of it he was on, and it may have baffled him too). I enjoyed debating against him, fellow guttersnipes as we were, and enjoyed even more our last meeting which closed in heartfelt embrace. But what he really represented was a fear in the hard Left that Nairn legitimised Scottish nationalism.

Even as it stood, Nairn hit hard in his essay in the *Red Paper on Scotland* (edited by G. Brown [1975] and today no longer listed in his personal bibliography) but the marksman was shifting even more than his target. He had begun to discover the very different forms of nationalism taking fire in Wales, where 'chauvinist' was a nationalist term of reproach, language rather than law was its most conspicuous card of identity, and Plaid Cymru's youth seemed to pride themselves on being left of the Labour Party by intention rather than like SNP members finding themselves there by accident. He had little difficulty in diagnosing the nationalism inherent in Ulster Unionism, whose rhetoric he compares today with Gordon Brown's 'Britishness'. I am less sure about this. Paisley always disliked the English, finding them hedonistic and snobbish, more so than ever after election to Westminster in 1970, and the Ulster Unionists at large lost their faith in their very 'British' vocabulary when Margaret Thatcher, who appeared to converse in the same noises, ratted on them under instructions from her darling Ronald Reagan, landing them with the 'Anglo-Irish' agreement of 1985. Anglos have been at a discount in those parts since. Nairn is quite right in assuming that Gordon Brown has appropriated the language of his Britishness from elsewhere, but it is Thatcherite rather than Paisleyite, as Nairn would certainly acknowledge for what political content it enjoys. As for the *Red Paper*, it was clear then that Nairn's full-scale prophecy of nationalism was not a case of 'whether' but of 'when'.

Nairn is less ready to express personal resentment in print than any polemicist I know, but this may have fuelled his theory. To me, when all due respect is paid to the giant that E. P. Thompson was, and the somewhat smaller stature of his associates, their high Marxist repudiations of Nairn and Perry Anderson were but little English nationalism writ large. Nairn has never said so, but he evidently realised it. He began to examine nationalism in its commentators such as the super-market wrapups by Hans Kohn, and the uneasy meditations of Ernest Gellner. Gellner fascinated Nairn, not least, perhaps because of his victimisation in another controversy in the early 1960s by the Philosophy establishment (ferociously rebuked by its maverick mandarin Bertrand Russell). Gellner's *Thought and Change* (1972) appropriately included nationalism, Gellner first dismissing commonplace anticipations of its decline and the Marxist version of that, acknowledging their plausibility however mistaken, then savaging fashionable reconsiderations:

> The history of the twentieth century testifies, apparently, to the re-emergence of the Dark Gods from their home in the bloodstream or in the intestines. (Romantic authors disagree about the precise physiological habitat of the Dark Gods.) These dark atavistic gods include, apparently, the call of ethnic or territorial loyalty. . . Those who oppose nationalism hope that Reason will prevail, aided perhaps by Student Exchange Schemes, the British Council, foreign holidays, re-written history textbooks and *au pair* girls. Those who favour nationalism, on the other hand, hope that a grey cosmopolitanism and a false bloodless ethos will not submerge the true sources of vitality, and they trust that the old Adam will out. This picture, which is so widely diffused amongst both the friends and the enemies of nationalism, seems to me utter nonsense (even when it occasionally includes some sensible premises – such as the importance of the human being to belong, to identify, and hence also to exclude).

If Nairn was to change course, it was essential that the positive source of change have a sense of humour. He may also have welcomed Gellner's admiration for works with which he disagreed, such as Elie Kedourie's *Nationalism*. Marxist debate usually conceded little or nothing to intellectual adversaries, as Thompson had shown Nairn all too well. Kedourie might begin 'Nationalism is a doctrine invented in Europe in the nineteenth century' which the Declaration of Arbroath and the *Scotochronicon* clearly belie. But he was nonetheless worth study.

Nairn was to advance the study of nationalism all along the line: it is simpler to note his impact on an allied but discrete topic, the monarchy. Monarchy in Britain has had many such critics, from Milton to Byron, and such prominent twentieth-century polemicists as Kingsley Martin, editor of the *New Statesman* 1931-60 and author of *The Crown and the Establishment*. The irony in Martin's title was that no more 'establishment' a form of Socialism could be found than that of which he was so prominent a pillar, nor no journal with so obvious a monarch as the weekly over which he reigned. What Nairn did was to show in *The Enchanted Glass* how monarchy had bewitched modern society, resulting in the creation of petty monarchies at all economic levels: the executive with the astronomical salary and the asinine specificity has become omnipresent. And it reflected his conviction that the working-class had allowed itself to be enchanted here as in the more obvious admirations for aristocracy and beguilements by the bourgeoisie. Having begun by charting Scots nationalist dreams, he had made himself foremost authority on the British nightmares' nests.

From the first he penetrated the empty resonance of the Blair project, and thus inherited the supreme Platonic tragedy: when Plato's pupil comes to power and the result is a Sicilian vespers. *Gordon Brown 'Bard of Britishness'* is a tragic work, although Nairn's austerity keeps the tragedy invisible to those who had not read the *Red Paper*. The subjoined critiques were to single out as the zenith – or nadir – of the Philippic Nairn's apparently pitiless indictment of Brown as:

> the Jeeves of Britain's last days, a courtier of self-abasement, sleaze, insanely false pretences, failed reform and neo-imperial warfare.

Nairn's friend Neal Ascherson read this with the pain it had probably given Nairn himself:

> Retaining affection for the bold young Gordon I once knew, I prefer to read this as a Nairnean trumpet-blast against the monstrosity of what he's chosen to inherit, rather than as a summary of what the poor guy has so far done on his own account.

And so said many of us. But it is so often Tom Nairn's way – or fate – to be right while the rest of us bootleg our doses of optimism. True to my place in Buchan's *MacDunciad* I wondered if either of them – indeed all of them – interpreted Jeeves correctly: the name is nowadays in wide ignoramus usage as merely meaning a servile valet, where Jeeves was in fact a dictatorial genius subjecting his nominal master to eternal thrall.

To return to the philosophical playground in which Norman Buchan zoologically gardened Nairn, Nairn would surely share Jeeves's rejection of Nietzsche ('fundamentally unsound') and admiration for Spinoza (expressed in *Joy in the Morning* written during Wodehouse's imprisonment by the Nazis). But Nairn and Neal Ascherson may not have undervalued Jeeves: Brown is intellectually so far above the empty

Blair and the moronic Thatcher that we must see the tragedy in his willingly – indeed wolfishly – devouring the dregs of their elixir, not even as a deplorable condition of employment but rather as the nectar bestowed by the gods. Nobody would be more ready to ridicule apotheosis than Nairn. But I am too old to learn new songs. If I wanted to find antecedents to his wit and wisdom, I would turn back to Swift and Shaw, and to Shaw's affectionate adversary Chesterton; more recently to Orwell or to Edmund Wilson, more recently still to Gore Vidal. This commits nobody to anything since they would have assailed one another's doctrines freely if ever given the chance. It also leaves plenty of room to disagree with what he wrote, as he has frequently done himself. And yet, and yet, it is not that I want to avenge the Church of Scotland, much more that I want to extol the faith so often weakened by the absurdities of its rabbis, priests and ministers. He is his country's prophet, with the usual limits on honour from the country – limits dictated by himself as well as his enemies, we will surely wait longer than Sir Patrick Spens's Lady before we see him rise Sir Tom Nairn. Instead he will continue to thunder reproaches at King Ahab for wallowing in the Baaldom peddled by his Jezebel, Thatcherism. Let us hope we have many years before the arrival of his fiery chariot. But when it comes, our Elijah will be good for an address from it of appropriate temperature, and if the S.N.P. prove unequal to his mantle they will – as they have before – take their turn in the curative heat. ❐

TARTAN PLINTHS

The Leviathan, (1651) Thomas Hobbes: The Maintenance of Social Order by rule of Law

Hugh MacDiarmid, poet

Harry Lauder: 'a fule like Lauder' said MacDiarmid
of the tartan-swathed music hall artiste

Seawards the Great Ships (1960) a gritty documentary of the heyday of Clydeside Shipbuilding, treatment by Grierson

STV logo (1980s) – light entertainment to turn Scots heads

Billy Connolly's banana boots: Clydeside Connolly acceded to Scotch Comic heaven in an only slightly less sartorially surreal fashion than Lauder

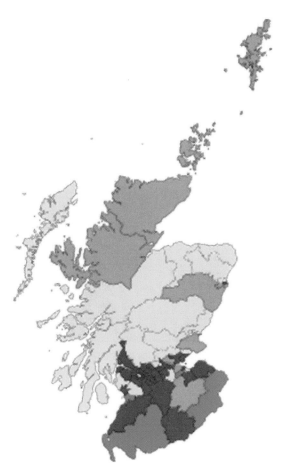

Electoral Map of Scotland: the SNP marching through the
heather in banana boots?

My Childhood (dir. Bill Douglas): This is the Modern World: a grim upbringing in industrial central Scotland

Trainspotting: This is the post-Modern World: sex, drugs and rock and roll in urban Scotland

UCS Shipbuilders demo (1971): 'Not a Man Down the Road', collectivist action to save jobs and communities

Rosie Kane swears (2003): an individualistic action, balancing the people in her hand before the sovereign

Ravenscraig Steelworks: the steelworkers failed to support the miners in 1984, then their industry went the same way

Oil Rig: A new economy – for whom?

Blair/Dewar/Steel : the triumvirate go home and prepare for the Parish Council?

The Holyrood Opposition: three non-party-political party leaders and an impartial professor?

A Scottish Leviathan, Alasdair Gray (1981): Who maintains the Social Order in Scotland?

THE IDEALISTS

Kilbryde Covenanter Flag, Courtesy: Kybo Theatre Co.

I. UP STOORIE BRAE WITHOUT A PATTLE

OR,

CAN THE SCOTTISH IDEAL BE BROUGHT DOWN TO PLANET EARTH?

O rake not up the ashes of our fathers!
Implacable resentment was their crime
And grievous has the expiation been.
> Matilda, Lady Randolph, in John Home's
> *Douglas, a Tragedy* (1758)

*S*COTTISH *Democracy?* – grab a bishop by the lapels, and shout 'Ye arena Mary Morison!' in his face. The thing is, the Scots usually call this easy liberality of manners by its doric nickname 'egalitarianism'. But if anyone were able to conceive of the weight behind Aristotle's judgement of democracy as the worst of all political systems, then surely it is the northern tribe of feeolosophers. The great age of struggle for Scottish democracy was 1560-1690. This was when the people, the real everyday peasantish people, *sometimes* got the chance to vote for their choice of local theocrat. He in turn would micro-manage on their behalf the legal contract which the National Temple had signed with the one and only fearsome and disciplinarian Deity. It was real democracy non-secular style (or let's say, for anachronistic argument's sake, Iranian style). And if you're looking for resentment – dish the bish! – and malicious and slanderous behaviour (ie. Antichrists and 'monstrous regiments'), namely all those drawbacks to poor people's rule that Plato and Aristotle claimed to see two and a half millennia ago, then you could have them by the pulpit-load.

Next came the age of Peace and Patronage, 1690-1830, when the wide ranging and armed resources of the newly convened and unwrittenly constituted British state could ensure that those nice people, the toffs and the profs, were kept in charge of those frightfully earnest folk at prayer, the Presbyterians. Under the urbane London-centric political management of the Argylls and then Dundas, the democratic zeal of the people and their resentments were swept under the drawing room carpet. And in the church, the energy and drive of those purist Calvinistic reformers was now directed by the moderates in charge (those toffs and profs) not towards godly discipline, but cultural pretension. Religious conflict and principled hatreds were ended for aye, or so Scott has it in his *Old Mortality*, while the two kingships were happily united, in that novel at any rate. But Peace and Patronage in the eighteenth century might not mean much to the starving and rioting townspeople, or the peasantry pressed to bloody service in the '15, the '45, or with the Brits – or their enemies – in America and continental Europe.

Happily for Scott, he was well dead before the 'good haters' of Scotch religion made a real comeback. The beginning of the period 1830-1960 brought the return of the demo-theo-cratic zealots like so many non-establishment undead emerging from the backwoods, and evangelicals and sabbatarians began to sleepwalk into places of power and influence in politics and education. This was egalitarianism alright, but only as long as you were a member of the slow-walking elect. Fortunately most people couldn't stomach another people's religious revolution. The hegemonic political parties agreed, Liberal for the first ninety years, Labour for the latter forty, and the idea of a self-managed Scottish polity was gradually dropped as education was realigned on a more anglo-friendly basis; and as for the dreadful Scottish history, it was consigned safely to, well, history.

The Tories do make a bit of a comeback in 1950s Scotland but there's certainly nothing cavalier about them – their most representative prime-minister was a publisher, and roundheaded Labour soon take over, forgetting most of their formative redness to become in their turn truly conservative and unionist once in power again. In the new

Anglo-British industrial state workers weren't supposed to be voting on the type of theology they practised, and nor were they welcomed in to clasp the lapels in the boardrooms – private or, later, nationalised – either.

In the 1960s however, the period of post-war austerity gradually faded and Britain entered a new age of prosperity. Philosophers, historians, writers and artists began to uncover the true unromanced versions of Scotland's histories again. It seemed at last, that maybe they had put enough time between themselves and 1560 to be able to live with heterogeneity, complexity, and dare we say it, heresy, without having to impose discipline and orthodoxy on themselves and their history. The cycles of Scottish histories seemed indeed to be wheeling around every 130 years or so: 1560-1690, 1690-1830, 1830-1960. Thus, if, as we propose here below, a new way of thinking and living in Scotland starts to take shape around the 1960s, what is its significance for a putatively new age, and what would the next 130 years or so bring?

One writer and artist prominent in this rethinking of life in Scotland is Alasdair Gray. His published personal motto reaches out with an exhortation to 'Work as if you were in the early days of a better nation', and carries an eerie resonance for the modern Scot. If the prickly egalitarianism of the official state motto *'nemo me impune lacessit'* ('No-one provokes me with impunity' – adopted, appropriately enough, in the seventeenth century) encapsulates in its epigrammatic classicism a whole ballad's worth of democracy's dealings with the bishop, then Gray's adopted words do it for many of our generation with their ringing together of irony, hesitation, resolution, modesty and patriotism. (A version of this motto has indeed been carved on the wall of the new Scottish Parliament in Holyrood.) But which example of 'better' should we take, it appears to ask us? (and is that only so that in kneejerk, as it were, we can reject the obvious one?) Is there indeed such a thing as a 'better nation'? And if we are to be patriots, if we are to do it for our neighbours and fellows, ought we not to work for some possible best, while still acknowledging that 'our' own past, was not as good as it could or should have been? And why the early days at all? – well, should we not work with hope? – for the next cycle. . .

Gray's words also encapsulate the steady and unapologetic determination which characterises the work of a whole raft of writers in the late twentieth century. The writings we examine in this section may have been unflinching in their patriotic modesty but that does not mean there is a fear of looking under the covers as it were. If the Victorian Age had found the masks of seventeenth century 'truth' so grotesquely challenging that they had to hide them below a gaily coloured plaid of fairy tales, then that meant the intrepid late twentieth century inquirer into Scottishness and its ideals had two layers of what Carlyle called 'Hebrew Old Clothes' to penetrate. It has always been easier for the Scots to stick to partisan 'truths' – this was where George Davie and Marinell Ash saw the nineteenth century 'mistake' – or to detach themselves from the truly enlightened and humane view through adopting a cynical attitude – as demonstrated in our own potted history in the first three paragraphs of this introduction.

What we find however, is that for so many of these writers here – even, apparently, the Glasgow poet Tom Leonard – the nineteenth century provides the key to understanding Scottish political conscious-ness and its ideals. Basically the distinct Scottish civil society, as recognised by Tom Nairn, had the unique opportunity in union with the great imperialist power *not* to develop through nationalism. This civil society undertook its own regulation and control by bourgeois and professional cliques (see Davie's universities and Ash's historical societies) which were, as Paterson (see next section) asserts, 'anti-statist and yet public, private and yet moral, depoliticised – in one sense of politics – and yet civic'. But this self-regulation began to collapse as the Industrial Revolution brought rapid urbanisation, immigration and mass proletarianisation. The keynote of the early union had been the institutional autonomy of Scottish civil society but this could not be sustained as Scotland through the nineteenth century became gradually incorporated into the centralising British Industrial State. But why did this phenomenon go so long unexamined, and what changed to make an examination possible from the 1960s onwards?

To understand why, and to get a sense of how an ideal – or if you want to exercise your democratic intellect, Platonic – Scotland changed in concept and purpose over the last 130 year cycle, you only had to visit West Port Books in Edinburgh, and its extensive collection of

Covenanter histories and folktales. 'History' may be more accurate, for these are red-topped, tabloidised accounts of events from the killing time, grand-guignolled to evangelical effect, for the benefit of nineteenth century audiences. Rev. Robert Simpson's *Martyrland: A Tale of Persecution from the Days of the Scottish Covenanters* could be taken as emblematic of this extraordinary literary subgenre. It articulates a sentiment that is, to paraphrase Smout's introduction to his *Century of the Scottish People*, alien and foreign to us (unless perhaps you are a member of some Pentecostal Super-Church in the American Midwest, or a clench-jawed white Southern Baptist). We could – and therefore must not – characterise the social/political imagination of our near ancestors as theocratic and death-obsessed. The formulation of ideal Scotland was complex and at all times, disputed. Restoring this complexity of incident and influence has been an important task of reconstruction for both left and right; Michael Fry, possibly the most surprising and individual of these writers, characterises the Scottish political climate as one in which an open discussion of first (political) principles has been impossible – 'it has usually been assumed that Scottish political history has been over and done with'.

The creation of a Scottish 'ideal' in the long-view has been the work of successive generations which extends far beyond the remit of *Tartan Pimps*. The oligarchic ideal encapsulated in the Declaration of Arbroath (yes, let's get that one out of the way) submitted the notion that the country was in a state of harmony when the liberties (of those who mattered) were guaranteed, and sketched a blueprint whereby disharmony could be amended by removing threats to that liberty – the same rhetoric was deployed against Thatcher in *A Claim of Right* in 1988, after nearly a decade of Scots getting hammered. Question then – do we therefore characterise Scottish democracy as a mass voluntary reflex against an unwelcome Daddy figure (and yes, that goes for the Thatch too. . .)? And lest we preen overmuch, wasn't it a Scottish monarch who subsequently theorised The Divine Right of Kings as an ideal state of paternal accord?

And then, as mentioned above, we have theocratic idealism, served by violent cycles of reform and covenant in favour of highly theoretical, abstract first principles. This latter explicitly favoured a textual imagining of the relationship between people, state, rulers and ruled, and hence, republics of letters, parish states and Whig fiefdoms vied for the soul of the people, and more importantly, actualisation in a distant political sphere by battering them over the head with charters, Kirk Sessions and dog-eared copies of *Das Kapital* (and that's gotta hurt. . .).

By 'the' we are of course being grammatically and historically definite; that political sphere was Westminster. Or at least publicly; as Michael Fry and James Kellas (see next section) confirmed from both right and left, there was a closeted Scottish politics, unseen but pervasive where power could be grabbed. They all, to a man, clambered into their coach or rail carriage, promised the earth and were never seen again, until someone found them at the palace of Westminster, sheepish and confused over which fork to use. It thus became very important for Scottish politicians, to disguise their own awkwardness down south, to the people doonhame.

If we have moved somewhat, from the dimensions of Plato to the grimy realities of Aristotle, it is only because Scottish idealism is technically minded and is dragged always, like it or not, towards the problem of internal and external constitutional relationships. In this chapter we present a number of reviews that consider the afore-mentioned reformulation of the Scottish ideal during the twentieth century, when so many of the concomitant threads – oligarchy, theocracy and Whig hegemony – unravelled or twisted in new and unexpected ways.

There is for sure, some new species of millennial thinking going on here, but it is not – it cannot be – completely unscathed by the centuries-old complexes – witness for example the resentments which surface most obviously in the writings of Leonard, MacDiarmid and Davie. Emerging from an era that had sated Scottish pride through handing us the fasces of the Imperium and bidding us to beat rivals and subalterns black and blue, twentieth century Scotland shook off the mad bad nineteenth with a crisis of identity and spirit. It was a *quiet* crisis; almost unnoticeable against the grand narratives, almost eccentric compared to the clash of labour and capital, or the horrors of World War II. It crept up even on the Scots themselves, who took a long time to realise that where the union was concerned, feelings, sentiment and reason were not always manifest in a given order. To Westminster and much of England this crisis remained mysterious and largely hidden, subsumed as it was in the great hegemonies of Liberal and Labour Scotland.

BedPan Babies: the curious birth of Labour Scotland

It is generally held that no one can write authoritatively on the political and social development of modern Scotland and omit to mention Tom Johnston. No argument here, but in *Tartan Pimps* we naturally, have sought out the Scottish Secretary's more scurrilous attributes. Johnston (1888-1965) achieved considerable respectability in later years as the most powerful and prominent custodian of the Scottish Office, architect of a limited devolution of powers to its committees and secretaries as part of a grand design to head off Scottish nationalism and focus on the really important issues at hand, of poverty and decay and land use. He is justly admired for his proto-environmentalism, belief in progress through industrial development and genuine concern over rectifying the injustices of the landowners.

Spanning as it did the foundation of the Scottish Labour Party by Keir Hardie in 1888, Johnston's lifetime is mostly contiguous with the creation of the single party pre-devolutionary non-state of Scotland he masterminded. Through public works and the creation of an intellectual framework for treating Scotland as a separate case, he accelerated Labour's rise to parochial power, its seepage into the niches previously dominated by Liberal grandees and its establishment as the party of 'getting on' in Scotland. But stolid as this background seemed, he was, to the very end of his life, attacked on a regular basis by establishment enemies who had caught wind of *Our Scots Noble Families*, his 'scurrilous tract', that got him blackballed out of the Westminster Caledonian Club by two unspecified Conservative MPs. As the introduction to the new edition of *Our Scots Noble Families* relates, an older Johnston spent many afternoons in second hand bookshops, systematically buying up copies of his first book. His given reason? 'Times have changed.'

More than he knew. Having raised the issue of a distinctively

Scottish form of capitalist exploitation that stretched beyond the Disruption and even the Union, the logic of containing the socialist struggle within A.J.P. Taylor's greater England (in which Scotland was mere anachronism) increasingly came into question. Johnston was sensitive to these currents, and his desire to prevent national issues from diverting the cause was a leading motive for his revitalisation of the Scottish Office, the apparatus around which the distinct Scottish political system, identified by James Kellas' analysis of Scottish electoral behaviour, spored and grew. And, just as Scottish Labour had shifted from insurgency to incumbence, so its *eminence grise* Johnston exercised considerable diplomacy in securing limited administrative devolution through the Scottish Office from of all people, Winston Churchill – a toff, but safely, usefully, English. (Half-American, actually, and trained in American politics.)

The irony was that the landowners had already lost most of their power, so that when Labour stormed the keep, they found the levers of power were either controlled elsewhere or there for the taking.

'Do you know your constituency?' the Tory Anstruther Gray was asked on TV during the election of 1966 when he was defeated by John P. Mackintosh (see below) in Berwick and East Lothian.

'Certainly!' he replied, 'Hunted over it several times!'

Like bedpan babies whose turn had come, they became the heirs of the Scottish ruling class; and yet, Johnston's position in Scottish Labour politics institutionalised resentment of the landowners while ignoring the bourgeoisie (who don't exist in Scotland, honest. . .) and emphasised the importance of land and housing as predominant issues, cues picked up by Smout and others. The Scottish Land Restoration League ensured that land issues became enshrined in Scottish socialist discourse – as, via Ian Carter's contributions to the *Red Paper for Scotland*, successive articles in the *Scottish Government Yearbook/Scottish Affairs* and successive reduxes of *Who Owns Scotland?*, it has continued to be. *Our Scots Noble Families* is at the head of strong literary lineage within Scottish political writing, one that unifies Marxian concerns over capital and land clearance with the peculiarly uneven ratios of Scottish land ownership (75% in the hands of less than 20 families). And, as with the *Red Paper*, *Our Scots Noble Families* boasted Prime-Ministerial associations, fore-worded by James Ramsay MacDonald who long before the National Government would make him and Johnston political enemies, praised the book as a 'weapon' to wield in the political sphere. The future PM also shows a keen historical sensibility:

> Have we for instance, ever had a true history of the Reformation in Scotland? We have had a gaily coloured pageantry of battle and execution, of political and ecclesiastical turmoil, but I know of no history of Scotland which traces any readjustment of economic and political power as the meaning and result of this wonderful time. The history of the people in Scotland yet remains to be written. . . The story of the people in history is the best handbook for the guidance of the people in politics.

The books reviewed below suggest that MacDonald's musings were neither idle nor singular. The return of Scottish history in the late 1960s indicated that this handbook was not only desired, but increasingly needed as a rhetorical tool. A history of the people of Scotland that the representatives of that people could get behind was a crucial deal-maker. Nationalist historians began it, but it was Smout, the anglo-liberal, who popularly re-conceived Scotland as a country with a relevant history. But he came late to the process, for it began in the amassed ranks of partisan Scotland. Gordon Brown had gone down the uni to study the history of unions in Scotland, and took this study all the way to the *Red Paper*, which he used as a discourse on recent history to diagnose Scotland's problems, just as Machiavelli did for the Florentines in his *Discorsi*. Tom Nairn used history in a similarly diagnostic fashion in his series of seminal texts on nationalism and the monarchy (the difference being his mirror of princes called for disaggregation, rather than unification). And all the time Christopher Harvie played a somewhat more Berlinesque than Machiavellian fox to Brown's Machiavellian lion: an intellectual sniffing hither and thither, forever on the lookout for a scent of the 'national destiny', and finally scarpering out from under the protective shade of the Labour hegemonic block altogether. There was more than one type of Machiavellianism active in 1970s Scottish politics, and it proved extra-ordinarily fertile.

A hotchpotch of essays, rants and nascent political theory, the *Red*

Paper currently enjoys pride of place in the 'canon' of Scottish political literature. *A Claim of Right* name checks it as a parent text and it resurfaces throughout the rest of the 'canon', which surely makes Brown (as noted above) the Moses figure of the devolved Promised Land (and like Moses, unable to enter it). The *Red Paper* is unquestionably, a *Labour* handbook. As suggested in the first chapter, Brown's collegiate editorship acted (intentionally or not) as a snare for the nats, so that the devolutionary ideal of the 1970s came to be guided by one partition of the Kirk – inclusive only insofar as it (the Lib-Lab unionist) was the largest.

Michty Me!

At almost exactly the same time as Brown was drafting his *Red Paper* his future predecessor was staging her coup of the Tory Party, and with it the country. It is tempting to see Brown and Thatcher as kindred spirits, both reacting against the cultural revolutions of the sixties in an archetypally Scottish and English fashion. We can imagine that they actually had very similar objections – all that Beatnik self-obsession, chaotic political organisation, cynicism against corporate/corporatist power, distrust of established symbols, smoking dope, dropping tabs and dropping out – a negative charge on either prong of the political horseshoe.

Throughout his stint as PM Brown struggled to head off the implications of the sixties either as a writer or a political actor. He also struggled to fill the Johnstonian shoes; whereas Johnston wore power and principle easily, Brown seemed cruelly exposed, a man in a constant state of existential crisis. But it is not because he is some lesser imitation of the great Johnston; it's just that Johnston, wisely, knew that the Scottish model of leadership should never be openly attempted in England. We need only look at the splendidly superficial Blair and his mammy figure Thatcher, whose solid and magisterial teat was constructed around an astonishing flimsy framework – yet succeeded for over a decade – to see why Brown gets bogged down in his own, jealously guarded substance.

Of course, all Thatcher could do was make that sixties selfishness and egotism seem natural, even eternal, but she was long gone before most of us realised. She was a shill but Brown's problems go much deeper, to the fundaments on which the Scottish principle of leadership is built. One of these, we should say, has a lot to do with his gender. Glaring by their absence in *Tartan Pimps* are the women. Is this because they have nothing to say though, or because they are actively discouraged from saying it? We have Marinell Ash of course, interrogating the origins of all that male-dominated Scottish Fundy fulmination in *The Strange Death of Scottish History*. But is that it? Look at the books in this section – Tom Johnston (*Our Scots Noble families*), Hugh MacDiarmid (*Drunk Man Looks at the Thistle*), George Davie (*The Democratic Intellect*), T.C. Smout (*A Century of the Scottish People*), Michael Fry (*Patronage and Principle*) and Craig Beveridge and Ronald Turnbull (*The Eclipse of Scottish Culture*) and you find a very macho gathering.

Is the chauvinism that of we authors? Has gender resulted in a very literary form of predestination? Of the many candidates for inclusion in this survey Liz Lochhead featured strongly. Not that she would describe herself as a political theorist perhaps, but the persistent questioning of male patriarchy in her work represents an important, alternative reality to masculine Scotland, in some respects taking up where Ash left off. The cabaret-inflected, anachronistic *Mary Queen of Scots got her head chopped off* has all the appearance of a modern 'Marian' text, a literary subculture of eighteenth century Scotland, aspiring to an alternative, feminine conception of authentic Scottish identity, as recently identified by Murray Pittock in figures as seemingly unlikely as James Boswell. The male, paternalistic and protestantistic response was more than ready for such dramatic recastings of our past and is none too diluted today: 'Aye, but,' you would say, 'Mary was a hoor, and incompetent, practically FRENCH – and a Pape (and did we mention she was a woman?)'

Lochhead creates a native voice for the Queen, wedding her by voice and expression to the country which would in a few generations, all but collapse politically and economically. Only religion preserved its purity and sense of continuity, making her anachronistic recasting of orange and green into the sixteenth century jarring but appropriate. Lochhead's Mary is confused and persistently incredulous not so much at the fact of masculine power, but its seething anger, and fear. Likewise, the Marian ideal as epitomised in Boswell's better nature – his generous, carnivalesque and humorous side, one that loved theatre in a country where it was banned so often that he needed London airs to breathe – was squashed by the more masculine, militaristic counter-tradition of the '45. Better the king over the water than the queen who came back.

There are other curious absences in our roundup of Scottish idealists. Why you might ask, in an age dominated by broadcast media, does our list stick to boring old fuddy-duddy makers of books? Where are the broadcasters? Yet neither Lord Reith nor his antithesis, John Grierson, figure large in conceptions of Scottish politics. Reith, especially, suppressed his fully Scottish aspects with no hesitation. Who wants to show themselves up in Hebrew Old Clothes, especially when adrift among cheerful and easy-going English congregations? Yet Reith moulded the BBC into a Kirk pulpit of extraordinary range and reach, and his teachings mimicked those of his Reverend United Free Church of Scotland forefathers:

> In the earliest years accused of setting out to give the public not what it wanted but what the BBC thought it should have, the answer was that few knew what they wanted, fewer what they needed.

This blend of messianic zeal and paternalist instincts had roots deep in the social hierarchies dominated by divines such as Reith and Grierson Senior. Grierson the younger, who cultivated a more maverick streak than Reith Junior, was in many respects the true successor to Carlyle – not the son of a preacher, but the son who should have been. His destiny was on the surface, a refutation of his roots; Grierson's parents only permitted him to watch actualities on the fairground cinematographs as they lacked the lying tendencies of fiction. As a grown man Grierson judged the merits or demerits of cinema on its ability to persuade; rather like Carlyle, he threw off the old clothes in disgust (favouring the Transatlantic and the socialist, as opposed to Carlyle's Germanic idealism). It took notable effect; Basil Wright, a filmmaker reared in the Grierson stable was brave enough to remark to his benefactor that:

> I realised that you used to have a Scots accent, you haven't got quite such an accent now, maybe that's because you've become an international civil servant. . .

But like Reith, Grierson found he could only wear his new breeks according to a given pattern, conceiving his cinema along the familiar pattern of the partisan line. Take for example, his exhortations to install 'dominies' and Kirk elders in Scotland who could steer a distinctive broadcasting and film industry and create activity in their 'parishes' along a 'Scotland-metropolis' binary.

> Making Scottish films or Irish films or Lancashire films is a necessary corrective to the pursuits of the artificial in the metropolis. . .

What is interesting here is that Grierson saw the creation of a Scottish cinema as beneficial to Britain as a whole, a means of reclaiming what Murray (quoted above, in an essay for the 6th issue of *The Drouth*) calls 'the real, lived experience' of national society from the caricatures of the metropolis. It still remains important that the metropolis occupy its central position, in order that the provinces should educate and improve it.

Compare that to Brown as you will, but Grierson nevertheless set up a hugely influential – some might say suffocating – film establishment in Scotland defined by a flinty, eat-yer-greens tone blended with virtuoso cinematography. The man himself looked outward, acquiring through hard work, diligence and a canny manipulation of the bureaucratic apparatus, a transatlantic reach. Grierson's deepest contribution to the Scots messianic impulse lay in engineering the creation of important and conducive images that impacted profoundly on the Scottish political consciousness. For many Scots the clang and heat of industry was a direct experience that moulded their personalities, but for the country as a whole, the image of steel plates riveted into a ship, or the orderly, efficient harvesting of the sea solidified a unifying idea of Scotland as workbench (or work-bank?), the great mechanism, a grand, sparkly cog in a massive infrastructure. The power of the massive, rust-red chain that uncoils and slithers into the sea in Hillary Harris' *Seawards* is the definitive image of Griersonian Scotland, where industry was a source of near religious awe. One of the first film critics, he wrote in a still new terminology of cinema speak and his own 'documentary value', but the rhythm, the style and the sense of drama were learned in the tent at the fair and in his father's Kirk.

Grierson engineered these images because he believed they were

191

good for us, but also for people elsewhere, and duly went to extol the benefits of Scottish medicine. He may not have theorised the Scottish state so much as its *de facto* problem-solving leadership ideal; the father figure adept in manipulating the machinery of state and corporation surfaced strongly in him and many other successful Scottish technocrats, who believed the Scottish way was a valid and widely applicable system for saving the world.

The great Griersonian rant, directed at everything from Hollywood's weak politics to the pressing needs for Soviet tanks in George Square post-Hungary 1956, show us Scottish patriarchy with its sense of mission restored and sins aplenty to exculpate. But it feeds off the implacable resentment of those 'true democrats' covenanted by peace and patronage.

Contrast this with Brown's wildly vacillating fortunes, removed from the devolutionary promised land he helped found, to go and run Egypt just as the peace and patronage succumbs to the seven plagues he brought about. Lurching from magnate to mummer, Brown emerged as a Scottish paternalist in crisis. Even the English noticed. But how best to characterise it? *Private Eye* ran a rather unfunny and somewhat off the mark strip, 'The Broonites' to lampoon the age of Gordy, but Archie Low and Dudley D. Watkins actually gave us a much more accurate depiction long before Brown began his ascent–because PM Brown *really is* Paw Broon. Vacillating from skinflint to rake, unable to affect cool, suave detachment, never quite able to get what he wants and often rueful when he gets it, Paw's bandy-legged trajectory in the long running comic strip describes the erosion of his own authority in the face of sarcastic females and precocious bairns and mad old Granpaws who readily put his gas at a peep.

'Save the world? Away ye auld blether.' (Dudley D. Watkins yearned to illustrate the Bible: his surviving sketches for Jesus Christ looked like Paw Broon.

So if we can't credit a Broon, who else do we follow? Is it maybe the impish, resilient, devious long-term eccentric Salmond, light on his feet, and possessed of that superficial charisma 'proper' English leaders possess? Times have changed fellow Broonites – enter, stage left, on his cartie – Oor Ally! ⊓

OUR SCOTS NOBLE FAMILIES
TOM JOHNSTON (1909)

Although outside of the 30-40 year range of *Tartan Pimps*, *Our Scots Noble Families* stakes its claim as an ancestral link between the subsumed Scotland of the nineteenth century and the emergent, dissonant 'shadow polity' of the twentieth. Its genetics are in fact, quite definite, as it was the direct inspiration for John McEwen's *Who Owns Scotland?* (1977), published when this was a vexed national question of political as well as economic importance, and even of CND tracts such as Malcolm Spaven's *Fortress Scotland* (1987). More generally – some might even say, spiritually – it marked a moment when a distinctive Scottish political conversation became detectable, though it was not necessarily respectable.

In later years Scottish Secretary Johnston publicly regretted the tone and fervour of the book as 'too harsh', and notably, did not usher it into reprint (as he did several times with his later *History of the Scottish Working Classes*). So it is tempting to see in Johnston's later drift from fervour to circumspection a microcosm of Scottish Labour's mellowing from movement-against-the-Grayne (the Border reiver kind) to an inert, self-protected vested-interest in its own right. Not that we should overstate the working class purity of early Labour – toffishness was difficult to avoid even when the young and hot-headed Johnston, only three years into the 27 year reign as editor of the political

and cultural journal *Forward*, gave over his paper for a series of essays that skewered aristocratic pretensions, one name at a time. Home ruler, Harrow graduate and fellow land campaigner R.B. Cunningham-Grahame (his family are lambasted in *Our Scots Noble Families*) was a *Forward* contributor, as were Wheatley, Maxton, Shinwell and the man to whom all owed ideological and political debts, David Keir Hardie.

The resulting book is on cold analysis, a slim, light tome, easily digested and easily attacked for its recklessly polemical tone and partiality to a cheap shot – but not for its research, which was hard to fault in breadth or depth. The book is laden with figures showing for instance, the annual income trousered by each family from its tenants. As clued by its title, the book can be conceived as an anti-*Burke's Peerage*, a text-only *Pitkin's Pictorial*[1] that strips these histories of their honeyed layers and indicts the legitimacies claimed by these families in honest terms, as the products of theft and rape. The complaints against the book rested on its sarcastic and scornful tone; many of Johnston's sentences seem to shake with barely suppressed rage and he can be brutal, here commenting on the debt collection methods of the Stairs:

---

[1] A series of popular historical picture books commonly found in the gift shops of Scotland's stately homes.

From this one sees there are still delicate and politic methods of describing the process of eating up widows' houses and grinding the faces of the poor.

The barbs are interspersed with vivid and often very moving accounts of poverty, especially signature case and *cause celebre*, the Vatersay 'land raiders', tenants who in 1906 'swarmed over unused land' rather than starve, and were ruthlessly prosecuted by the Gordons of Barra ('land raider' seems uncomfortably reminiscent of the 'land grab' terminology employed by Tory MSP Bill Aitken in response to the Scottish Parliament's Land Reform legislation). Johnston thus arranges what he calls 'stray leaves from the past' into a manual of iniquity, to be tapped into on future campaigns, which places *Our Scots Noble Families* into the sphere of sophisticated, diagnostic histories such as Machiavelli's *Il Principe* – except rather than hold up a mirror to princes, it proposes to melt them under a magnifying glass.

As with *Il Principe, Our Scots Noble Families* defies such easy description; it is a negative exhortation to a national ideal, altogether too pointed for it to count as a *bona fide* work of social science, too prosaic to make it a work of philosophy and too instrumental in its intentions to qualify as satire. Few satirists enclose *bona fide* graphs, tables and diagrams into their attacks. Nor is Johnston – not here at least – protecting any sort of status quo or accepted gold standard, the basis upon which most satirists work. The old moral standards that underpin the more wistful satires, as held by the nobs are dismissed as distinctly sub-par:

They scorned every principle of

morality *we* [our emphasis] hold dear; they gambled and murdered and robbed and foisted numerous children of illegitimate lusts on the granaries of the common people.

So instead of satirising, the young Johnston surges upwards to grab the silk lapels of his 'betters' and in classic Scots fashion, drags the wearer downwards into the realm of common sense judgements. For such tasks satire is much less effective than highly informed *sarcasm*. He drew on something very old and authentic, detected by Boswell when he complained to Rousseau of Scots' 'warm sarcastical vivacity'. It was to such grandees a threatening heat, one Scotland's greatest conservative thinker, Carlyle, called the language of the devil.

Oh aye? (as *Private Eye* would never say). Quick wits are fine between social equals, flytes flown within a position of relative security. What use is that to the pawky Scots subaltern summoned to the big house? P.G. Wodehouse well understood that sarcasm was a verbal weapon with which the lower classes can rake at the psychological flesh of their apparent betters while leaving no discernible – or rather provable – traces. Before he himself took over the big house, Johnston found in 'Sarcire' a rhetorical weapon of some force, a low vivacious form that drew upon ideals and standards foreign to English satire.

It is probably significant that Johnston emerges from the nineteenth century as a willing carrier of such a seditious and pathologically Scottish disease for the sake of class and nation. The age of the *Sarcaste* was upon us, and they had no time for more 'elevated forms of humour', as one online style manual puts it. Though written in English and guided by Marx, *Our Scots Noble Families* is peculiarly Scottish in rhythm, if not in lexis or voice. But like all sarky bastarts, Johnston skelped his targets without giving too much of himself away, a tactic that only entailed consequences when he went up in the world (Westminster, that is). Thus he set the tone for his heirs in Scottish politics for a long time to come.

A DRUNK MAN LOOKS AT THE THISTLE
HUGH MACDIARMID (1926)

The kneejerk recourse in assessment or criticism of any Scottish cultural or political phenomenon is comparison with a supposed English equivalent. MacDiarmid's *A Drunk Man Looks at the Thistle* (DMLT) sets out his stall as *the* long poem in modern Scots, and as such the obvious English language 'equivalent' must be Milton's *Paradise Lost*. Indeed a comparison of content and structure of the two works is instructive and enlightening. In Milton's epic the sober narrative involves various independent characters and personalities, and the argument between them is carried out closely within an ordered social hierarchy. In the Scots poem a solitary drunk collapsed on a hillside performs a dramatic monologue before an audience of an imaginary and fleeting series of phantasmagorical characters, including the personal ghosts of his international literary heroes. There could be no starker symbolic contrast between the political conditions of the *chosen* native territory within which these two most political of poets operated. We find in one poem the discussion of concrete rights, duties and privileges while a new young Republic struggles to be born into the world of states ruled by divine right; and in the other are solipsistic dreams, visions and nightmare while the respectively dormant and not quite fully assimilated quasi-state has no real political relation as such to the world or any other states beyond its confines.

To be fair we are not strictly comparing intellectual like with like: the English seventeenth century epic and the Scottish early twentieth century monologue. But can the ligaments and musculature of the body politic that automatically bind and pull the would-be free-willed puppet into the obvious comparison be so easily discounted? MacDiarmid's monologuing drunk might in any case be considered – at a lang loup – to satisfy Aristotle's epical condition for a 'single action', as long as the whole contextual Trojan War, as it were, could be taken to be in this case the context of the full historical and spiritual development of the facts of Scottishness.

Like Dunbar, Fergusson and Burns

before him, MacDiarmid believed that the would-be Scottish literary *pater* maun assume the burden of his nation's patter. Unlike his above-named predecessors though, MacDiarmid makes us, his readers, feel that burden too. As with the Tom Johnston work above, so the MacDiarmid poem is published some thirty or forty years before our proper period of study here in *Tartan Pimps*, yet its importance in the ongoing debate as to how Scots assess, express and weigh up the relevance of their nationality cannot be denied. As MacDiarmid put it in a preface to six extracts from the poem published in the *Glasgow Herald* on 13th February 1926:

> . . . its preoccupation with the distinctive elements in Scottish psychology . . . depend for their effective expression upon the hitherto unrealised potentialities of Braid Scots.

MacDiarmid thus considers and works from a notion of language as a repository of spiritual values. His essentially imagist exposition of the Scottish condition seeks to blaze a path of wild speculative freedom 'whereo' the fules (*who speak under the burden of this fragmented, suppressed and ambitionless lexicon*) ha'e never recked.'

But MacDiarmid's drunk man, plundering dictionaries for obscure, forgotten, but enlightening terms, is no mere high priest of linguistic communion here. If he is. . .

Tyauvin wi' this root hewn Scottis saul

then he is also, most certainly, *tyauvin* agin it. For the Scots spirit, if there be such, surely operates in language not by the seductiveness and glamour of occult charms but by what we have called

elsewhere (*Fickle Man*) the 'power of the reductive tone'. MacDiarmid himself for example, claimed that Burns's greatest line was 'Ye arena Mary Morison'. If the Scots tradition of 'flyting' did not predate the Reformation then we might almost be convinced that a Calvinistic levelling, flinging of Jenny Geddes stools, and institutionalised popular interrogation of the theology of ministers of religion, were at the root of this phenomenon. But perhaps they are indeed a symptom rather than a cause? At any rate, throughout the whole DMLT, by manipulation of language and image – moon and thistle – MacDiarmid not only invokes Nietzsche's notion of man as a 'hybrid of plant and ghost' but raises the notion of Scottish egalitarianism to a cosmic condition where things spiritual and material are both met with the same reductive (and inebriate) verve.

The poem is in this way so idiosyncratically Scottish that any comparison as mentioned above is rendered irrelevant, and of course, MacDiarmid gloried in T.S. Eliot's contemporary description of a Scottish literary tradition as 'alien'. But it would be too simplistic to claim that MacDiarmid's nationalism drives him to straightforward corporate aims, and that such lines as:

The thistle rises and ever will

envisage a saviour for the nation. As David Daiches points out (in *Oxford Companion to English Literature*), MacDiarmid's nationalism did not go in for 'crude sloganising', and immediately after that section of the poem he goes on in a species of Nietzschean disgust to berate the spiritual barrenness of his homeland. If anything the sheer contradictory and rationally inconsistent power of the monologue convinces us that his poem is taken up entirely with the path to salvation of the individual. The drunk man gazes on the thistle and says:

This horror I writhe in – is my soul!

– hardly the reaction of the true-blue patriot to the national symbol. Instead the protagonist looks deep into the possibilities for the 'soul's increase', into human potential and self-realisation, and meditates on how to optimise these possibilities for the individual existing within a given spiritual and material heritage. Indeed Tom Nairn calls it 'that great national poem on the impossibility of nationalism.'

THE DEMOCRATIC INTELLECT
GEORGE DAVIE (1961)

A history of nineteenth century pedagogical method may seem an unlikely choice of text to add to the canon of works decisive in the formation of a certain late twentieth century political consciousness. On the face of it George Davie's *The Democratic Intellect* is stuffed full of abstruse scholastic nit-pickings – on the relative merits of geometric and algebraic exposition; on the necessary and preferable relationship between mathematics, physics and philosophy; and on whether university professors, tutors or written examinations ought to bear the curricular strain. We readers must bear in mind however, that we refer here to a Scottish political consciousness, and that *the* constitutional document enshrining the position of the quasi-submerged Scottish state, *The Treaty of Union*, guarantees the three untouchable pillars of Scottishness as law, religion, *and* education.

Davie's contention is that Scotland's once independent academic tradition, which was more akin to some continental traditions rather than the English tradition, suffered a series of attacks and setbacks in the nineteenth century designed to assimilate it, and indeed to subordinate it to the English, and in particular the Oxbridge, model. Davie's title for this Scottish tradition is contracted from 'Walter Elliot's felicitous phrase "democratic intellectualism", ' and the democratic aspects as he reads them can roughly be summed up as follows.

Until the nineteenth century, boys would attend Scottish universities typically as young as 15 or 16, and there would be no matriculation exam in order to gain entry. The basis of any university course there was given with general classes in philosophy in order to train the youths in metaphysical aspects of truth and under-standing, how to analyse and argue from first principles. The boys would pass through university socially as one class, with their professors not only lecturing but engaging in several hours of 'examination' through a species of post-lecture Socratic dialogue around the class. There were in fact no written examinations, nor were students given 'marks', and indeed awards and merits for the students were often, so Davie tells us, given not by the professor but by the vote of the class.

The claims made on behalf of this tradition, and in contrast with the alleged social exclusion, elitism and specialism of Oxbridge, are that it was more humanist, at once principled and pragmatic. Basically Scottish education was, at least in the ideal, supposedly available to the highest levels for all (men), while Oxbridge education was only for the English ruling classes. The question must be though, how that democratic ideal – evidently absent in Oxbridge – and the mythology of 'the lad o'pairts' which universalised the ideal through society, played out in the reality of a nineteenth century Scottish civic realm which was as class-ridden as any other?

Nonetheless, under pressure from Westminster government and others, the Scottish system was to be dragged towards some form of assimilation with England. Four special government Commissions (1826, '58, '76, '89) were set up in turn, to deal with the problem of Scottish university education. These Commissions may, as Davie sometimes alleges, have been stuffed full of Anglican placemen and enemies of the Scottish tradition. They all in one way or another agreed that Scottish universities were too generalist, too much importance was placed on first principles, with philosophy as a compulsory basic study; not enough emphasis on specialism, or on classics (particularly Greek language);

and too much emphasis on professorial care rather than written examinations and marks. These commissions implied that this led to premature intellectualism in the young students, to the Scots reputation as being committed to abstruse metaphysics in argument, and to their always enjoying unnecessary and wasteful debate over first principles.

Although some young Scots Professors – including J.S. Blackie, J.F. Ferrier and James Forbes – seemed to profit from an anglo-moderniser alliance partly in order to institute some modicum of change which they felt was required, in general the Scots could initially mount a spirited defence of their traditions. As they saw it, the English system led to premature specialism which produced mere technocrats with supreme facility in unthinking dogmas, whereas the general, more culturally wide-ranging Scottish degree allowed an attitude which could distinguish sharply between necessary or essential, and contingent or accidental features in any subsequent field of specialism.

The 'love of lucid argument' as they would put it, was not a problem for the Scots, but a necessary precondition for any specialism. Indeed one great dispute which typifies the debate was over whether geometry should be taught through the traditional European spatial method from the Euclid (as in Scotland), or through highly developed Cartesian algebraic-geometry (as done in Cambridge). The Scots saw in the Cartesian method of substituting symbols for objects of discussion (lines, surfaces, solids etc), a removal from the present physical world into abstract mechanical procedures. For the Scots their mathematical inheritance was a metaphysical meditation on actual spatial relations, and mathematics was a branch of liberal education, part of the European humanist legacy, whereas the complex algebraic calculations of the Cambridge school could be for many students simply a 'mechanical knack' with no obvious immediate relation to the world around them.

Ultimately Scottish universities were unable to face down British Establishment pressure. As Davie says, 'a nation noted educationally both for social mobility and fixity of first principle gradually reconciled itself to an alien system in which principles traditionally did not matter and a rigid immobilisation was the accepted thing.'

Davie thus has a barely-veiled partisan view of this 'reconciliation', and the whole book reads much as a 'traditional' Scots litany of defeat and resentment. That makes it at once difficult to get through, and easy to understand why Scots MPs, vocal and supportive at home, were near silent when it came time to regale 'the finest club in the world' with their concatenation of northern resentments. Davie's work has also been criticised for being disingenuous, or plainly inaccurate, as regards equality of access to this education – of completely ignoring women – and of preaching a generalist

conception of democracy while dealing only with one elitist and sheltered corner of society. The great irony however, must be that while Davie has been popular and influential with the nationalist thinkers (eg Beveridge and Turnbull, see below), he depicts in his study of Scottish universities some of the ideally autonomous operations of a particular civil society which was necessarily anti-statist and non-nationalist.

What is vital however, from this greatly important work is that Davie gives us a thorough grounding (from first principles no less!) in one of the major pillars and all its ramifications, of the phenomenon of Scottish democracy. The great significance and surprise of his exhaustive researches is that this democracy is almost exclusively a European renaissance inheritance with long roots into the Greek Enlightenment, and hardly a mention at all of Calvin, Knox, or the Reformation. Having said that however, it was side by side with Presbyterianism as an integral part of the Scottish political constitution that this educational tradition had survived; and indeed it's no coincidence that they also fell together in the 'anarchic disintegration' of the Scottish institutional inheritance over the 1843 Disruption of the national church and the failure to develop an authentic response to the rapidly industrialising society of the nineteenth century.

THE STRANGE DEATH OF SCOTTISH HISTORY
MARINELL ASH (1980)

The regenerative heart of Ash's short book refines our ideas of some embarrassing facts. It asks us in particular, obliquely but insistently, to re-examine two most powerful twentieth century myths about Scottish history: namely, one, that Walter Scott turned Scotland's past into nothing but a plaid-clad Boys Own fantasy, and we've never been taken seriously since; and two, that there's no real Scottish history taught in our schools and that's all because of the English, the Unionist quislings, and the Labour Party – those three operating either serially, separately, or in collusion to keep us in ignorance of our grand heritage.

This book tackles head-on that notion, expressed vaguely above by Ramsay MacDonald, that Romanticism ruined historical scholarship. Ash shows us that a powerful writer like Scott could, by investing as much emotion and intuition as well as reason and balance into his work, wrest history away from the interested parties of philosophers, politicians, and other teleologists, and portray a historical 'society which worked on its own terms and not those of the present.' But Scott's legacy to the world of historical research and scholarship did not end with his poetry and novels where heart and head had co-operated, as it were, to create pictures of living societies.

Late in life he conceived that in clubbable Edinburgh, a new club of jolly fellows, both bibliomaniacs and scholars, could be got together socially to work up, research and publish historical documents at once for posterity's sake and for their own delectation. The Bannatyne Club was duly constituted with members and connections in the law, publishing, printing and government departments, and work began in seeking out, editing and publishing important historical manuscripts and records which otherwise might never see the public light of day.

Edinburgh's anomalous situation as governmental and royal ex-capital of a former state meant that there was much work could be done by such private clubs in securing and publishing historical documents on politics, religion and monarchy, which in other modern countries would be performed by state functionaries. For Scott, product of Enlightenment education, tory with a small 't', and convert to non-established religion (Episcopalian), the state was well kept out of such enterprises, and the organic development by morally committed individuals of private institutions to meet society's needs was the ideal. Other clubs were duly set up on the same model – like the Maitland in Glasgow – and it seemed that the future scholarship and publication of historical researches was secured.

Yet if by the time of Scott's death (1832), the private but collective effort to thoroughly research Scottish history was set on a confident, sure and certain path, then only some twenty years later all seemed suddenly lost. In referring to this collapse – the Strange Death – Ash explicitly places her findings within the same narrative scope of 'anarchic disintegration' of Scottish institutions as found in Davie's *Democratic Intellect*. She misquotes his judgement 'intellectual failure of nerve' replacing the first word here with 'historical', and gives us to understand with this easy substitution that this was a culture-wide crisis and collapse of values.

'The spirit of Scott's historical revolution,' says Ash, 'was deeply utilitarian', but why did Scots evidently lose their interest in their history just when, in the heat of romantic nationalism, other small nations – Ireland, Hungary, Finland etc – began to find and revive theirs?

It is, of course, a complex story, but three dates can immediately put us in a miniature picture: 1829, the emancipation of Catholics; 1832, the Reform Bill; and most important of all, 1843, the Disruption of the Church of Scotland. The truth is that nineteenth century Scottish society was undergoing enormous changes, with rapid industrialisation and the rise of a new middle class, urbanisation at a rate never seen before, and accordingly mass immigration, especially of Catholics from Ireland.

With the Reform Bill and the break away to form the Free Church at the Disruption, the Liberal Party and the Evangelicals could be seen as rejecting the old aristocratic, land-owning order and facing up in some measure to this great social upheaval. The Liberals and Evangelicals – there were strong connections between the two – became ever more powerful in local and national politics, and as noted by Davie, town councillors often had the vote in appointing university professors. (The Provost had the power to appoint university principals, such as George Husband Baird, the longest serving Principal of Edinburgh University who was appointed by his father-in-law the Lord Provost of Edinburgh.)

As the evangelical Presbyterians with their uncompromising beliefs and Calvinistic self-righteousness became more influential, the old intellectual elite (which had comprised men of the calibre of Scott, Adam Smith, and William Robertson) with their concentration on unsectarian historical values and learning rather than denominational religious history, and with their ties to the old landed aristocracy, were being weakened and shoved aside.

In this new rapidly changing order, Catholics were emancipated, Evangelical Presbyterians despised both them and the patronage of the predominantly Episcopalian landlords, and sectarianism flourished.

'Scott had helped to foster a historical consensus with which all Scots could identify,' says Ash, but by mid-century it was impossible to find one agreed history of Scotland. The failure of nerve was in effect a failure of the old Moderate order in the face of both a changing society and a popular fundamentalist response to that change. To make a crude simplification of the new conceptions of history – either John Knox was a murderer, or Mary Stuart was murderess. Apparently no compromise was acceptable.

The new Scottish middle classes, intent on profiting from the opportunities offered by the expanding British Empire, did not want to be weighed down by this dreadful history. Thus what was presented by and for the middle classes as Scottish history was 'highly selective images of Scotland's past' – a series of emotional and sectarian heroes like William Wallace, Robert the Bruce, Mary Queen of Scots, John Knox, Bonnie Prince Charlie, and Rabbie Burns – and these prettified images 'did not endanger the new-found freedom from the past of which many imperial Scots were proud.'

In this sense it may indeed be accurate, as alleged in myth no.2, that the Labour Party of the twentieth century in some way sought to suppress, or at least to ignore the study of Scotland's authentic history. But if so, was it really reprehensible, in the given political climate, to act like a Tito-of-all-the-slavs in putting a brake on the flourishing and flaunting of sectarian histories in order to achieve a modicum of consensus on social progress?

A CENTURY OF THE SCOTTISH PEOPLE T.C.SMOUT (1986)

A Century of the Scottish People is a book with a troubled heart. Why it asks, when the development of industrial capitalism conferred social mobility in America and spread wealth much more evenly on the continent, should Scotland suffer some of the most appalling social deprivation in the then-developed world? In answering, the English-educated Chris Smout flouted both the triumphalist narratives of official economic histories – the myth of Scotland the workshop – and the systematic analyses that defined the world according to Marx (at least, insofar as his disciples understood it). He places his Liberal interpretation front and centre:

My Marxist colleagues, whose labours have done so much. . . to save Scottish economic and Social History from tedium, will be inclined to scoff at my amazement at the rigours of the Scottish nineteenth century. For them, it is inherent in the capitalist system that manufacturers should be rich, get richer, and be celebrated as heroes by the bourgeois intelligentsia, while the workers stay poor, or become poorer. . .

Smout argues that Scotland presents social and cultural features that diverted the effects of capital in a fashion very different to those patterns of development experienced by its southern neighbour. He also goes on –

The Strange Death Of Scottish History • Marinell Ash

courageously, given our setting is the mid-1980s – to argue that Britain's adherence to class conflict seems 'positively perverse' given that in other countries, more conciliatory approaches had ensured a more equitable spread of wealth. Scotland in particular, had excluded itself by attachment to two extremes; at one end militancy in the workplace, at the other a fabric of reformist clubs and gradualist movements – i.e. moral force Chartism – that paradoxically, prevented the working classes from baring their teeth at the most opportune and advantageous moments.

A nationalist might look at Smout's material and conclude that these twin tendencies had also arrested any possibility of a national consciousness emerging as it had on the other side of the Irish Sea. So while not *nationalist*, this was, in its quiet way, a powerful reimagining of the creation of Scottish modernity –and it got him into trouble. His brother historians have smote Smout frequently and often, but that is testament to the central position he occupies in current Scottish historiography. His *History of the Scottish People 1560 to 1830* raised the ire of George Davie (see previous) who criticised his over-emphasis on the power and influence of the Kirk Evangelicals in shaping Scottish political and intellectual institutions at the expense of Scotland's secular traditions. An easy mistake (if mistake it be) to make for an Englishman confronted with the seemingly monolithic presbyteries – monolithic at least, to English sensibilities.

But Smout is generally frank and credible and can write clearly and lucidly on material that can be otherwise, near impenetrable. He discredits many fondly held pieties; showing how 'traditional' rural areas, such as Banffshire, had a much higher percentage of illegitimate births than the urban centres and that bad housing, rather than a tendency to drink, had much more to do with the inability of the Scottish working class to improve its lot. Indeed, the 'Tenement City' chapter, while beset with some very Anglo prejudices and bigotries over social housing, makes a strong case that poor quality builds and an almost pathological aversion to spending money on accommodation was one major crinkle in Scotland's development as a modern industrial society.

Another thing rarely mentioned of Smout is his strong feel for visuals. The illustrations he has selected for the *Century* are vivid, articulate and polemical in tone. The selection is guided by thesis and antithesis; the kilted laird lounging amid his stuffed kills is contrasted with a single end, lush ladies taking the country air with Glasgow mothers in dank tenements, and the clean limbs of country kids contrasted with those of slum children bent with rickets (something of an obsession of Smout's, judging by the captions). It is arch and yet endearing, for however you respond to Smout's ideology, his compassion for the suffering of ordinary folk lends humanity and purpose to the text.

Smout's book is perhaps most significant as a synthesis of historiographic archaeology. The nineteenth century saw the subsuming of Scotland and the twisting of

A Century of the Scottish People • T.C.Smout

203

national sentiment into the strange faux-baronial forms of 'patriotic unionism' (never more absurd than when a giant penis was erected atop a pap near Stirling by Scots who were 'Englishmen' under the Empire). To our modern sensibility and despite recent efforts, the nineteenth century is for Scots an embarrassing and obscene dark hole. Yet Smout drags us in, showing it to be an essential prologue to the seething energies of the twentieth, a bridge between our mythicised early modern and medieval eras and our own – not least the transmission of all that uncomfortable, colourful, medieval madness.

And who could doubt that such acts of historical repair are needed? Scotland worked and is worked through terroristic myths. Smout makes a good case that these fuelled the rise of Scottish Labour, which deliberately resurrected exorcised demons and devils, as in the 1915 Glasgow rent strikes, when the rhetoric of evil factors was called back from clachan to tenement to receive a good doin'. A daring point to make, as public

intellectuals rallied around Scottish Labour against Thatcher's Westminster. Equally adventurous, given that last ditch efforts were being made to retain shipbuilding on the Clyde, was his judgement on the Red Clydesiders. Remarking on their ultimate descent into *Pimp*ish quiescence on the Westminster back benches he states, simply and laconically, that 'The story of the Clydesiders is not edifying.'

A Century of the Scottish People is in a sense, a post-Union, post-trade union, history which builds into a swatch of what a complex, textured – some might say grown-up – conception of Scottish history looks like, and perhaps only an outsider – nationally and politically – could have done so. Until Devine or any of the post-devolutionary eminences of Scottish historiography produce something as readable, timely and intellectually important, we will still smite Smout who showed us that the Scottish nineteenth century made of us more than we'd ever like to admit.

PATRONAGE AND PRINCIPLE
MICHAEL FRY (1987)

To suggest Tory historian Michael Fry as Scotland's pre-eminent post-colonialist is surely pulling the leg. Yet this now overlooked history argues that subsuming Scottish political history *a la* A.J.P. Taylor makes Scots 'incapable of acting in awareness of their past as the English so often do'. It was a problem created by

followers of Sir Walter Scott, who regarded pre-1707 Scotland as a barely coalesced patchwork of interests. But the lack of nuance and subtlety among his immediate adherents saw a veneration of history degrade into indolence and nostalgia.

The stated purpose of this 'Tory Home

Ruler' – 'about as significant in the affairs of their country in our own day as the Auld Licht Burghers were in theirs' – is not only to correct the historiographical gap, but also perhaps, to change consciousness (not something Tories are really supposed to do). If it seems an odd preoccupation for a Tory it is largely because Labour Scotland has been so effective in formulating certain received wisdoms, not least that there is no right of the non-existent centre in Scotland, or its literature. How could there be, given Scotland's stately progress towards the independent Scottish Socialist Republic that plagued Tom Leonard's dreams (see *Situations Theoretical and Contemporary*, 1986) and so stubbornly refused to emerge post-1997.

Rich in occasionally surprising detail, Fry's extended essay concludes that Scotland's political system has for 200+ years been locked in a stasis of Patronage vs Principle, and that the former would always overcome the other. 'Oligarchic' rule exercised by a chosen Unionist elite working out of sight of the public is a constant of this thesis, reinventing itself according to the prevailing fashion, from Kirk to Whig and then to Labour. Commenting on the tenure of his colleague Malcolm Rifkind as Scottish Secretary (he who famously referred to the post as that of Colonial Governor), Fry remarks:

'The apparatus he took over had been showing its ample capacity for stifling through institutional inertia all radical impulses, whether of Left or Right. The local oligarchies continued, as for the last 200 years, to mediate between central authority and a clamant populace with jovial venality.'

There are similarities here in tone at least, to Tom Nairn's, and Beveridge and Turnbull's analysis of a political and economic elite who, while not colonised, acted as if they were. Scottish politics being our compensation for having proscribed theatre for so long. Fry's surprising conclusion is that whatever its benefits the union is corrosive, as Scots political interests will cluster around the cyclical question of how to respond to their 'perpetual friction' against London power, creating a closeted system of secretive government in absence of a public forum in which to resolve them. 'Congress' style political movements thus overcome natural partisanship to form and entrench themselves as Dundas in the late eighteenth century, Liberal in the nineteenth and Labour in the twentieth. The result, while occasionally galvanising, was ultimately sclerotic.

Fry's thinking is simple; rearrange the London-Scotland axis, so that natural partisanship can manifest itself and a healthier political culture can emerge.

'Partisan spirit and alternation in power do, if rather self-consciously, foster constant critical scrutiny, diversity of opinion and efforts at reform. In Scotland by contrast, government is conducted behind closed doors.'

Correcting this involves retrieving the Scottish right from its subsumation into single party state politics, which Fry believed would find its own authentic voice with the creation of Home Rule. A Scottish Tory party cannot flourish in a unitary British state – especially when they are so identified with its core interests, but it could if the single party system was broken up and politics

Patronage and Principle • Michael Fry

conducted publicly in Edinburgh, rather than on the fringes of Westminster; successive Scottish elections have in fact, borne this out – for sure, the Tories have yet to win Holyrood, but they have in many respects looked much more comfortable in its environs than Labour.

But to leave it at that would condemn Fry as merely a cynical, if erudite pollster; he speaks also of the 'tradition, liberal and individualistic, but generous and progressive, which has its crowning achievement in the creation of Modern Scotland' but admits that it is viewed with hostility not only by Johnstonian collectivism, but Scottish Conservatism.

Even if you take this to be so – and it is a persuasive argument for any non-aligned person with a basic belief in the toleration of dissent, the dispassionate observer of Scottish politics since 1979 must look, amazed, at how an entrenched establishment (Labour) so grouted into every cranny of Scottish life, believed, with customary 'jovial venality' that they could open up its politics yet lord it over a secret Congress-state. Fry did tell them so:

'I do not assume that Scotland can only be saved by an Assembly under a Labour Administration, as the portal of a participatory socialist paradise.'

The morbid fear among Labour activists of the 1970s and 80s of Home Rule as a betrayal of the socialist ideal, led the Labour front bench in Holyrood to raise the spectre of Toryism resurgent at every opportunity. But the Fry model extends to elsewhere in the chamber; if the current First Minister were to win a referendum on Independence what splits and fractures would show in the SNP's makeup? Can we ever imagine an *independent Conservative government* in Edinburgh, headed by someone very unlike Sir George Younger, 4th Viscount of Leckie, but not unlike Annabel Goldie, which latter to be sure, speaks with a voice not thrown from central office in London, but one (like it or not) authentically, undeniably centre-right and Scottish?

At the risk of sounding pious, if we genuinely believe in parliaments, or even a milder form of the Leonardian notion of political dialogue then this possibility must surely remain open to us? Otherwise we descend into dangerously facetious special pleading. The Corsican Leader Gen Paoli said of the suggestion – endorsed by Rousseau – that post-Genoese Corsica should retain its Genoese hangman to preserve the purity of the Corsican republic, 'as we have Corsican tailors and shoemakers [or Grocer's daughters. . .], so we should also have a Corsican hangman'. The alternative as he well understood is mere terrorism of a quiet – you could say jovial – sort.

THE ECLIPSE OF SCOTTISH CULTURE
CRAIG BEVERIDGE AND RONALD TURNBULL (1989)

Beveridge and Turnbull give us, in their *Eclipse* a very recognisable Scottish prickliness. These bare-knuckle bonny fechters want at once to sweep the intellectual board clean, and to carry on cultural business exactly as it was when we left it off in 1706. They speak of the 'task facing nationalists' and unlike many other sympathetic critics, they are not afraid to boldly include themselves under that denomination.

The most lively and provocative part of their analysis is, ironically, not their invective (which H.T. Buckle might recognise, see below), but their exposure of a lack of intellectual sophistication in the nationalist surge of the 1970s. This is related to their adoption of Frantz Fanon's theories of colonialism for the case of Scotland. There is, as they say, no doubt something recognisable to the Scot in the Fanon description of the colonised native being led to doubt the worth and significance of their inherited ways and to embrace the superior and civilised ways of the coloniser. Thus far we are in fairly well-known and -trod territory, but Beveridge and Turnbull are then prepared to go further than Fanon's generalised warnings about the dangerous 'cultural' ground on which the 'native intellectual' treads, and develop the critique into an out and out *trahison des clercs*.

When they defend Scottish traditions against Trevor-Roper and Scottish Calvinism against H.T. Buckle we tend at once to nod our heads along with Beveridge and Turnbull and shake them in despair at their 'metropolitan' targets. Trevor-Roper it was, after all, who in the Hobsbawm *The Invention of Tradition* volume denied the Highlanders all their traditions including Gaelic poetry (which he could not read), and Buckle said in his history, 'In no country is toleration so little understood as in Scotland'. But Beveridge and Turnbull soon broaden their attack to include the more surprising target of the native Scottish intelligentsia, who have apparently internalised the coloniser's views, and 'have a deep aversion to everything native and local'.

Thus when the intellectuals bemoan the stifling effects of Scottish religion and education and its alleged effect of Scottish 'inarticulacy', the *Eclipse* mounts a spirited, totally unexpected, highly unfashionable, and thus usually unheard-of defence of the Scottish Calvinist tradition. Articulacy, they say, 'cannot be equated with verbosity' (they should know!), and inarticulacy ought not to be conflated 'with quite different phenomena, such as taciturnity and unwillingness to communicate'. For, they go on, the metropolitans would understand nothing of behaviour consistent with the Calvinist inheritance of 'moral seriousness, distrust of complacency, passion for theoretical argument'.

What is most surprising and provocative however, (again in comparison with Fanon's abstracted and generalised drift) is when the accusations against the native intellectuals here are carried out *ad hominem*. Tom Nairn for example, merits a chapter of his own in this small book, and in his analysis of nationalism as a way forward for the left, is dismissed as a union jack underpant-wearing British Socialist, who is 'closer to the ravings of a Trevor-Roper than to what might be expected in a literary figure of a nationalist bent'.

In fact the book largely descends from a challenging initial critique into a *cri-de-coeur*, with its heroes (principally Scottish twentieth century philosophers like George Davie), and its villains, which latter include everyone else in *Tartan Pimps* except Margaret Thatcher and Tom Leonard (and what an odd pair of bedfellows by omission).

This is a pity because the thesis is insightful, and despite the failure to develop it, has been influential and promised a sophisticated and bracing analysis of Scotland. Unfortunately its authors forget that as the Frantz Fanon model can only be a conceit in Scotland's case, taking it too literally causes them to become conceited. It is a mere conceit here in particular because of these authors' lack of material. And in fact a much stronger and more realistic case for this sort of thesis is made by for example, Charles McKean, the architectural historian, in *The Scottish Chateau*. This history of one particular building type – the country house – marshalls exhaustive research and a wealth of empirical evidence towards the unavoidable conclusion that a vital and once flourishing element of indigenous culture – Scots Renaissance architecture – was denigrated, denied and ignored not only by English commentators but by native cosmopolitans and Enlightenment improvers alike.

Fanon also had *matériel* to hand: he squared up to the *pied noirs*, the French military and the collective weight of a vast, abstract intellectual establishment that had dominated his assimilationist upbringing. Dying from leukaemia as he dictated *The Wretched of the Earth*, his ruthlessness was spurred by impending mortality, his outsider status as a non-French non-Algerian and an acknowledgement that the system he attacked had already depersonalised everyone who spoke for it. In contrast, while Turnbull and Beveridge nominally square up to London they soon lose sight of the system and take square-goes with anyone they regard as shouting against the team.

The crazed Sir Who Terrible Raver, (a 'metropolitan' but perhaps only insomuch as Bedlam is sited within the London city limits) is a deserving target. Otherwise, texts are rifled and the offending, 'reactionary' sentences singled out – and no one is too short, or innocuous, or out of context to qualify for their disapproval. It is more than a little sinister.

Take for example the case of R.H. Campbell, who initially comes out well as a disciplined economic historian who established important continuities between the 'darkness' of the seventeenth and the golden eighteenth – but is still condemned for acknowledging the importance of the great changes signalled, if not solely caused, by the

The Eclipse of Scottish Culture • Craig Beveridge and Ronald Turnbull

Union. Worked this way, the Fanon analysis becomes a benchmark for some 'perfect', 'pure' response from native Scottish culture that everyone is doomed to fall short of. As a result, the *Eclipse* feels less of a reading of Fanon (or even his source-spring, Gramsci) than of Kafka, with the court inventing new crimes and new possibilities of guilt as successive Jock Ks fail to meet standards of perfectibility defined by a law no-one ever defines or clarifies.

A CLAIM OF RIGHT FOR SCOTLAND
OWEN DUDLEY EDWARDS (ED), (1989)

Was it humility, timorousness, or ambiguity that led the authors of *A Claim of Right for Scotland* to opt for the indefinite article? Maybe it was *historical correctness*, recognising the pre-eminence of the original *Claim of Right* of 1689, which exploited the contractual concept of Scottish kingship to oust James VII in favour of William of Orange and the other fruits of 1688. Or perhaps it was an instinctive legalism that tempered their language, as *Claim of Right 1689* was an Act of Scotland's previous Parliament, whereas *A Claim of Right 1988* held no legal force whatsoever. In any case, reviving the title seems bound to arouse suspicion among nationalists of upper or lower case as it defers to an original that, though it had called upon native Scottish legal precedents, further tightened links with London on the eve of Union. Either *Claim of Right* could be accused of that recurring wee-small-c-conservative recoupment in Scottish politics, where we grouse at London because nagging reminds them there are still two of us in this marriage.

So was the SNP right to call it 'a devolutionist trap'? The 1989 book of essays of the same title is edited by Owen Dudley Edwards (Irish revisionist, Welsh nationalist and cheerful contrarian) provides a commentary on the earlier 50 page document that embraces positive and negative reactions. The document was created by a volunteer committee of academics, union leaders, technocrats, politicians, 58 out of 65 local authorities and members of the Edinburgh literati, more a critical mass than a mass movement. They were what any student of our then recently re-gifted modern history (see everything and anything in the preceding reviews. . .) would recognise as members of a post-colonial 'elite resistance' stirring up the subalterns of the non-colony by yanking peevishly at the ropes they learned from their masters.

The committee could at least argue its narrow Lib-Lab political legitimacy as broadly representative of civic Scotland, but the absence of Tory and SNP thought is taken up by the commentators. Putting the fundamentalist SNP position is Chris MacLean, who is scathing over the committee's self-imposed restrictions. Fumbling for a truly withering put-down, lone Tory Michael Fry calls his essay 'A Claim of Wrong' and attacks the document's 'dreary corporatism' and its belief that political autonomy ensures economic growth because it allows politicians and institutions to create an alternative centre of patronage outside of London (a dogma carried through into Labour's first term on the Mound). Now, these Tories and the Nats surely have a damned cheek given they didn't even turn up for the meetings, but Edwards salutes the courage of these few in stepping over solid party lines.

Overall, the mood is pragmatic and conciliatory; even Tom Nairn comes out for cautious corporatist gradualism, donning his Carlyle-cum-Burke habit to excoriate a 'girning' SNP. The decision for him clearly, was to focus on what was achievable and play a long game.

But many of his colleagues were clearly fixed on the short term, as the document stated:

> Scotland faces a crisis of identity and survival. It is now being governed without consent and subject to the declared intention of having imposed on it a radical change of outlook and behaviour pattern which it shows no sign of wanting.

The true cynic might observe that the Tartan Leviathan moved (but to pounce? or cringe?) because Thatcherism – the 'radical change of outlook and behaviour pattern' – was a competing elite ideology flexing formidable bulges of Westminster muscle. There is an element of turf war, but it's about more than just her disregard for Consensus politics:

> The comments of Adam Smith are put to uses which would have astonished him, Scottish history is selectively distorted and the Scots are told that their votes are lying: that they secretly love what they constantly vote against.

O Tempora! O mores! This articulates not so much a constitutional argument but collective disgust at the whole of the Scottish 1980s which is why it struck a chord beyond the tight inner circles. We have only dim personal recollections of what Stephen Maxwell calls in his essay 'the cruel mould' of the decade but we still feel, as many others did, that *A Claim* tapped into authentic popular sentiments – at turns prophylactic, at others profound. There is the feeling that various strands of the Great Scottish Argument – historical, legalistic, political and moral – are finally being woven together into something coherent. And that this need not exclude native conservative thought. To prove it, Edwards quotes from Scott's *The Letters of Malachi Malagrowther*:

> The Scottish Members of Parliament must therefore lose no time – not an instant – in uniting together in their national character as the representatives of Scotland.

This question of what Scottish representation as it stood, could achieve is echoed by Dennis Canavan, described by Edwards with admiration as a 'Parnellite obstructionist':

> 'Is our first loyalty to the British state or to the people we were elected to represent?'

Canavan here confirms that the notion of a distinctive Scottish *political* system – and not Scott's concept of a cluster of vigorous and independent civil institutions – has come to be widely accepted as not only existing but as the mechanism for protecting Scottish interests. Observing that 'the Scottish conscience is spread more widely and thinly than before' Charles Kennedy makes this question one of collective soul, badly strained by the prevailing madness emanating dahn sahrf (and there is every

grounds to argue the spread is still as thin today). The consensus at the heart of *A Claim of Right* is that such a conscience could not be left to the mercies of an alien, inimical political creed with no respect for old-fashioned Scott-ish political clusters.

On this at least, 'the resistance' was in broad agreement, which is why *A Claim of Right* remains an important (if indefinite) political Scottish political landmark. True, it represented – to quote arch-sneerer Jaroslav Hasek's mockery of 'democracy' within the Austrian Empire- no more than 'moderate progress within the bounds of the law'. Sure. But in an unconquered colony there are far worse alternatives.

RADICAL RENFREW
TOM LEONARD (1990)

Some readers might wonder why we choose *Radical Renfrew* as the volume typifying and characterising Tom Leonard's expression and influence on political formations. For *Radical Renfrew* is an anthology of work from eighteenth and nineteenth century poets largely of low (if any) national profile, which was collected, and introduced by a short essay, by Leonard.

Tom Leonard's own body of poetic work while highly significant and influential is a slim one. The most important and

successful individual poems, those which have brought him great respect and a large following of enthusiastic readers and listeners, number perhaps around three dozen short pieces. Most of these poems were written around the 1970s in a phonetic representation of Glaswegian languagewhich stresses the actual sound of the spoken words, and they were published in various pamphlets and samizdat editions, and finally collected in *Intimate Voices* in 1984 by Galloping Dog Press, a one man garage-publishing type outfit from Newcastle.

Not only is the body of poetic work a small one butLeonard still givs regular readings of these works he wrote some thirty years ago. Yet as is evident from the hushed and appreciative crowds (especially Glaswegian ones) these poems seem to be possessed of some special incantatory or totemistic power for their audience. On examination of the texts – short pieces of everyday dialogue, often banal even when ostensibly dealing with such themes as 'The Good Thief' – one might be at a loss to explain their hold and their power over the listeners. It is indeed tempting to reach impishly for a comparison with the eldritch sway held by the Black Dwarf, described in Scott's eponymous novel as having,

> qualities which made him appear, in the eyes of the vulgar, a man possessed of supernatural power.

But happily the gnomic qualities of his poems have had some light thrown on them by Leonard himself in the introduction to *Radical Renfrew*, where he sets before the reader what amounts to a species of artistic mission statement. By taking a broad selection of local poetry which has largely been rejected by the 'canon' of literature as discussed in critical material and taught in schools and universities, and bringing it into the public eye, Leonard demonstrates how literature can and ought to play a central role in universal democracy. Leonard means to reaffirm that people ought to have the right to read and write what they want in their own and any other language. That the canon of 'taught' literature depends heavily on a special literary language – usually a representation of Received Pronunciation (RP) – which not only does not allow the

vast majority of people just to 'be' themselves, but by codifying literature with certain social and political values often deprives the majority of access to the dialogue.

Leonard's own poetry is thus written in a phonetic dialect, which not only is based on an everyday spoken language of the people, but on a language he speaks himself. For Leonard 'democracy' would not entail politicians listening more closely to the electorate, or bringing more institutions into intimate and intricate contact with the people or any such top-down, ultimately patronising gestures – he has said in comment on the setting up of a Scottish Parliament in 1999 that it was 'a sweetie shop where people could argue over the Mars bars and the Rollos' – but about people having the right to speak of themselves in their own voices to one another. And perhaps that is one key to the enormous reverence that greets Leonard's public readings: the performance might be termed as an *ecce homo*, as it were, the man, his own voice, his own things; he present naked, unapologetic; his everyday sufferings and triumphs the equal of all others.

But by use of this 'phonetic' script and his insisting on the everyday speech of the urban working class of Glasgow, Leonard makes radical assertions of worth in the face of the institutional-isation of Scottish dialects which, according to him, placed similar restrictions on content as does the standardisation of the 'canon' in the RP voice of those in control. For Leonard much of the nineteenth century post-Burns Scots poetry has been controlled by a middle class whose conventional and conservative political agenda worked to exclude the often radical and heterodox expression of the working classes.

'The angry became the pawky,' says Leonard, and this history led the Scots language movement inexorably from Burns to the Kailyard and Harry Lauder. This linguistic understanding is very much analogous to the nineteenth century historiography of Marinell Ash as seen above. We might indeed term it 'The Strange Death of the Scots language' as literary monuments were raised in a meaningless and highly selective language which could ignore the living, wild and unpredictable speech of the new urban working classes, and would provide a quaint, pawky picture of pre-industrial happy peasants of which the new imperial middle class could be the proud descendants.

This pawkiness was of course a phenomenon that MacDiarmid too struggled against in his attempt to renew and reinvigorate the Scots lexis. As we saw above, MacDiarmid took on this task with specific political aims in mind. But for Leonard everything is about the word as spoken, and having the right to speak it, to be as he says 'a' person, rather than adapting to be 'the' ideal literature reader or writer complicit with all the values and morals inherent in the language that dominates that discourse.

So MacDiarmid's heavy dependence on the dictionary, on obscure, researched, and often redundant terminology is for Leonard at once too elitist rather than truly democratic, and too centred on the idea of the propriety of the 'nation' and the 'national'.

The negative aspects of this work ('fuck thi lohta thim') may bring us back to Aristotle and the 'resentments' which he maintained would surface in democracy. But there's more to this connection, for with Leonard poetry truly demonstrates its relation to both logic and the political by continually affirming and redefining what it is possible to say. The intract-ability of his humane expression is, moreover, recognisable in its relationship to a native egalitarianism of the type noted by Nairn in his *Red Paper* essay when he quotes MacDiarmid, saying in 1927 'the absence of nationalism is, paradoxically, a form of Scottish self-determination.'

Radical Renfrew • Tom Leonard

II.

THIRTY-NINE STEPS WHICH WAY?

I

IN the last weeks before the Referendum on the Scottish Assembly
of 1979 there appeared a 14-page tract. *A Voter's Guide to the
Scottish Assembly and Why You Should Support it*, keeping for page
two the italicised information that:

> This guide, which is non-profit making, has been compiled by
> Gordon Brown and Christopher Harvie, as a contribution towards
> the endorsement of the Scotland Act.

Granted that our utterances of thirty years ago will often wallow
in what President Grover Cleveland called innocuous desuetude, yet
this sentiment sounds if anything even more remote than President
Grover Cleveland. Tell me, grandpa, did the Labour Party once venerate
the principle of 'non profit making'? Yes, my child, all that was before
President-expectant Blair taught us that New Labour Is But Old Capital
Writ Large. We know that Gordon Brown rationalised this proceeding
by the conviction that Labour would retain its principles provided he
was at the centre of power, however unsavoury his bedfellows. And I
for one believe he reached this conviction with no more cynicism than

might sustain chit-chat unwinding after hard campaign slog.

Professor Christopher Harvie, then his fellow intellectual in Scottish/British Labour, has found a new destiny in Holyrood rather than the doorsteps of Downing Street, but his new master, the SNP, has also been at pains to befriend occasional fat cats.

Their readers in 1979 were given brief biographies, space presumably preventing the inclusion of Labour Party membership, and in any case the content held a faint aroma of penitence for the Labour Party's indifference to what the pamphlet saw, viz, that:

> The mass of the Scottish people have indicated time and time again they want, not separatism, but the greater degree of democratic involvement in Scottish life that the Assembly will permit.

> Since the Scottish Office was created, nearly a century ago, there has been an insistent demand for responsible government in Scotland, which has brought the issue of home rule frequently to the fore. . . The time has now come for the issue to be tackled directly, and for the machinery of government in Scotland to be made accessible and responsible. This isn't an antiquarian ideal; the need for greater regional autonomy is accepted throughout Europe; it makes no concessions to the sentimentality of traditional Scottish nationalism.

The inference was plain: Brown-Harvie accepted the SNP claim that Labour, like the Tories and Liberals, when in government, had kept government in Scotland inaccessible and irresponsible. How far did they realise that their formula excluding the sentimentality of traditional Scottish nationalism committed them to the unadulterated sentimentality of British nationalism? Yet their perception was profound. It was Scottish intellect *versus* British emotion. And so, it has largely remained.

The biographies, bereft of political affiliation, played the intellectual trump cards:

> Gordon Brown is a lecturer in politics in Glasgow College of Technology, former Rector of Edinburgh University and editor of the *Red Paper on Scotland*.

> Christopher Harvie is senior lecturer in history at The Open University and author of *Scotland and Nationalism*.

The pamphlet's chief argument for the Assembly was that the power of the Secretary of State for Scotland had increased, was increasing and (again by implication) ought to be diminished:

> The Secretary of State is now, in Scotland, Home Secretary, Environment and Energy Secretary, Minister for Health, Housing, Agriculture, Social Services (excluding Social Security), Transport and Education. He has a bigger staff than the Foreign Office, the Home Office or the Treasury and handles a budget for 1978-79 of more than £3,500m per annum – more than 5% of all government expenditure and more than that handled by most of his ministerial colleagues.

> But the growth of the Scottish Office has never been based on well-defined principles. Indeed its haphazard expansion is a remarkable illustration of the prevalence of *ad hoc* responses to the problems of the day.

Both Brown and Harvie must have known the historical conclusion of the Regius Professor of Modern History in Cambridge, Sir John Seeley (1834-95) that 'We', the English. . .

> . . . seem, as it were, to have conquered and peopled half the world in a fit of absence of mind.
>
> *The Expansion of England* (1883), Lecture 1)

There was more truth in this than Seeley's superficial imperialism fully comprehended, and its relevance to Scotland indicated that the Scottish Office expanded on the same imperial principle. Brown and Harvie had heard in their infancy of the great battles against imperialism in Africa in the 1950s, and the Labour Party's conviction that it made passionate politics on the anti-imperial side. Their rage against the Scottish Office is easier understood when we add up such individual items. (Seeley's other famous judgement, 'History is past politics, and politics present history [*The Growth of British Policy,* 1895] appropriately divided Brown and Harvie: Brown grew increasingly sympathetic with that view, Harvie increasingly hostile to it.)

The painful truth was that from Labour's return to power in 1964 (as Harold Wilson would make clear in his memoirs) Willie Ross, the Secretary of State for Scotland, was valued for his ability to deliver every Labour Scottish MP into Government lobbies, and there his value climaxed. In the comparable context of Mayor Richard Daley's

Chicago in 1968, the *Sunday Times* book on that year's Presidential election (*An American Melodrama*,1969) quotes Joyce's *Ulysses*:

> And by that way wend the herds innumerable of bellwethers and flushed ewes and shearling rams and lambs and stubble geese and medium steers and roaring mares and polled calves and longwools and storesheep and Cuffe's prime springers and culls and sowpigs and baconhogs and the various different varieties of highly distinguished swine. . .

Here the authors of *An American Melodrama* (Lewis Chester, Godfrey Hodgson and Bruce May) ended their quotation, but for our purposes the next lines have their apposition:

> . . . and Angus heifers and polly bullocks of immaculate pedigree together with prime premiated milchcows and beeves.

If anything, Brown today would deny the passage was in his mind, Harvie today would deny that it was not in his. Their morose recital continued in 1979:

> Today there are five departments – agriculture and fisheries, home and health, education, development and economic planning. The number of civil servants under the Secretary of State was 7,000 in 1767, but stood at 10,000 in 1974.

> An empire, but a secretive one. If Whitehall discourages parliamentary enquiry, its mushrooming Scottish satellite exercises power with minimal responsibilities.

'Satellite' in 1979 was a word most used in allusion to the Iron Curtain countries bullied, defrauded and forced to prioritise Russia above themselves; its other immediate reference would be to Russian projectiles in space, dog-bearing or cosmonaut-peopled, but absolutely dependent on Russia to whom satellite achievements were vauntingly ascribed.

> As well as the departments, there has in the last thirty years been a proliferation of agencies even more remote from democratic control . . . For this web of power and patronage, making more than 4,800 appointments – 500 of them paid – the Secretary of State is responsible. In Parliament there are few major debates on Scottish affairs. The Secretary of State answers questions only once every three weeks.

So Secretary of State for Scotland Ross, prodigal son of his people, kept the swine, delivering them to their Westminster destination to ensure his personal reward of the fatted calf. (The Church of Scotland minister's son would have known the text: but the Selkirk school-master's son would have known it also.) Ross's replacement by the colourless Bruce Millan made for little improvement, for all his grooming in lower ministerial office:

> While the number of civil servants has grown, there are now only four additional ministers of junior rank, who are scarcely able to take any legislative or even executive initiative. So is it surprising that the Scottish Office has continually failed to live up to its expectations, despite its wide remit and its location in Scotland? As for the 'patronage state' does this settle on the best people of the best policies? Or does it simply promote the party hack or 'safe' delegate of a powerful interest group and acquiesce in the decisions of officials and highly-paid consultants? What we know of it – urban motorways, nuclear power stations, oil rig building yards, and the controversies that decisions about them have generated – doesn't promote complacency. But we know little enough.

> The accountability of the Scottish Office to parliament may be bad, but its accountability to the Scottish people is even worse.

All this was officially hostile to the SNP whose followers were nevertheless expected also to vote for the Scottish Assembly, come the Referendum. But the sibilant song of nationalism animated these passages as thoroughly as any SNP audience might expect. The crackle of anger is if anything greater. SNP orators might call the Labour Party traitors (or declaim, as did one SNP Conference speaker at this time, that if Keir Hardie were alive today he would be turning in his grave). But the Labour Party devolutionists knew the market value of that treachery and felt themselves to be its victims. To turn from Joyce's *Ulysses* to Milton's *Lycida*,

> The hungry sheep look up, and are not fed
> But, swoln with wind and the rank mist they draw,
> Rot inwardly, and foul contagion spread.

Or, as Brown and Harvie put it, elegantly derivative of Christian *Catechism* and *Communist Manifesto*:

> Did Glasgow people really want to live in thirty storey blocks, or to see their cities swathed by motorways? Were the Borderers allowed

to decide whether or not they wanted to keep their railway lines? Was there any public discussion of the long term planning of onshore oil extraction activity, or of the local government system?

Silent though their biographies were as to their Labour affiliation, they addressed their audience as though the only voters were Labour Party supporters, or as though Labour Party supporters were the only voters in need of guidance (or, more paranoid, the only voters Brown and Harvie thought capable of listening to them.) The Labour Party in Scotland was so riven with dissent on devolution in 1979 that the need to preach to its unconverted might seem the only necessity of victory, what with Tam Dalyell thunderously opposed, and Robin Cook, revving up his 'No' to become tomorrow's 'Yes' after suitable huckstering, and Norman and Janey Buchan ferociously non-committal, and back in 10 Downing Street Prime Minister James Callaghan hostile to his own government's proposal, telling the Scottish voter through the mouths of Brown and Harvie why 'you' should support it: you should, he wouldn't.

It is hardly surprising that at the subsequent General Election Gordon Brown's Election Address (Edinburgh South) showed a picture of the candidate apparently about to slug the Prime Minister in the solar plexus, Callaghan taking what cover he could behind his spectacles, his expression more one of alarm than surprise.

But for all the need to convert the Labour Party to its own Scotland Act, *A Voter's Guide* seemed almost to imply that it would be blasphemous to address arguments to anyone capable of voting for any other party in any other election. Yet within 18 years the UK Labour Party would frame its appeals almost exclusively to Tory voters possibly capable of their first defection to Labour, and all the more would it crawl before the newspaper tycoons whose newspaper no decent Labour Party person should read.

While *A Voter's Guide* shuddered away from ecumenism, it rejoiced in cosmopolitanism. It explained to 'you' that 'many have voted' for the SNP 'out of sheer frustration at a system of government whose operations, in Westminster, the Scottish Office and in the local councils, have been remote and secretive – and can never be anything else.' Its assumption that its readers would accept its authority on voter reasons for voting for another party might strain credulity, but this would save the briefly wayward voters from damnation where belief in Scottish independence would show the brand of Cain on their brow, and predestination to the Inferno for their souls.

But their cosmopolitanism could even extend beyond Geneva (and its Jansenist equivalents owing allegiance to the Vatican). Brown and Harvie sought divine mercy for rebel tendencies among the Labour Party:

> The issue of accountability and decentralisation is acute in Scotland but it is certainly not unique. Throughout the West there is a growing division between a centralism which remains obsessed with maximising material satisfaction and a radical opposition which is more concerned with freedom and the distribution of power. . . self government for Scotland is. . . a means of revitalising the democratic involvement of the individual. The more political power is acquired, the more it must be given away.

II

What became of Gordon Brown we know. And it is hard to believe that he consciously repudiated *A Voter's Guide*, although these last sentiments are harder to equate with where his Government has gone now. He may be much more true to it than his associates realise. It may be that he really would prefer not to get votes from anyone who has not at some time, voted Labour, or at least whose parents have not: it would explain his obvious dislike of a snap election when he assumed the Premiership in 2007, so obviously dependent on fair-weathered friends. Even if his cosmeticians dragged him to the foot of the altar of Rupert Murdoch, his face may have shone its disgust through the protective powder and patch. Behind Mr Murdoch's repudiation of Brown, there is all the ageing bitterness of the *roué* who knows he can only buy Mr Brown's lips, never his heart. The vicissitudes of the Murdoch prints towards Mr David Cameron spit more of the bitterness: Mr Murdoch knows that David Cameron is merely a mechanical toy, whose fidelity depends on his clockwork winder, where Mr Brown was a real man, once.

And yet even David Cameron's clockwork can accommodate

wheels within wheels parodying that ancient rhetoric of freedom and accountability. It is as though Mr Cameron has adopted Brown's Chanel No. 5, original perfumier having no apparent use for same (to judge by the destruction of human rights of refugees, asylum seekers and non-violent Muslims by Mr Brown's Home Office and the *agents provocateurs* stirring up death in the name of security). We know that if ever in office Mr Cameron will deodorise the aroma of civil liberties out of his every pore and every armpit, but he knows that the rhetoric may swing a vote or two still, at least until he can inherit their state power he so bleatingly denounces. Gordon Brown is left as a Cinderella whose Ugly Sisters intend to make a hit at the Prince's Ball wearing her 30-year-old castoffs.

This may leave Professor Harvie as Buttons the page, true to Cinderella's old Principles however discarded by Brown and made over by Cameron. There is more to the analogy than mere derision. Buttons is a sympathetic figure in the Cinderella story, but essentially as Cinderella's equal, colleague, sidekick, not simply a devoted old retainer still true to the former Mademoiselle of the castle. Hence the happy ending cannot require Buttons to take a somewhat egregious place among the Prince's retainers. Buttons remains true to the prenuptial Cinderella, just as the Seven Dwarfs are to the pre-nuptial Snow White, but neither should intrude on post-marital domesticity. So Buttons went away to slay a Tartan Monster using cartography provided by the prophet Nairn, whose *The Break-Up of Britain* he would describe in his history of twentieth century Scotland *No Gods and Previous Few Heroes* (1981) as the 'central text of a new and unsentimental intellectual nationalism'. This made explicit the anti-sentimental implications for future Scottish nationalism already diagnosed by *A Voter's Guide*.

Harvie's credential for guiding voters has been *Scotland and Nationalism* whose vicissitudes tell their own tale. The book won its second edition some fifteen years later, and Buttons, while enlarged, had if anything increased his appeal to the balcony (in his preface):

> Revising a book after fifteen years is a vertiginous business, a partnership with an immature, cocky younger self who occasionally manages feats of generalisation and insight which middle age is no longer up to. . .

The book was prolix, young Harvie apparently having Lloyd George's idea that an argument could only be got across the politicians by endless repetition. In an ideological sense, it was also strongly anti-nationalist, or at least hostile to what it saw as the simplicities of the nationalist picture of a martyred nation. This led some reviewers to regard it as opposing the devolution policy which eventually foundered on 1 March 1979.

A Voter's Guide in addition to all else was thus a bibliographical corrective. Happily Harvie had only to correct and revise: the credential cited for Brown, the *Red Paper on Scotland*, had to be disappeared. Harvie's second edition continued:

> Where it succeeded, the book did so for reasons which were collective rather than individualistic: the 'common sense' which possessed a generation in Scotland that its own past had been forgotten, as much by nationalists as by unionists: that the culture of the country was the result of a peculiar dialogue between community and enterprise, Calvinism and rationalism, Scotland and 'Britain', between the peoples and regions of a complicated, argumentative nation.

> . . . There was a feeling that if Scotland was in contact with anywhere else, it had to happen *through* England – something the 'renaissance' itself fed by being so dependent on London publishers and publicity. The 'British' experience was the necessary catalyst, but matters didn't stop there. Two things have happened to this view. One: Britain was never only England, but a construction which, by opening out to the Empire and to America, rather dissolved the constrictions of conventional nationalism. Two: The European connection remained much more important than I judged in 1977, both through Scots' experiences of Europe and through the world of the immigrant communities.

Harvie modestly refrained from adding that the latter perception was owed largely to his own translation from Senior Lecturer in the UK to Professor at the University of Tübingen. *A Voter's Guide* had remarked that as the 'commanding heights' of the UK economy had 'receded, into. . . the Common Market. . . we have had to regain our democratic traditions.' If this was not a direct manifestation of the British Left against Europe, as denounced by Tom Nairn, it was both cold and fearful, above all with the implication that 'the Common Market' was alien from our 'democratic traditions' whose being regained would be in spite of 'the Common Market'. Harvie's academic experience not only made him a European: it released him from the Platonic cave in which so many British socialists continued to shiver at the shadows of what they took to be Europe. From all we can gather, especially in his contribution to the totem that the Treasury made of the pound sterling, Brown remains in that cave.

There were other instruments of change. Harvie never needed to acquire an Irish sense: he had written profoundly about Irish cultural history while still an undergraduate. But he had yet to discover Wales, so natural a harbour for him with its affinity with his own cultural priorities in history. *A Voter's Guide* had shown that he shared the Welsh nationalist guru John Osmond's suspicions of what he termed 'the centralist enemy.' And he also discovered common perceptions (and tragedies) with Kenneth O. Morgan, foremost historian of modern Wales which his own work so brilliantly contextualised in the history of the entire archipelago. Harvie would be welcomed into a part-time chair at the most national of Wales's university colleges, Aberystwyth.

Harvie (whom it seems impossible for any rational person to dislike) mixed modesty, self-mockery and constructive reappraisal so well in his subsequent editions of *Scotland and Nationalism* that it seems ungracious to notice further solecisms. There is indeed a danger of neglecting the first edition now that we have its successors, and each edition has major perceptions of their times needful for us to remember. For instance, in 1977 (when Harvie was not a lone anti-nationalist but, as noted, left some readers of at least some intelligence (book reviewers in fact) with the belief he also opposed devolution), *Scotland and Nationalism* began a conclusion (entitled 'Forward from Nationalism', embarrassingly reminiscent of Stephen Spender's *Forward from Liberalism* (1937) whose heralded sequels were to be (a) the Communist party, and (b) the editorship of *Encounter* subvented by the CIA):

> In 1977 the main question in Anglo-Scottish politics is no longer what to do about the Scottish National Party or about North Sea oil, but how to prevent a total disintegration of the relationship between the two peoples. While this book was being written, layer after layer of the paintwork which overlay the Union settlement has been

shaken off. What has become visible is not a mechanism for the systematic exploitation of the Scots complex range of institutions and assumptions which have in the past linked, not fused, the two nations. . . . the rise of political nationalism [and] the discovery of oil. . . were only catalysts in the dissolution of a relationship which pivoted on the joint exploitation of industry and empire. . . (272-73)

That this was the conclusion of a Unionist in 1977 is a landmark of significance in today's perspective. (One may, somewhat irrelevantly, differ about its specifics: what I have always found startling about Scottish nationalism was how little, not how large, whines about English exploitation echoed in the SNP mentality, the centre seeming to be that English (or English-dominated) rule of Scotland was held inefficient for Scotland's needs.)

The objections to that final chapter of 1977 is simply that Harvie forgot his own profession:

> . . . in the economic changes that will follow independence the party's performance is bound to betray its promises. (278-79)

> . . . George Orwell noticed in 1947. . . 'an English or anglicised upper class' and 'a Scottish working class which speaks with a markedly different accent, or even, part of the time, in a different language. . . a more dangerous kind of class division than any now existing in England'. After independence, the more opportunistic means of polarising politics along lines which do not threaten the distribution of wealth. And by then the rocky road to freedom may have set the stage for the sort of ideological paralysis which gripped Eire for forty years (280)

> . . . the Scots will unquestionably call the assembly in the old Royal High School their parliament and the leader of its majority party their prime minister. (280)

> One thing can certainly be guaranteed: devolution will not bring tranquillity to the Scottish political scene. Indeed, the first years of the Assembly will be occupied largely by conflicts with its competitors, the secretary of state on one hand and the regions on the other.

Harvie is a historian to trade. His field is therefore the past. But such youthful solecisms expelled into exterior darkness in his later editions remind us how many similar errors have been predicted by British Unionists at every stage of what Harvie charmingly entitled 'a dance to the music of nationalism'. Nor are attempted historical parallels more reliable technology for prediction than the entrails of birds, *Old Moore's Alamanack*, &c. 'Eire' owed its ideological paralysis to winning independence by violence, something the SNP tabooed with implications Unionism has never understood, much less acknowledged, Tory Party Unionism (if not its parasite graft, Labour Party Unionism) was at any rate consistent in this, since the core of Unionism lies in celebration of Scottish regiments in desirable slaughterhouses.

III

Any doubts about Harvies's support for devolution were answered by *A Voter's Guide*, but even more telling was the depression clouding his textbook in the New History of Scotland series, *No Gods and Precious Few Heroes –Scotland 1914-1980* (1981). The book is useful – Harvie could hardly write a line which was not, either by intention or by admission – but the grey shade of defeat clings over it like an Edinburgh haar clamming around tourists. There was some tawdry intellectualisation of the Labour Party attempts to assure the public that the SNP was at heart anti-Catholic:

> . . . Protestant Action in Edinburgh . . . became in 1936 the second-largest party in Edinburgh, with 31 per cent of the vote, returning a maximum of nine councillors. This movement remains mysterious in several respects although the rise in the overall poll which it caused – had some similarities to the SNP's municipal impact in the 1960s (see p. 148). It had some vaguely Fascist overtones . . . (p.100)

P.148 did little to amplify this delicate discovery unless the allusion was to SNP activists in the 1970s often having no previous political experience, but that is a feature of new movements: in the early 1980s the Social Democrats attracted activists who had never been members of any political party either. In any case if Harvie wanted to fish for anti-Papists in SNP waters, it would have made for more reliable history to compare like time with like time. The results would have been entertaining enough. The SNP had some quite outspoken anti-

Catholics among the midwives attending its birth – George Thomson and Andrew Dewar Gibb, for instance. It also had some outspoken pro-Catholics among the midwives – Fionn MacColla, Compton Mackenzie, Moray MacLaren (all Catholics), Hugh MacDiarmid (an atheist, but a pro-Catholic atheist when Anathema stakes were burning). It also had some profoundly anti-anti-Catholics. Labour also had its anti-Catholics such as Sam Campbell, and its anti-anti-Catholics as well as its Catholics. So did the Tories (put that in your wee drum and bang it), and the Liberals. Anti-Catholicism, pro-Catholicism and anti-anti-Catholicism were simply factors of Scottish political life between 1919 and the Pope's visit. Where the Labour Party differed from the others was in its readiness to charge its rivals with anti-Catholicism as the means for keeping its Catholic followers faithful, which from time to time it recalls with less and less success (one of the more ludicrous recent attempts to pump up fear of anti-Catholics resulting in its local MP preventing the Irish Taoiseach from appearing at a Roman Catholic shrine).

But the issue is dead, apart from the generous wrath of a few Catholics because nobody is persecuting them; it was killed by the remarkable coalition of John Paul II and the Church of Scotland. Harvie was thus premature in his textbook title: there were Gods all right between 1914 and 1980, and fairly contentious Gods too, especially in the 1930s. It was the sequel, however, which testified to divine survival. Not only did the Church of Scotland ensure the Papal presence in Scotland, but it also brought Thatcherism tottering down in vengeance for her gatecrashing the General Assembly, inspired a Methodist Canon to lead the revolt (or, if you prefer, devolt), whipped all opposition parties into facing the enemy instead of one another, and nailed their commitment to a far stronger devolution than the Unionists among them were demanding (while drawing the SNP from the Cave of Adullam into which its fundamentalists had consigned it). God had not enjoyed Scottish politics so much in decades, all the more with the Church of Scotland supplying several heroes from its own ranks.

We have to leave Harvie in the academic life of T‚bingen while the Gods resurrect and the heroes return. We can accept such symbolism as naturally comes his way by his introduction in John Buchan's *Witch*

Wood (1988, Canongate Classics 17, reprinting the original 1927 edition): its subject is a Church of Scotland minister who also goes off to the European continent while being popularly reputed to have vanished with the fairies. He would produce a much more substantial introduction in 1993 for Buchan's more famous metamorphosis, *The Thirty-Nine Steps*. It cannot claim to be Buchan's greatest fiction – surely that must be awarded to his last novel, *Sick Heart River* (1941) written as he was dying about a hero making a bonfire of his own vanities and championing the survival of what his previous world would deemed the unfittest. But it is his greatest success, materially speaking, winning his widest audience. And it seems impossible that Harvie's edition for Oxford's World's Classics, can be bettered. It is much more sensitive than his previous work to religion and this seems a logical consequence for the Kirk's salvation of the cause of Scottish nationhood from the years of the Thatcherite locust. From the very beginning Harvie affirms the underpinning of the book to spiritual implications, first in his epigraph (p. vii); from Buchan's hero Richard Hannay facing his final ordeals:

> Here was I, a very ordinary fellow, with no particular brains, and yet I was convinced that somehow I was needed to help this business through – that without me it would all go to blazes. I told myself it was sheer silly conceit, that four or five of the cleverest people living, with all the might of the British Empire at their back, had the job in hand. Yet I couldn't be convinced. It seemed as if a voice kept speaking in my ear, telling me to be up and doing, or I would never sleep again.

Unspoken, that for openers of his introduction tells us one thing about Harvie as a critic: that this will be good partly because his critique accompanies his identification, that Buchan's success depends on your fleeing from Scudder's dead body when you have disguised yourself as a milkman, followed by adventures in Scotland including meeting Buchan himself (a splendid perception on Harvie's part) in the role of a literary innkeeper, then other encounters in which Harvie again scores by seeing the best of them to be (what is also morally the finest) the initially half-drunk spectacled road-repairman, and then your supreme moment of horror, when you place yourself under the protection of the bald archaeologist:

'Have they gone?' I asked.

'They have gone. I convinced them that you had crossed the hill. I do not choose that the police should come between me and one whom I am delighted to honour. This is a lucky morning for you, Mr Richard Hannay.' As he spoke his eyelids seemed to tremble and to fall a little over his keen grey eyes. In a flash the phrase of Scudder's came back to me, when he had described the man he most dreaded in the world. He had said that he 'could hood his eyes like a hawk'.

I, like Harvie, enjoy identification with that scene. The trouble is that in reading it I sometimes identify with the bald archaeologist. I seem to remember, having first read it as a boy then standing in front of a mirror, and trying to convince myself I could hood my eyes like a hawk. Fortunately I didn't know any hawks. Harvie's introduction makes the startling point that this way may be closer to the author's intention than we might guess from the book's being written early in World War I, and hence as war propaganda, Harvie argues – and to my mind proves – that Buchan based the German masterspy on the only masterspy he knew, Admiral Sir Reginald ('Blinker') Hall, head of naval intelligence, whose biography by a subordinate, Admiral Sir William James, was entitled *The Eyes of the Navy* (Harvie takes James's epigraph whence he entitles his book to be James's own words, but in fact it was the ambassador from the neutral USA who gasped 'Such eyes as the man has!'). Harvie quotes James's notice of Hall in the *Dictionary of National Biography*:

> [Germans] who had failed to respond to ordinary interrogation often became as putty in his hands. There was a hypnotic power about his glance which broke their resistance.

It's important that it's not only James's reaction, but also Ambassador Walter Hines Page: this strengthens the case for Buchan having the same reaction. Harvie quotes Hannay's weakening under the eyes:

> There was something weird and devilish in these eyes, cold, malignant, unearthly and most hellishly clever. They fascinated me like the bright eyes of a snake. I had a strong impulse to throw myself on his mercy and offer to join his side.

And Harvie notes Hannay's reaction at the end of the story when Hannay has trapped the man who had so nearly trapped him:

There was more in those eyes than any common triumph. They had been hooded like a bird of prey, and now they flamed with a hawk's pride. A white fanatic heat burned in them, and I realised for the first time the terrible thing I had been up against. This man was more than a spy; in his foul way he had been a patriot.

But if Harvie has seen so well how deeply Buchan's enlistment in British intelligence gave him a propensity to contemplate trading loyalties, what does that tell us of the erosion of Harvie's own British Unionism of the 1970s? His introduction's initial epigraph from Hannay and the part he realises he must play can be a libretto for Harvie's thoughts on the emergence of a Scottish nation and his growing doubts as to whether he really wanted to sit out the dance to the music of nationalism. Also Harvie's later use of it has resonance for us (p. ix):

It seems straightforward: a piece of propaganda for individual responsibility at a time – in 1915 – when the war machines were physically crushing individuals by the thousand. And yet it is also charged with elements of Bunyan and Shakespeare, the Quaker's 'inner light' and the 'conscience' of Scottish common-sense philosophy.

This was to accept the lesson of the Church of Scotland's transformation of contemporary Scottish constitutional history with a vengeance, and Harvie having assimilated and aggrandised the religious implications of his country reborning, courteously noted the cruder agreement of an authoritative historian of espionage, David Stafford:

Buchan found . . . a vehicle [to] transport his readers to a land of . . . adventures, but maps guide them on their secular pilgrimage through the tortuous ethical and social landscape . . . they were sermons as well as yarns.

Stafford was speaking of the Hannay novels in general (and religion, especially Bunyan's *Pilgrim's Progress*, is unavoidable in *Greenmantle* (1916), and *Mr Standfast* (1919)) but Harvie zoomed in on its less recognised but even more vital foundation for *The Thirty-Nine Steps* :

With the head of intelligence, the kindly but complacent Bullivant, ignoring Scudder's and Hannay's warnings; with [one of] Scudder's murderer[s] walking coldly out of a meeting of the Allied high command with the mobilization plans in his head, the power of the prophets is sorely needed. Even at the most breathless moments of *The Thirty-Nine Steps*, the Free Kirk pulpit is – literally – never far away.

Harvie having grasped the religious lever opening up Scottish politics in the 1990s as well as *The Thirty-Nine Steps*, follows its machinery to the heart of the novel's meaning and purpose, utilising the very device superficial critics might naturally question, viz. why should the South African Hannay take refuge on the Scottish borders (other than that Buchan knew them better than any other rural landscape)?:

> . . . Hannay's Scottish pilgrimage . . . establishes a sense of place and a frame of literary and topographical references which nurture a sense of menace and what the Germans would call *Schicksalskampf* : a conflict in which personal and national destiny is decided . . . at the Galloway inn . . . the young in keeper repeats a passage from Book Two of *Paradise Lost* as Hannay approaches
>
> As when a Gryphon through the wilderness
>
> With wingéd step, o'er the hill and moory dale
>
> Pursues the Arimaspian.
>
> The gold stealing Arimaspian is Hannay, and the gryphon, otherwise Lucifer, is the 'fallen angel' of Germany, in whose cultural ambience Buchan had largely been raised. Hannay's confrontation with the Black Stone gang on the moors of southern Scotland is thus a modern-day restatement of the Calvinist confrontation with the powers of darkness, and subsequent regeneration: in short, a 'creation myth' applied to the origins of the war.

The Church of Scotland had jettisoned much of its formal Calvinism (though its removal of the Westminster confession still lay a few years into the future) but Harvie's grasp of the religious hinterland of *the Thirty-Nine Steps* showed from what terrain was hewn the Kirk's summons of the Scots to a Constitutional Convention in 1990:

> The Border landscape, of which Buchan knew every burn and dry-stane dyke, was one revered in Calvinist history. It had sheltered the Covenanters in the 'Killing Times' of the 1680s, and Buchan had already explored it in three early novels . . .

Ultimately the Kirk's defiance of the Thatcher Government, on the Calvinist principle of the superiority of Church to State (unlike the English order, so comforting to secular authority), resembled Hannay in flight from the police, with the world of Mammon all around us an appropriate analogy for the highly modern militarism of the Germans in 1914-15. Naturally Harvie did not make so irrelevant a point to his work on the novel, but that work helps us to see the evolution of his political thought on the evolving Scottish present. His contemporaries had witnessed a 'creation myth' for the new Scotland, in this case a myth that was also a reality. Even his footnotes gently signalled his appreciation of the character of the Kirk's achievement. He explained the General Assembly (which the currently secularised Hannay is neatly distanced from his author by calling 'some ecclesiastical spree'):

the annual 'parliament of the Church of Scotland'

– who better to set in motion the means to demand a parliament than a parliament itself?

IV

If Harvie's rethinking of old texts by new light illuminates the progress of his own perceptions and convictions, his revisal of *Scotland and Nationalism* for 1994 and then for 1988 became a cool observation of intellectual transformations one of which had been his own. He mocked the confidence of the first edition whose prisoner he could now see he had been; the second and third were the work of an observer all the more because of his academic profession in Germany and Wales. He saw the erosion of the Labour Left as the formidable figures of his own time opted for what they thought as realism and he called surrender. He kept literature as his spirit rather than his handmaid, and consulted the back of Scots luckpennies to some purpose:

The Murdoch-Neil agenda put Scottish internationalism in a different context . . . One could look at Wall Street, Microsoft or News International . . . and see a lot of this Social Darwinism in place: James Hogg's Gil-martin on a global level. (3rd edition, 228-9)

Reappraisal included doubts about the value of others of his diatribes than where it was most predictable, e.g. nationalism (as a *Tribune* reporter he had studied the SNP in Conference at first-hand, with the usual result of being startled by its friendliness: on such occasions it was a party having a party, when it was not too preoccupied with moving the remit back). But Harvie also doubted the value of his 'demonisation' of Thatcher, and his cooler head and more scientific hand dissected her nationalism:

> Was she an English nationalist, as she told Michael [Earl of] Ancram? But English nationalists around her wanted the Scots to clear out, carrying with them the toxins [should that be 'toxics'?] of Celtic collectivism. Was she a British imperialist? Is so, was she an incompetent one, letting the Scottish Unionists collapse when some superficial devolution compromise (of the third chamber sort entertained by Edward Heath) might have given them room for manoeuvre. [In the light of the Holyrood Parliament as it came into being, this was a true prediction, all the better for not being one, and Tories survived in Scottish politics only by grace of the legislature Thatcher had rejoiced in denying for so long.] Or was she, on this as on other issues, a typical Westminster product, aiming at party advantage, unconcerned as to ultimate ends? (p.230)

He had already written her epitaph (p.203) and that of her successor 'Thatcher and Major were clueless rather than nationalist'. Harvie was, and always would be, a man of the left, but his growth into nationalism, in the midst of reappraisal of Buchan, meant recognition that something great had died with the passing of his 'cultural nationalist/political unionist' ideology, something going back to Stevenson, Scott, Hogg, the Gaelic Jacobite poets, the great medieval singers and chroniclers. After all, *The Thirty-Nine Steps* had been frank enough in so oddly setting Hannay on a long voyage home: Buchan's Toryism was at home in Scotland, and returned to it (in such tales as *John Macnab*) for some sort of reScottification (via staghunting or fishing – or befriending orphan boys). The Toryism realising itself through international capitalism was its own orphan. Buchan had found heirs as far afield as MacDiarmid and Muir, and cultivated them with pride.

Harvie's books, essays, articles, Open University coursework, and so forth, reached a vast quantity by the time of his fourth edition in

2004, and many were remote from Scotland. But with this last revision of *Scotland and Nationalism* he returned to his earlier work, one of the deepest studies of the history of political ideas in Britain, *The Lights of Liberalism* in which he illuminated, amongst other extinct volcanoes, the constitutional theorist A.V. Dicey. Harvie had penetrated the post-literate Thatcherism (citing such illuminati as Secretary of State for Scotland Ian Lang who explained his anti-devolutionism on the terrible consequences of the Liberals having given the Irish Home Rule in 1886), and the realities of what misunderstood echoes they entertained of Dicey (who had played some part in ensuring the Irish never got Home Rule): and if he could show the self-delusion of Dicey, what was left to be said of Dicey's heirs, Labour borrowing from the Tories the rhetoric they had fragmented from Dicey? Harvie once again re-examined himself as remorselessly – and as amusingly – as he did others:

> It's difficult not to see 'my young university friends, who were the lights of Liberalism – Matthew Arnold's epitaph on the Liberal intellectuals of the 1860s – behind my own approach, coupled with the belief that the national cause now gave a concrete element to intellectual involvement that Victorian Britain had lacked.

> What had gone wrong? Had I underestimated the weakness of Britain? The Whitehall Scots were an elite unused to conventional democracy, too eager to exploit new and dynamic external circumstances, with few questions asked. The New Labour 'project furthered such opportunism, but at the cost of its own health; at the end of 2003 Blair was still in power, but increasingly weak and directionless. Major's watch had shown how easy it was to go from hero to zero, and Blair – frustrated in Europe, bogged down in Iraq, hitting increasing economic turbulence, and under concentrated attack from an (at last) competent Tory front bench – looked like imitating him. (4th edition, p.245).

With no particular intention of doing so, Harvie charted the diverse fates of the guides to the voter of the 1979 Referendum. What Harvie had described for Blair, Gordon Brown felt himself only able to inherit with no ability or perceived means of going back to the premises of 1979. Whatever his contribution to it Brown needed a new card game: all he gave himself was the same deal with cards whose marks to ensure dealer's victory had become increasingly illegible since the pack had first been shuffled by Thatcher for action. Above all he seemed to have lost the gift of self-reassessment where Harvie prospered so well:

The 'come to Jesus' bit of earlier editions of *Scotland and Nationalism* had been the need to plan a national recovery, and the specifications for the class which could do this. Over time, though, the author realised that his own generation had missed the bus, even if the agenda for positive planning persisted.

So he entered Holyrood much less convinced of his hold on all the answers, but with confidence in the national identity which he had now embraced and from which he could play his part in the future in the light of the past rather than by dictates to that future from a rootless present. In his *Mending Scotland,* published also in 2004, Harvie showed with what little history we equip that future – 'islands of emotion . . . in a sea of ignorance'. And he warned 'If history is checked at the door, it will come slithering over the windowsill, in forms trivial and formidable'. Above all he wanted the nationalism he now endorsed to take its international inheritance and potentialities with the seriousness which the British chauvinism in power since 1979 has rendered all but impossible in the UK.

And amid all the fortune-telling of pollsters it is clear that Scotland has now shown intrinsic acknowledgement of a European as well as a Scottish identity, where English votes for morons like UKIP or bigots like the BNP are rising. But if Scotland is to maintain and increase its respect for its international surroundings it will need a new history to tell it what, intellectually, this has meant, for all of the archipelago, and Harvie has given us the nourishment on which to build our future in his masterpiece *A Floating Commonwealth: Politics, Culture, and Technology on Britain's Atlantic Coast 1860-1930.* ❐

THE PRAGMATISTS

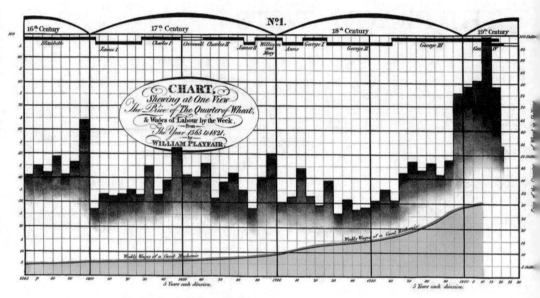

Playfair Graph, William Playfair

I. FLAT EARTH OR SCOTCH PANCAKE

FIGURES ARE FUN: WEIGH THEM BY THE PUN

HARDLY out his diapers, so the legend goes, and Kirkcaldy's most famous son (no, not that one) was kidnapped by a band of tinkers. It is an ancient biographer's trope, the kidnap of the hero as child, but no doubt it was an auspicious and formative experience for the boy who would go on in maturity to establish the disciplinary groundwork for the social sciences. We might imagine his captors sitting around the campfire with the callow Adam Smith, grumbling about property rights and ownership, about work practices and the supply and demand for itinerant labour while they passed the billy-can around from horny hand to horny hand.

But we *would* have to imagine that scene, for the point is, nothing of such details has come down to us in the legend itself. And thus what is made clear with this traditional mere outlining of the picturesque aspects of the tale is that the moral cast is the driver of it all. It is the bare fact that Smith was abducted by tinkers or gypsies or 'travelling people' that is telling. And the intended shock value of this fact seems to make, as a secondary effect, a mockery of the much vaunted egalitarianism of the Scots. In order 'to get' the interest of the story, we have to tacitly sanction a social apartheid and the concomitant set of prejudices against one particular group of folk which has existed in Scotland since time immemorial.

It is doubly meaningful that this 'myth of origin' is told as the founding – or foundling – chapter in the life of the father of the social sciences. For what we have here is not so much a counter-myth, but a supplementary myth which could deepen while complicating our understanding of those myths of ethnicity – Highlandism and Kailyard – which David McCrone (below) sees as 'cultural formations' organising and supporting the belief in an inherent Scottish egalitarianism. McCrone's pleading is that it is more important to understand how and why beliefs like these are sustained by a particular society rather than to attempt to debunk them. But what does it mean then that the travelling people of Scotland are not only held on the one mythical hand to be (somewhat like the Highlanders and the *volk* of the Kailyard) Scots avatars, bearers of real and true tradition, resonant with all the values of echtness, purity and authenticity, while on the other more mundane hand, they are at the same time seen as criminal, untouchable, and of mysterious, dark and foreign origin? It is at least significant as such, that the wise one, the clear thinking moral philosopher and social scientist is fabled into a rite of passage with this holy of holies, this taboo made of gold and dirt, the pure and the untouchable: the tinkers.

There is at any rate, arguably a symbolically shamanistic element to the operation, within the Scottish context, of those most humdrum of individuals, the social scientists. They are pushed, reluctantly shrugging their bureaucratic shoulders, into the middle of the political 'arena', and just like the aboriginal people of Australia with their songlines, they conjure up a territory out of nothingness: a nation – or for instance 'a political system' in the Kellas example – is spun out of words: myths, talk, history, facts and figures. The songs – from the litany of the *Red Paper*, to the howl in the wilderness of *A Claim of Right* – must be sung to keep the land alive.

The social scientists expose how the words work their way through this territory, forming and deforming, constituting and unravelling a particular set of ways of living together. Take egalitarianism, that most vague of notions; it adapts disguises, takes a leap of faith from simple 'equality' out to right and justice. And so we find an obsession with egalitarianism's radical sister, democracy, arising persistently like a bad smell, and in the strangest of places: from George Davie's algebra and

Flat Earth or Scotch Pancake

geometry and the democratic intellect, to Scots religion and the presbytery, from Tom Leonard's minor literature of the provinces, to the designation, by among others, architect Isi Metzstein, of the Glasgow merchants' urban design as a 'democratic grid', and to the 'claim', famously in Edwards's 'Right', that:

> we . . . hereby acknowledge the sovereign right of the Scottish people.

Perhaps this desperation to read 'democracy' everywhere in the Scots body politic is so marked precisely because 'officially' it is, or was, nowhere. In the much quoted judgement from the case of *MacCormick v Lord Advocate* 1954, Lord Cooper stated that:

> The principle of the unlimited sovereignty of Parliament is a distinctively English principle which has no counterpart in Scottish constitutional law . . .

This is, of course, merely definition by omission, creation of negative space, as it were, a posh dealing of the what-the-English-are-is-not-us hand. And as such it is dismissed by James Kellas – he ever with an eye and ear for any distinctive and autonomous political rumblings – as of 'academic interest' only. Besides, in the fifty odd years since the challenge against Queen Elizabeth's right to sport the Roman 'II' after her name in Scotland, which case occasioned the pronouncing of Lord Cooper's sentence, the question of the principle, or principles of sovereignty have become enormously more complicated. Membership of the EU (1973), the signing up to the European Convention of Human Rights (1996), and the setting up of the Scottish Parliament (Scotland Act 1998), amongst other constitutional adaptations, have left even the English principle severely compromised.

And the resultant subtle gradations and limitations placed on legislative and executive capabilities are the stuff, as Midwinter and Keating would no doubt remind us, of everyday administration. They are also the stuff that the ever decreasing band of Tories who ruled Scotland for Thatcher throughout the eighties failed miserably to comprehend. Why let the banal realities of administration get in the way of a superior ideology, seemed to be their attitude. **Who cares if that ideology is so unpopular that we cannot attain the numbers** of representatives necessary to staff the Scottish administration, never mind gain majorities on the Scottish Committees in Parliament? We have 400 MPs in Westminster – does that mean nothing to the Scottish people? And if the school boards we insist are appointed then side with the schools against us, then that is their problem! And if we want to do away with big regional local government because it's Labour, Labour, Labour, then how were we to know that the lack of large scale organisation and economy across the country would make the setting up of a dreaded Scottish Parliament (yet more Labour!) a necessary and inevitable administrative consequence?

Even when it came to one of their greatest heroes, Adam Smith, the Tories let their own rhetoric get in the way of understanding. Why didn't they just take a lesson from the first episode of Smith's tale? Sure, the pale skinned young swot would have been an ideological plus: he could be put out to beg in the marketplace in his nice posh voice from the douce burghers. But the administrative realities of the deal were not promising. How could the small band of tinkers, as outsiders, convince the people that they met that he belonged to them? They knew a real majority when they saw one. A mere consensus convinced them, and they handed the world's first economist back to those that understood him.

As mentioned above, exact information on Smith's time among the tinkers or gypsies is patchy. Officially, it was a kidnapping, a myth of peril and rescue in which sinister interlopers descend from the hills to snatch baby Adam and a posse mustered from the community catch them up and retrieve him. The plot is almost identical to that in S.R. Crockett's swashbuckling novel *The Raiders*, in which God himself, via a snowstorm, punishes the gangrel perpetrators. But, anthropologists tell us that when times were hard in traditional European societies, it was fairly common (pan-European) practice for Gypsies to be given an endowment to take 'kidnapped' children off the hands of families in dire economic straits for a period, or indefinitely. Did the grieving and likely impoverished relatives of the late Adam Smith Snr. put Jnr. in hock until conditions improved? And did the Smiths, like other families who arranged such a lease, protect their good name by claiming the contract was a kidnapping?

But such cynical conjectures dispel our fable in the making; outsiders steal native Scottish genius and with the forces of law and establishment (Edinburgh) standing helpless, the community collectively acts to rescue it. One might call it the rescue myth of Scottish power-play, one taken up by Labour – the posse-cum-real administrators of Scotland – who protected native Scotland from the Tories– that London cabal of false claimants who encroached, stole and appropriated, without so much as a receipt.

If we were really in an allegorical frame of mind, we might wonder if in dispelling, or countering the myth through anthropological means, we have here the makings of a countering *unionist* parable in which a Scots kindred shows its duplicity through engineering an outrage to balance the books, then stages a timely rescue scene to show that their ancient, but flawed, notion of self-reliance still endured. Are, as some of our deepest, darkest fears whisper to us, the rescuers of Scottish liberties, the Scottish home, and the Scottish commonwealth in fact the *original perpetrators of whatever crime Scotland fell victim to*? (as is the case, to a degree, in Crockett's *Raiders*). This question is the same for the amateur folklorist as it is for the social scientists profiled here; did Smith, or Scotland, ever really *need* rescued?

In *The Autonomy of Modern Scotland* Lindsay Paterson writes:

> In effect, if not in constitutional theory or political rhetoric, Scotland has been autonomous for most of the three centuries since the Union – not a fully independent state, of course, but far more than a mere province. It has been at least as autonomous as other small European nations, for which the reality of politics has always been the negotiation of partial independence amid the rivalry of great powers.

It pays then, as Paterson notes, for a small country to observe what happens in practice rather than what the rules said *should* happen. In this, he sees a particular species, or doctrine of autonomy at work in Scottish political history. It is in some regards persuasive, even attractive – an organic form of self-determination persisting in spite of 300 years of a unitary state. Paterson drew multiple lessons from his studies of Scottish education, an ecosystem that maintains its autonomy by recognising that the need for autonomy – and level of such – changes over time and circumstance. Accordingly the system that managed to neuter the anglicising potential of school boards – a triumph, in both senses, of practice over principle (or perhaps of practice in service to a much deeper, ingrained principle?). Likewise, the rules at Westminster, as so carefully described by Mackintosh, did not prevent the Scots acting and responding to events quietly, privately, on their own terms. And then again, there are surely dangers in complacently putting faith in what is *in effect*; it provided no defence for Scottish rules against Westminster interference – and, as Mackintosh pointed out, something as clandestine as the Privy Council might be able to counter rulings of a Scottish Parliament. In such a climate the belief in the prospects for compromise with England tends to diminish, and so the case for nationalism increases.

To be fair to Paterson, he never claims to have arrived upon a fixed truth, but only to give insight into the procedural challenges facing Scottish democracy, wherever and in whatever forms you might purport to find it. Since Paterson wrote Scotland has acquired structures and rules that reshape where events happen. Not that the questions necessarily change – in 1976 Clarke and Drucker asked if an independent Scotland would be more prosperous, and how it might disentangle itself from its many interdependencies. The promise of oil money was since replaced with the power of Scottish banks, and in the event, ideas of autonomy have had to change, as they must now in the light of recent crises. But the questions, necessarily, will continue.

The flow of knowledge and experience has worked to maintain a notion of Scotland in effect or otherwise. The efforts of the devolutionists, emerging from the wreckage of the 1970s might bear lazy comparison to the 1750s-70s. Then, the first generation of Social scientists, led by the Gypsy refund himself, recovered a sense of distinctiveness and autonomy irrespective of the political vacuum by anatomising the structures of society and examining the nature of states, not as eternal truths but a construct, a case in point. In the 1970s this level of autonomy seemed flimsy and ad hoc. Their successors turned the tools they inherited to a search for permanence through building a new apparatus. As the *Scottish Government Yearbook* shows, the base structure – actually, the only available structure – to hang this crystalising politics around was contained in the academies. With jobs and hierarchies to sustain them, these scholars accrued a public profile unusual in the capitalist west that made them participant observers in the emergence of a Scottish politics. They did so through the identification of 'patterns of influence' in policymaking, framing the constitutional debate as an exercise in systemic problem solving. To these systems analysts issues of Englishness and Scottishness were secondary to what Keating and Midwinter described as a 'relentless trend of centralisation which is damaging both the efficiency of Scottish governmental arrangements and the quality of Scottish democracy'.

So while in Ireland, folklore celebrates the intellectuals who strapped swords to their backs and occupied the Post Office (a step beyond attacking the numerals on post-boxes. . .); a post-independence Scotland will recognise the fathers of national liberation as the first to have been thoroughly peer-reviewed, referenced and cited. From the lauded Republic of letters to a Republic of Vivas may seem a stretch of the imagination, but it illustrates the point that the Scottish intellectual climate has really only produced two types – the autonomist and the anatomist. These are not mutually exclusive – far from it. The Enlightenment produced anatomists who were at heart autonomists, attuned to Smith's campfire realities. The social scientists are autonomists who proved it by anatomising an administrative and political system (Lindsay Paterson, incidentally, began his career in medical research) to the point where its contradictions and weaknesses could no longer be denied by almost anyone except the Tories).

The autonomists' conclusion was that even before the last Constitutional Convention met in 1989, the need for autonomy was changing. By the time the *Scottish Government Yearbook* became *Scottish Affairs*, the need to express autonomy in the system had shifted to a need to speak in an autonomous voice on the issues that would comprise the future legislative programme for an Edinburgh assembly. Reaching Scottish solutions to women's issues, equality and diversity, sectarianism, and economic development – the anatomy of Scottish *current affairs* became more important than the epistemological question of whether they existed, and equally, the ability of Scottish politics to address them became the primary basis for judging the worth of Scottish autonomy in either effect or theory, parliament or not.

The social scientists' contribution is thus a little Frankenstein in character – or, if you prefer your horror home grown, then imagine that the Scottish autonomist Hyde confirms their own existence through the systemic classifications and divisions of the anatomised Jekyll; separate, diverse organs are contained within an admittedly thin, but definable, Hobbesian skin. By 1999, when Holyrood met for the first time, fears of encroachment had been replaced by a desire for solutions over institutions, a shift in thinking that would be to Labour's eventual cost. They were not needed to swoop in and rescue Scotland anymore.

Whether that is to the good or the bad is probably not the subject of any ultimate, summative truth; such permanence is a myth. For this lesson we must thank the number-crunching Mackintoshes, McCrones, Kellases, Keatings, Patersons and – yes – even the Midwinters. Their anthropology, or folklore, triumphed, and killed the myth of timely rescue. At least, for the time being.   ❒

THE GOVERNMENT AND POLITICS OF BRITAIN
JOHN P. MACKINTOSH (1970)

Whatever your politics, you might regret that you can no longer vote for John Pitcairn Mackintosh, Labour MP for Berwick and East Lothian. Erudite, collegiate and free-spirited he seems cast from a type rare among the much-caricatured Scot-Lab rank and file. Splitting his duties as MP with Professorial duties at Edinburgh and the University of Strathclyde, he could easily be imagined taking a seat as representative for the old 'Combined Scottish Universities' constituency in parliament (abolished in 1950). As a politician he is best known for his insistence that Scottishness and Britishness could be separate yet simultaneous identities – so commonly understood today we would be shocked to think this was ever a difficult concept. He also posed a pre-emptive East Lothian answer to the West Lothian Question in defence of both devolution for Scotland and of 'dual nationality' for Scots in Britain. 'People in Scotland want a degree of government for themselves. It is not beyond the wit of man to devise the institutions to meet these demands'. Alas, John P succumbed to a wasting disease on the eve of the Devolution Referendum, and in any case possessed brains that were too well known (especially for Harold Wilson's liking) for him to transcend his maverick status.

He left us other, possibly more valuable legacies. *The Government and Politics of Britain* was first published in 1970, and remained in print until constitutional changes finally outpaced it. A follow up to his most acclaimed work *The British Cabinet* (Mackintosh's contribution to the spirit of '68), *The Government* is almost certainly better read, the text where most students of politics- including many who have since entered public office – encounter him. It was the 'classic' textbook at Mackintosh's old department during the 1990s, deployed as an update and corrective to Walter Bagehot's *The English Constitution* (1865).

Few textbooks convey 'personality' but much of the appeal of *The Government and Politics of Britain* rests on Mackintosh's authorial voice, able to convey complex and potentially boring knowledge in clear and unfussy prose. Mackintosh had an excellent opportunity as a participant observer in British politics at house and constituency level. Given that the classical concept of the 'British constitution' is of an accumulation of customs and habits (or as Mackintosh puts it, 'custom and awe'), where everything is legal until said otherwise, accounts of it inevitably resemble works of Social Anthropology. Such accounts are pitched somewhere between shamanism and particle physics, incantations that ensure the phenomenon described is really there, actions that need to be observed to actually exist.

By accounts we of course mean first and foremost Bagehot's rhapsody of 'Cabinet

247

Government' as a perfected form of government, very much taking the Francis Fukuyama role in the heyday of 'Liberal England'. A later by-product of Whig tradition (via Labour) Mackintosh takes a similarly descriptive, anthropological approach, but his prime concern is to correct and counter Bagehot, who once famously wrote;

> I do not consider the exclusion of the working classes from effectual representation a defect in THIS aspect of our Parliamentary representation. The working classes contribute almost nothing to our corporate public opinion, and therefore, the fact of their want of influence in Parliament does not impair the coincidence of Parliament with public opinion.

Given Mackintosh's Labour affiliations we might expect him to denigrate and debunk; with *The British Cabinet* he effectively claimed Bagehot's own territory. But in *The Government and Politics of Britain* he (sparingly) discourses on Bagehot as Machiavelli to his Livy; he respects the foundation, but builds his own constructs. A pivotal chapter 'Why do people obey the government' takes on Bagehot by engaging his theory of why the masses prefer 'a man they can imagine' to the complexities of fiats and constitutions;

The monarchy had tremendous traditional respect from the aristocracy, the middle classes and illiterate masses. It was a symbolic or dignified government everyone could understand. Behind this distinguished monarchical front, the real (or 'efficient' in Bagehot's terms) government was free to operate through the Cabinet and the House of Commons.

Note the past tense (and see review above of *The Enchanted Glass*). To Mackintosh, Bagehot's meaning is that only the spread of education beyond 'the ruling ten thousand' can pave the way for widening knowledge of the constitution. As Mackintosh said, several aspects have changed, not least the monarchy's introversion, diverting its efforts to sustaining its own position – it can no longer 'cloak' controversial actions and people feel on the 'receiving end' of government. Through the iron discipline of party loyalty cabinet has gone from being the 'buckle' that fastens legislature to executive to a shackle on parliament. Local government is in crisis (the Welsh and Scottish nationalists representing a proposed solution) and the real legitimacy of the British arrangement is really, as Mackintosh remarks – 'satisfaction, tradition and inertia.'

From there, Mackintosh counters Bagehot indirectly, describing, depicting and outlining surpluses and deficits of democracy in a far from perfect system, not much 'perfectly balanced' in the Bagehotian sense as constantly in flux and frequently one occasion de-stabilised by political expediencies. He also shows that the House has not been able to keep pace with administrative developments, mostly because it lacked a method for collecting information on the social side effects of legislation. This seems prophetic (it explains how party political mechanisms such as New Labour's focus groups could become so powerful) and sees especially relevant to Scotland, where administrative realities long outstripped the political (a lesson the Tories never learned).

It's tempting to conclude then, that the

current Scottish politics is the by-product of a doomed trust in Bagehot's inertia over accepting certain extra-Westministerial realities. As a textbook (rather than a sacred text in the Bagehot sense) *Government and Politics of Britain* shared Bagehot's synthetic values but escaped said inertia. It has been reprinted 5 times since his death in 1978 and undergone frequent revisions by other political scientists who attempt to cleave to Mackintosh's realism and clarity of style. He became in many respects, a Socratic figurehead for political anthropology – a 'man we could imagine', epitomising efficient analysis of frequently exasperating tribal politics.

THE SCOTTISH POLITICAL SYSTEM
JAMES G. KELLAS (1973)

Kellas is something of a minor Plato figure for late twentieth century Scottish political science. It would be an exaggeration to assert that 'the rest' of the commentators provide mere footnotes to his musings, but nonetheless he assuredly started the most persistent political hares from the couthy long grass of Scottish backwoodsism. Until he came on the scene, that is, the principal academic and 'serious' questions for the Scots disciples of Machiavelli's science were all British ones.

Post-Kellatic Caledonia obsesses, more or less, as one startled bunny, on: how systematic is the cabbage patch? (though, for consistency's, not to mention mellifluency's, sake, perhaps we should call it the 'kailyard')

Basically, Kellas's thesis is that there is a recognisably defined Scottish political system. His idea of a system here is painted broad brushstroke as comprising multiple and heteronymous agents operating across a wide ranging 'political' field. (From the STUC to the SFA, from the *Scottish Daily Express* to the Scottish Grand Committee.) For 'political' we may thus read something of the original Greek meaning, as anything to do with the civic and cultural life of the citizens – although perhaps we mix our antique etymologies too far into woolly-headedness here). At any rate the political activity which constitutes a 'system' for Kellas is exercised through a structure of recognisable institutions, organised groups, media and so on, and is based in a politico-social 'arena' which is distinctive and can be defined by key features such as national feeling, religious beliefs and organisation, education, the legal system, and socio-economic factors (housing etc). The important aspect vis-à-vis the Bagehotian sense of 'tradition' in the 'British' system is that the Scots developed these 'political' institutions (eg the Scottish Office and the system of Local government) themselves.

One problem with Kellas' approach is that it blurs the distinction between a political system *strictu sensu* and what Nairn calls the 'Gramscian category' of 'civil society' (can the national footballing association really be considered as part of a *political* system?). In the *Red Paper* Nairn makes the case that to 'understand any society as a whole one must always distinguish between its 'State' or political and administrative structure and its "civil society".' He goes on to show why such a distinction is particularly important in the case of a stateless nation like Scotland. Yet despite the somewhat all-things-to-all-men nature of his 'system', Kellas cannot but help returning to pick over a number of particular bones of interest to him; namely, the Scottish Legal System, Scottish nationalism, and the need for a Scottish Parliament.

As with Bagehot, so Kellas makes out a near totemic virtue of constitutional inheritance. For the Scots he says, the 'rights outlined in the Act of Union are important psychologically'. But first among psychological equals (education, religion), is the indigenous Legal system, which is 'one of the strongest clues' to a Scottish political system, because 'separate laws engender separate politics and administration.' And while on the one hand Kellas dismisses as merely of 'academic interest' the argument that Scots Law reflects a different notion of democracy in not sharing the English doctrine of the 'sovereignty of parliament', on the other he pronounces it 'odd' that the Act of Union, as guaranteed *for all time* should be subject to amendment by parliament.

When Kellas speaks of 'nationalism' he is at pains to point out that this does not mean merely voting SNP, but that the whole Scottish Political System as he defines it is underpinned by a wider conception of the phenomenon. Just so, he can point to nationalistic tendencies emanating from the most unlikely quarter (as imagined by the party-minded), when George Younger, as Mrs Thatcher's Secretary of State for Scotland, on being asked about Barnett formula differentials by the Select Committee on Scottish Affairs replied:

> Scottish needs are very often different. Scottish priorities are very often different. I would not wish to have my priorities dictated to me by my Whitehall colleagues. I now have complete control over these priorities by myself.

(This might on the face of it sound like playing 'hard ball' in the corridors of Westminster, but a near literal American translation of the beer-magnate's bravado is surely pitched by Marlowe in Chandler's *Farewell My Lovely*, as 'I go to the bathroom alone and everything.')

An undercurrent of 'nationalism' in the wider sense is also made manifest when Kellas demonstrates using figures from 1970s elections that the SNP surge in that decade, contrary to popular myth and the jibe 'Tartan Tories', was achieved by gains equally from all other mainstream parties. And he all but says that it was precisely these gains that called the major institutions' (Labour, Liberal, Tory, STUC, Church etc) fair-weather bluff on a hundred year long nominal commitment to self determination. But it is also that decade that gives us the answer to Mackintosh's now strange seeming assertion (see above) about British- and Scottish-ness.

For Kellas shows us that in surveys in Scotland in 1970 over 70% of respondents to a question about nationality gave the answer as Scottish (with only around 20% as British), whereas by 1979 only around 50% were giving the answer as Scottish, and he asserts that this was probably the result of politicisation and polarisation of the question of national allegiance as a result of the devolution campaign.

For Kellas a Scottish parliament is a touchstone for democracy in this political 'system'. There is a need for a democratic institution which is not remote, often reluctant, uninterested, lacking in time, or unsure of its role in underpinning and keeping checks on the administrative and legal autonomy of the system. Westminster clearly did not fit the bill, but neither did the 'pro-consular' role of Secretary of State for Scotland in the British Government. This much was obvious for those who accepted that the 'system' existed and was largely as Kellas saw it. But it was also obvious to a sizeable constituency at large in the country who, as the 2 million signatories to the 1949 Covenant had demonstrated, considered seriously at one time or another, that 'reform in the constitution of our country is necessary'.

Did Kellas, however, in his enthusiasm, go too far in envisaging how a Scottish parliament would be a balm unto us and ease the stress of our conflicting loyalties? Again and again he stresses its virtues – a parliament would: lighten the legal burden on the Scottish secretary; solve the inequity of having a constitutional representative who is also chief public prosecutor (Lord Advocate); provide a legislative body to balance the existent executive and judicial branches; remove elites from power and promote a less authoritarian and patriarchal society than the present one which was 'heavily weighted towards administrative and legal activities' but with no legislative body; do away with complexity and secrecy of decision making in the Scottish Office and provide a more open form of government; and vitally encourage more Scots Lawyers (as Edinburgh based) to engage their professional expertise in legislative procedure.

The list is not endless, but very long; yet by now it could probably be fairly accurately assessed as to its achievability. The assessment should put paid to an absurd aside found in the text, of a type uncharacteristic of Kellas, the political scientist, but heard often enough in the cynical byways, namely:

> A large residue are probably indifferent as to how the machinery of government is shaped – they are concerned only with the results of policies.

The Bagehotian critique of this sentence would be to say that it gives all attention to the strategy for battle without any consideration for the task of raising an army. In truth however, it is as depressing an utterance for its day as was Bagehot's judgement that the majority of the people are 'narrow-minded, unintelligent, incurious'. But what can we say about the manifold versions of this sort of patronising comment, except that people are interested in many things, and give them different priorities according to differing times and situations. Or as Owen Dudley Edwards once said of human residues, 'I would believe polls more readily if 5% told us to fuck off.'

SCOTTISH GOVERNMENT YEARBOOK 1976 – 1992/ SCOTTISH AFFAIRS 1992-PRESENT
HENRY DRUCKER, NANCY DRUCKER, MARTIN CLARKE, DAVID McCRONE, ALICE BROWN, LINDSAY PATERSON, JOHN MacINNES, EBERHARD BORT (EDS)

The editorial roster of the *Scottish Government Yearbook* reads as a who's who of late twentieth century Scottish social science. Founded a year after the *Red Paper for Scotland*, this annual publication collected the output of the Unit for Study of Government in Scotland (USGS), located within the University of Edinburgh Politics department and headed for its first six months, by John P. Mackintosh. Henry Drucker and Clarke edited the first volume under the title of *Our Changing Scotland: A Yearbook of Scottish Government* (dedicated to 'the much maligned governors of Scotland') and from there it appeared regularly before becoming the quarterly journal *Scottish Affairs* in 1992.

The 1979 issue was dedicated to the memory of Prof Mackintosh and was issued just before the devolution referendum. At this point the 'constitutionalists' had learned from Mackintosh and Kellas a fine appreciation for the Scottish strands within British politics, with James Naughtie providing a blow-by-blow account of the devolutionists' manoeuvres within parliament. At the time, it must have felt as if the momentum was with them;

within a year, the next edition was wondering where and what next. Yet they continued with their careful, robust and detailed analysis of Scottish administrative and political affairs. Broadly speaking the importance of this contribution can be interpreted in either of two ways; was the tenacity of USGS and its affiliates a form of protest that reflected Scotland's wider pre-millennial tensions, or was it a devolutionary vanguard – persistent, pushy and buoyed by their shared enthusiasm- that would conspire to foment and create a climate conducive to home rule?

There was certainly a vibrant and committed network of worthies involved; James Kellas, Arthur Midwinter, James Naughtie, Catriona Levy, Walter Humes, Iain McWhirter, Christopher Harvie, Pamela Munn, O.D. Edwards, James Mitchell, Hamish McN. Henderson, Michael Keating, David Raffe, Neil MacCormick, even Cardinal Winning were all contributors. Most came from departments of sociology and politics, but departments of economics, law, education, history and the journalistic mainstream were frequently represented. The tone and sheer intensity of this activity lend credence to the 'vanguard' argument; the social sciences, born of the pragmatic intellectualism of the Scottish Enlightenment, set out to create a new Scottish political system by describing it into being, detail by painstaking detail.

To get a sense of the agenda, one can do worse than look up 'Towards a Scottish Politics', Drucker and Drucker's Introduction to the 1979 yearbook.

> Despite the arguments of James Kellas (*The Scottish Political System*, 1973) "system" is precisely what Scottish politics lacks. Perhaps it is foolish to expect system in British institutions; but Scottish political life carries the normal British flair for *ad hoc* arrangements to an extreme. Scottish politics find expression in a series of practices and institutions some of which have been thought out in relation to each other, but most not.

We see here most clearly, the lead taken from Mackintosh (an *Appreciation* of whom is the next item in this particular edition) and even from Sir Walter Scott; if Scotland itself would not provide system, then they, the devolutionists would be systematic in shedding light on this sorry state of affairs. If there was no *Hansard* for Scotland then Hamish McN. Henderson would, every year, provide a detailed record of Scottish legislation passing through Westminster. If there was no Scottish budget, then Scottish economists would dutifully tease out Scottish accounts and projections from the 'national' legers. With facts and figures they created a 'feeling' of Scottish public life, and giving voice to civic Scotland in ways previously thought of as impolite, or a la Johnston, overly harsh. Ultimately, their most powerful legacy was to incubate the Whiggish idea of 'a

path to Home Rule', almost everywhere cited, no matter how much their patience was tried and tested by years of stubborn Tory hegemony. Alan Lawson even saw the 1987 election as a 'very significant milestone' to constitutional shakeup. Even before that, a consensus seems to form that logically, given the weight of administrative and political evidence, devolution had to happen.

All of this could at times, be dry and highly prosaic, but was occasionally relieved by touches of humour; Owen Dudley Edwards appears in the '92 yearbook to ask 'Who invented Devolution?' in a rich, densely lyrical and comprehensive history of limited home rule as an active political idea (where else but in pre-dev Scotland could the Tynwald of Man be taken so seriously?); comparative politics, including Quebec and Luis Moreno in 1988 writing on 'Scotland and Catalonia', and even literary; reeling from the devo-killing Thatcher victory in 1987 Alan Lawson references Hamish Henderson (the other one. . .) in the title to his analysis of electoral forces 'Mair nor a rouch wind blawin' that sums up the mixture of forbearance and hope. Lawson diagnoses the Tories' problems in Scotland as symptoms of 100 years of the British 'system' offering ad hoc response to national sentiments. It had left a number of important anomalies, such as a hugely powerful, and hostile Scottish Grand Committee as a source of political pressure that could at every turn, embarrass the Tories, a position they (yet again) seemed incapable of recognising.

By 1992 there is the sense that much of Scotland's patchwork polity founded upon the 'jovial conviviality' described by

Michael Fry has been described and fully understood. The '92 yearbook is more compact and has been reworked as a forum for ideas, where high level debate on the social, moral and legislative issues set to bedevil a putative Embra Parly can be examined at length. Women's political representation, Sectarianism, the Howie committee on Post-Compulsory Schooling and Mental Health are all extra-constitutional issues covered in this volume, a trend that continued into *Scottish Affairs* under a rotating editorship from Yearbook pool. *Scottish Affairs* was more thematic in its approach, publishing a whole issue, edited by MacInnes and D. McCrone, on 'Stateless Nations', and recently, half an edition on the 'demographic timebomb'. Prominent contributors reviewed books from outside Scotland about Scotland that effected the 'To a Louse' manoeuvre and took advantage of the four-a year format in responding quickly to emerging topics. In a change from the barely hidden machismo of the early yearbooks, when Midwinter and Kellas bristled at each other over their moustaches, *Scottish Affairs* was more feminine in taking Scottish politics from the collective to the domestic sphere – Alexandra Howson's 'No Gods and Precious Few Women' (Winter 1993) is especially scathing on the absence of women from Scottish cultural identity. *Scottish Affairs* also kept its profile high, attracting contributions from Andrew Marr, Gavin McCrone, and Bernard Crick. Recent issues have featured Brian Taylor on Scottish Social Democracy and a detailed analysis of what 'One Scotland, Many Cultures' actually means; it is now nearing its 70th issue and every year, the editor gives us 'Annals of the Parish; a roundup of the past year in Holyrood'. One wonders whether the devolutionists see it as ironic that, in describing the ad hoc institutions of Scotland they had themselves become one.

THE GOVERNMENT OF SCOTLAND MICHAEL KEATING AND ARTHUR MIDWINTER (1983)

'No politics here' is the flag of convenience which Keating and Midwinter sought to raise above both St Andrew's House and City Chambers across the land in 1983. The question, to whom or for what it was convenient, is a moot one. Both writers have strong connections with Labour (Keating having written several species of Labour history, and Midwinter going on to become advisor to Wendy Alexander), a party whose all pervasive presence in Scottish civic life seemed to gather strength with every day of Thatcher's rule.

In many ways these two were principal players in the articulation of the genuine moral force and right that belonged to some sections of Scottish Labour in its struggle with the alien creeds of Thatcherism. Yet is there not indeed something of the palpably political (albeit a petty and churlish politics), in *The Government of Scotland*'s blank disavowal of the groundbreaking work of Kellas (above)? The project to deny the existence of a Scottish political system, viz:

> It is doubtful whether Scotland can be considered a political system . . . [since] . . . ultimately authority lies outside Scotland.

and to affirm instead the importance of 'a distinct Scottish administrative system' is as explicit a counter to Kellas' argument as it is possible to make, yet the latter's name appears nowhere in the text, notes, index, or bibliography (there is none) of Keating and Midwinter's book.

Having set their limits and horizons for discussion of Scottish government in policy making at departmental (Scottish Office), local authority, quango and party level, these two lower their eyes to the grey grey tarry ground in a study of 'effectiveness, democracy, and accountability' of administration in municipal and regional Scotland. As an assessment of local government in the wake of the 1975 reorganisation into large regional units (Strathclyde, Lothians etc) and constituent district councils, this book was timely and the authors claim it as,

> the first full text book treatment of the Scottish local government system

In 1983 municipal Scotland – largely Labour run – was still holding out against the imposition of Thatcher's new policies. It was time, in the face of the Tory onslaught, for those who still believed in consensual local government to look to the operation of policy making. They would have to understand how effective or otherwise were what Keating and Midwinter (in the avowed absence of a political system) call the 'complex networks' of institutions and agencies at delivering services, and how they could continue to deliver under threat. From this point of view the book could almost be described as a training handbook for the members of the Convention of Scottish Local Authorities. And the supreme targeted bean-counter, bumbling into managerial action with this encheiridion neatly packed in his briefcase, might be someone like the former Labour Party Secretary of State for Scotland, Bruce Millan, now all but forgotten, but praised (note *praised*) here as 'a pragmatic administrator rather than an ideal politician.'

Naturally pragmatism is a principle to be admired in a network of policy makers with no 'ultimate authority' of their own but with aims and standards which largely differed (in the Thatcher age at any rate) from those of the external source of authority. Keating and Midwinter make some fairly accurate predictions about problems which the pragmatist will have to deal with in the Scottish administrative system in the future: – including a dismissal of the relevance of the once current myth of ring fencing of the Scottish economy (two acronyms, HBOS & RBS, have us laughing all the way to the bank over this now. . .); and the observation that the Barnett formula introduced in 1978 is no more than a 'holding operation' before

The Government of Scotland • Michael Keating and Arthur Midwinter the big battle on funding (– we're still waiting on that one but surely it won't be long now . . .)

In their conclusions about the government of Scotland however, Keating and Midwinter seem unable to avoid becoming 'political'. Mind you, when they call for a Scottish Assembly with tax raising powers, the cynic (viz., Michael Fry) might well say this again is consistently *not* to do with political justice (ie adjustment for the situation where the majority representation in Scotland is not of the same party as the majority at Westminster), but precisely to do with pragmatic *control* (and keeping Scotland for the Labour Party even when England votes Tory). But then again, the true Scots pragmatist might equally retort, that given Labour's erstwhile apparent permanence as elected spokesparty of the people, the making of a distinction between 'Labour Party' and 'majority representation' is (or, was) a theoretical, and mere quibbling, irrelevance.

At any rate these two found it convenient to be much more 'political' in their criticism in subsequent books. And faced with the new right Tory ideologues of 1987-90 who would blame them for such an apparent about turn into mobilisation of political consciousness? Any weapon to hand, as it were . . . Midwinter in particular subsequently

made a devastating critique of the Public Choice Theories – ratecapping, poll tax, school boards and opt-outs, and direct charging – forced on Scottish local authorities, and demonstrated how out of touch was the ideological rhetoric of late Thatcherism in attempting to redefine citizens as consumers and establish pure simple and direct relationships between economic behaviour and political behaviour.

In the final analysis it may be that Keating and Midwinter were right in 1983 that we could not then talk about a Scottish political system but just an administrative system, if only because, as Mackintosh says elsewhere – there was no 'focal point' to such a (political) system in Scotland. Keating and Midwinter point out that 'politics is the weakest part of the policy process', but there is no value judgement as to whether such Scottish governmental exceptionalism is a good thing, and why. Just an acceptance that that's the way things are. Depending on one's purely political party standpoint one may find this reluctance to speculate suspicious : do they really only keep their eyes down for the opportunity to control? Perhaps that is too cynical, but at any rate things are different now: for the moment we do have such a focal point, and it is not the type ever imagined in the 1983 dreams of these two promoters of a tax raising but non-political Scottish parliament.

The Government of Scotland • Michael Keating and Arthur Midwinter

UNDERSTANDING SCOTLAND: THE SOCIOLOGY OF A STATELESS NATION DAVID MCCRONE (1992)

If for some, like Tom Nairn, Scotland is a 'psychiatric condition' then for David McCrone it is a post-modern sociological case study. As a late contribution in this series of influential works, *Understanding Scotland* marshalls its figures in the widest sense (ciphers, tropes and personalities); and it draws most all of the writers analysed here in *Pimps* into its own survey and analysis of the field. (indeed only Leonard, Tom Johnston, and perhaps most tellingly, Gordon Brown, are absent from his index). But with Thatcher already ditched, Kinnock sunk in the tides at Blackpool, and the Iron Curtain torn back across Europe, McCrone pitches in to a very different arena from some of those writers above.

Where many of the others here are largely concerned with analysing Scotland's nationhood in terms of its economic, political and social coherence, and taking stock via economic and political indicators of its performance, development and well-being, McCrone is more interested in the question what *is* a nation, a state, and a society? And what, if any, is the relationship between those three?

To put it in more simple, journalistic terms we might say that for modernist thinkers in the mainstream of the post-war period the principle around which all social problems cohered was how to deal with the process of industrialisation; but for the post-modernist the question howling insistently through the post-industrial brownfield site is one of 'identity', of de-alignment from the centralised state, and broadening of social questions.

Thus the relationship of McCrone's approach to that of say, Kellas, Midwinter, or Mackintosh, is analogous to the relation between the projected 1979 Scottish Assembly, with its would-be planning and policy making aspects, appearing as grey suited and bureaucratic as any other agency of industrial control (viz. the SDA); and the 1999 Scottish Parliament as instituted with its world-firsts of a Policy on Architecture (2000), a long term aim to house all homeless people (Homeless Act 2003), and its debates on repealing repressive laws against homosexuals (Section 2 A).

McCrone draws heavily on the work of previous writers, but his criticism of such theories as Hechter's 'internal colonialism' and Smout's 'dependency' in explaining Scottish historical development show that this is no post-modern compendium of 'anything goes'. Indeed perhaps the most original and powerful analysis is the one he applies to the hoary old chestnut of Scottish egalitarianism.

He analyses what might be the role of myth for any nation (or 'imagined community'.) A myth, he tells us in full po-mo flow, cannot be disproved by confronting it with facts. Instead McCrone urges us to ask why such and such a myth might persist in any certain society?

The myth of the inherent egalitarianism of the Scots has several layers of interest and significance in these terms. In the first place, not only is it pointless to attempt to disprove the myth, but it's notable that this myth adapts for everyman through its innate ambiguity. Take the culturally pivotal Burns's poem *A Man's a Man For a' That:* on the one hand it can be claimed by the radical as a call for action on social equality and democracy, and to do away with social hierarchy; but equally on the other hand, it could be viewed as a confirmation of the status quo, that no action is needed on social reform, as essentially all men of all classes are the same anyway.

McCrone goes on to examine how this working notion of inherent egalitarianism is maintained by certain myths about social structure, namely that Scots were always more literate and more socially mobile than were their neighbours. He proves, more or less, that these particular myths are unsustainable by use of historical data. But he then goes on to show how these structural myths are in turn sustained by powerful ethnic myths of Scottish identity: Kailyardism, with its pawky peasants (see Tom Leonard) and the lad o' pairts; and Highlandism, or tartanry, with its primeval social organisation and individualistic and spontaneous subjects.

The question of how those myths arose and were exploited from the nineteenth century is connected to complex cultural and political questions which McCrone examines at length. It seems straightforward now, to say that this complex network of myths exists as some sort of ideological device for 'marking Scotland off from an equally mythological England', no doubt the latter being one of hierarchy, social immobility and snobbishness. But unlike some modernist theorists (eg Tom Nairn) McCrone does not take fright at tartanism and all that. Understanding is the title of this book and putting in new contexts is one of the themes. He quotes Renan 'Getting its history wrong is part of being a nation', and claims that when writers and intellectuals, like Colin McArthur, seek out a more 'authentic' discourse on Scottish identity, they search in vain. They can, that is, only reproduce the problem of having everything Scottish subsumed under the one dominant and limited rubric, as in 'tartanism'. Why indeed, is it necessary to define 'Scotland'? For McCrone says, 'in modern pluralistic societies, it is increasingly the case that no single 'national' culture is to be found'.

We may wonder though, what exactly is meant by 'modern' here. For surely it is at least since the publication of *MacPherson's Farewell*, Scott's *Old Mortality*, and Stevenson's *Kidnapped* that we have had the possibility of general public awareness of that cultural plurality as a living reality. But perhaps it is reassuring nonetheless to see the message has at last echoed through the sombre halls of academe. For we remember that around the same time that Burns was rejigging the poetic expression of Macpherson's alien non-conformity, the philosopher Hume, who denied a singular essence of personal identity, was rejected by the academy. But then we're all post-modernists now. . .

EDUCATION AND A SCOTTISH PARLIAMENT/ THE AUTONOMY OF MODERN SCOTLAND LINDSAY PATERSON (1989/1994)

Scotland has, apparently, not existed politically for a very long time, and yet political rhetoric claims that its traditions are under uniquely serious threat.

Are our schools a 'tradition'? A custom? A habit? In Lindsay Paterson's *The Autonomy of Modern Scotland* the Scottish schoolroom – which in 1989 was set to be administered by school boards – is presented as a leading example of one such tradition (which Paterson points out, has been constructed within the last generation) that comprises a 'Scottish autonomy' that existed in spite of the unitary state.

In this book, one of the last, important contributions to the devolutionary debate Paterson examines the various forms of Scottish administrative and political autonomy within the UK system, and in comparison to other informal and formal systems of autonomy in America and Europe from the eighteenth century to the present. It is perhaps no surprise that an educationalist should begin his argument with an account of the fierce cross party resistance to the introduction of school boards, prompting members from all sides to oppose what was seen as an attack on the "distinctive 'virtues of Scottish Education.'" Nothing else in Scottish political life was so bipartisan or as totemic that so many unionist politicians could unconsciously describe challenges to it as 'alien to Scottish traditions.'

As described by Paterson the language of the politicians takes on mythical, even spiritual overtones. Could we imagine English MPs rallying to defend the distinctive virtues of the English schools system? (More importantly, could we imagine such unity in today's chamber at Holyrood?) It was easier, and more important to link arms in those days; in the late eighties Thatcher swished the tawse (via, God help us, Michael 'Mad Dog' Forsyth) in ever more savage strokes against Scottish sensibilities, and school boards seemed to be a particularly symbolic attempt to decapitate a source of Scottish resistance to the centre. Everyone knew 'Scotland' existed without being able to pinpoint what it was; but the local school and perhaps also the college was a tangible, definite, identifiable and *different* civic institution that schooled them and their children.

But it was not the same institution for all of them. For Labour the universal schools system was a bulwark of egalitarianism, especially as Scottish comprehensives for the most part functioned fairly well. For Nationalists, schools incubated the native genius essential to national liberation, and for Tories they represented intellectual and personal independence. In numerous essays over the late 80s and summatively in *Education and the Scottish Parliament*, Paterson exposes the myth-making process to show the Scottish education system as tangible if complex, and the aforementioned popular and tribal perceptions of the same order as those gained from blindly fondling an elephant. That being so, even if we detect no definite Scottish educative 'self' beyond Hume's accrued bundles of customs and habits, we can at least acknowledge that there is a distinctive, touchable form that is Scotland/Scottish Education. Weird and oddball it may be, but it's still better than designing a horse by committee, or indeed a sacred cow.

As a historian of education Paterson well appreciates the distorted perspective through which one generation regards another; autonomy in one era looks like dependency to another. Scotland is autonomous in practice, but such practices can become flawed, and will occasionally need to be changed. Accordingly Paterson favours an approach based on responding to events rather than upholding constitutional theories, which sounds very much like an appeal for Kellas' politics over Midwinter's administrative culture. But, he warns, even if national independence is gained, inter-dependence with other nations will nevertheless dictate a great deal of said country's aspirations and capabilities (as Alex Salmond has found post-banking crisis).

This also sounds rather like his analysis of Scottish education, which has maintained an enviable degree of autonomy through careful compromise and renegotiation. Along with Pamela Munn, Walter Humes, Roy Canning, Gwynned Lloyd, Elizabeth Jordan, Rowena Arshad, Brian Boyd, David Raffe and Cathy Howieson, Paterson studied the Scottish system as more than just a technocratic problem,

but a dynamic, mutable effigy of civic Scotland. Over three decades the educationalists worked in tandem – but occasionally in opposition to – the technocrats at the Scottish Office and later various agencies and quangos, to steer the Scottish system from a renowned, but narrow conveyor belt of parts and lads to an all-encompassing framework based on 'parity of esteem' between academic and vocational learning. Compare Paterson's accounts of schools in the fifties in his 2003 Opus *Scottish Education in the Twentieth Century* to the late nineties and you will appreciate the irony contained in various politicians' efforts to defend the sanctity of the Scottish system.

And to return to Hume, there comes further heresy; in the 1992 issue of the Scottish Government Yearbook Paterson went so far as to praise the new school boards as 'anything but the tame poodles of the Scottish office'. He effectively vindicates Forsyth's intervention, noting in the *Autonomy of Modern Scotland* that Forsyth had himself adopted the language of an 'autonomist' in the 1989 debate to defend his proposals, describing the boards as a return to the 'traditional type of education in Scotland', based in the local community'. For Paterson such ironies and ambiguities (who were the real conservatives here?) only underline the importance of paying attention to the event over the underlying principle. For, as he writes of the new school boards 'It seems, when Scottish society is given new voices at the moment, it speaks in surprising ways.'

II. IT'S SCOTLAND'S EUROPE:
MacCormick and Ascherson

I

A GOOD bouquet of modern Scottish nationalism flowered when it became clear that various agenda were more easily fulfilled by concentration on Scotland: environmentalism, for instance, was Scottish long before it was fashionable. Perhaps the main undertow drawing the prophet Nairn from his hostility to Scottish nationalism to his place today as probably its foremost intellectual, derives from his realisation that the Europhobic Left did not hold Scottish nationalist allegiance. The obvious figure at hand in such instruction was Neal Ascherson, Nairn's flatmate in the 1970s, in some ways as startling a convert to Scottish self-realisation as Nairn himself. But an equally formidable evangel of the internationalism of Scottish nationalism was Neil MacCormick, later SNP MEP, and inheritor of Scottish nationalist ideology by blood, rather than by perception of Scots Europe in contrast to English – or even British – England.

MacCormick's case began before Ascherson's, although for all his piety he did not join the party until 1967, while previously a defiant nationalist voice in Glasgow University Union when the John Smiths and Donald Dewars were benchmarking future Labour Party careers. His father John MacCormick (1904-61) had founded the SNP in 1934 but had left it in 1942, never to return, when Neil was few months old. Glasgow in the 1950s and 1960s held the greatest debating society in British and Irish Universities, and possibly the world. Its camaraderie contextualised its combats, as Neil MacCormick showed when piping his old friend John Smith into his Iona grave in 1994. The last mournful notes symbolised the depth as well as the height of the tribute: had John Smith survived, it would have been at the expense of Scottish nationalism of which he embodied enough to draw off SNP momentum. For Blair to attract Scottish nationalist sentiment he would have had to be born again in a different skin; for Brown to attract it was to plunge himself in torment at becoming so unBritish a phenomenon. They Britified their Englishness with total lack of conviction: Smith was the last British statesman, and was mourned by MacCormick – and Ascherson – as such.

John Smith was the best Prime Minister we never had, at least for the twentieth century, and, from start to finish, a gentleman, but the pain of his death was a public one, and one liable to get worse in the light of subsequent events, for all of Blair's success in airbrushing him from official history. Blair was true to his nature in so doing, and had every reason to dread so superior a lost leader, although he certainly deserved the airbrushing he won in his turn. Mourning Neil MacCormick is too personal to keep up academic assessment, po-faced. Some writers you have known never lose their voice as you re-read them, and in his case the great speaker had often preceded the profound writer, and what is hardest though also happiest to remember, the little gurgle of laughter that seemed perpetually to underscore his words. It was a courteous, self-mocking laughter, a laughter which however passionate its owner about his subject was never to be set aside. He virtually laughed his way to death: I saw him week upon week, when we could manage it, in his last months and the laughter never ceased, nor did the courtesy. He was genuine through and through, and no doubt Charles II was not, but he virtually echoed Charles in politely regretting taking so long to die. Naturally when he did die obituaries flowed with the usual superlatives, but one thing was certain. Nobody ever heard him say a bad word of anybody else. Nobody ever seems to have said a bad word of him. He was not only a good man – as teacher, legislator, politician, lawyer, philosopher, orator, diplomat – he was a good man in the truest sense of the word.

It was in 2008 that we last performed in public together, commentators at the launch of *Scotland and the Union 1707-2007* edited by Tom Devine. Fellow-pundits were Joyce McMillan, determined that wherever Scotland might go, it was to be cultured, and Magnus Linklater, standing forever on the burning deck as the Union disintegrated around him. Neil was the last of us to speak, head back, comradely smile (did any academic or politician or philosopher or lawyer have the ghost of a competitive chance against his charm?), lightness of touch, courtesy of dissent – but now his obvious and just admiration for the essay of the conscientious Ewan Cameron, possibly the most promising of all modern Scottish historians, was unveiling a characteristically gentle but definitely steely criticism. Ewan Cameron had termed *MacCormick v The Lord Advocate* (1953) as having 'failed as it was found' that whether Elizabeth the Queen called herself First or Second of Scotland was a matter for her (not for simple arithmetic). Neil MacCormick in genuinely friendly manner denied the case's failure, save on the specific numerology (where in any case the Queen for the future avoided all numerals in relation to Scotland). But Cameron agreed that the case had won Lord Cooper's denial from the bench that the Act of Union had simply meant the adoption of surviving legislation passed in the English Parliament and dismissal of all in the Scottish. That had all too frequently been practice. But *MacCormick* finished any pretence of its legality. What lay behind this, in Neil MacCormick's last public appearance, was the vindication of his father, so often accused of having wasted Scottish chances.

At the same time there appeared a new edition of his father's autobiography *The Flag in the Wind* with an introduction from Neil himself (Birlinn, 2008, original edition 1955) the book is an admirably lucid and constructive account of John MacCormick's life, probably the best memoir by a Scottish politician in that century. The last words of Neil's introduction, 'He was a fine man and this is a fine book', are true with all the emphasis that rich voice would have given the repeated 'fine'. The book goes out of its way to warn readers of its writer's biases and inviting the reservation of judgement until other views are heard. But it is clear that John MacCormick was a colder man than his son, weaker in intellect, more limited in horizons, and proud of himself where Neil was proud of his father. His SNP followers knew him as 'King John', and the term had equal force as compliment and as indictment. No father has ever been better defended by his son than that introduction and none has been more eloquently hymned in love. Yet there seems curiously little similarity. *The Flag in the Wind* carries a back cover photograph showing John MacCormick 'addressing a Scottish Convention Meeting, St. Andrew's Hall, Glasgow' in 1949, as part of a campaign which won two million signatures for a Scottish Parliament. MacCormick was evidently addressing an audience with a large platform party seated behind him: yet it absurdly suggests a speaker so self-entranced that he has forgotten his audience's existence. Arms are outflung, hands open with palms uplifted in a cross between an eagle and a conjurer. Neil MacCormick never forgot his audience, and in that last exchange with Dr Ewan Cameron the great teacher was in supreme command of the traffic in ideas. He was holding the George Square theatre in his hand, and yet his whole intent was zoomed into anxiety to win Cameron over to the larger view of the case's outcome. Neil would never address such an audience again. Ewan Cameron, we may hope, may have many great audiences to instruct in future years. And Neil, knowing what he knew, was giving all his conviction to making his father's real achievement a part of Ewan Cameron's future (an acceptance readily granted by Cameron). One of John MacCormick's nationalist followers who helped to elect him rector of Glasgow University in 1951 was told by the victor that he, John MacCormick, had done it all for the Scottish people, only to be hurt when his youthful attendant sincerely assured him that so had all those supporting him. Neil MacCormick would have howled with delight if such a retort had been given to him, but he would never have drawn it by so self-righteous a claim. Fortunately he may never have heard the story.

The irony therefore remained that in their entry into the party their proud father founded, Neil and his brother Iain (SNP MP for Argyll, 1974-79) were at loggerheads with paternal politics outside their infancies. But with a dexterity as generous as it was brilliant,

Neil lived to congratulate his party and his country on having fulfilled the aspirations of his father. For all of his angry departure from the SNP when he lost control of it in 1942, John MacCormick was not displeased at its small, steady growth in the years before he died. But Neil's final verdict was no cautious *amende*, however *honorable*. Today's readers of *The Flag in the Wind* were told by its author's son, now clearly teaching the appropriate lessons of his dead father as well as to the party that abjured him:

> Since 1999, we have had a Scottish Parliament sitting in Edinburgh, still as a 'home rule' or 'devolved' parliament, yet even as such a transformational force in our society and indeed, in its very being, an expression of a transformed self-understanding of Scotland and its people. Since May 2007, the Scottish National Party under the leadership of First Minister Alex Salmond has formed the government in that parliament and over its first year in office made great progress in the judgement of most observers of the Scottish scene.
>
> . . .
>
> It has certainly turned out that both the political ventures on which John MacCormick embarked were essential forerunners of the journey Scotland took since his death. The Scottish Parliament would not have come into being without a strong cross-party commitment to the project, such as achieved through the 'Constitutional Convention' established in 1988. Probably without the external catalyst of, and potential threat from, the Scottish National Party, the Convention itself might not have sufficed. And certainly, when it came to the referendum campaign of 1997, it was vital that the SNP brought its full weight in with the Liberal Democrats, Labour and non-aligned forces to secure the greatest possible – and a more than adequate – majority for establishing a parliament with some tax-varying powers, and with full-hearted popular support behind it. Truly, it took both what one might call the 'Covenant tendency' as represented in the clear stand-out for a more fundamental long-term solution, to bring about the great transformation of Scotland's place in the UK and the wider world since 1707.

Few sons have the greatness to show where Father knew best despite Father's failure to realise or indeed witness it, or to show how in one of the greatest intra-party battles of his own political life both he and his opponents were right. As a matter of fact he did it at the time. A gradualist by conviction, and a peacemaker in contrast to his father's battles on all fronts, he spoke with the highest of admiration for one of his own pupils, Chris McLean, for denouncing Neil's support for the Convention. Neil's youth had been passed among omnipresent sneers at his father's failure to get further results for the two million signatures backing a Scottish Parliament. Yet he lived to show that all paths to a Parliament included that one, and he may well be right in thinking that without that apparent failure there would have been no ultimate success.

But I am thankful that the MacCormick I knew and loved was that son.

Neil MacCormick's generosity of heart was thus a Godsend for Scottish politics, above all in his perpetual zeal to find the best anyone had to say and to make the best use of it for the public good. It followed that his place as an MEP was one of perpetual awareness of the benefits other cultures had to offer. He had always been a figure of cultural enthusiasm. Hugh MacDiarmid had been one of his father's bitterest enemies: Hugh MacDiarmid's introduction to the *Golden Treasury of Scottish Poetry* was regarded by Neil as the cultural agenda of Scottish nationhood. At the heart of MacDiarmid's doctrines was the insistence that interwar England was stifling Scottish respiration from the world. Neil MacCormick had far too great a sense of humour to complain unduly against English parochialism, although it is significant that he became a formal Scottish Nationalist after study at Oxford. But in seeking to build up Scottish self-realisation by European, and indeed global, experience he was MacDiarmid's man. Hence to him the much-abused European constitution was a fascinating web of varying participant cultures, although needing more Scottish input.

To Neil MacCormick globalisation, the world-wide web, the increasing common cultural currency, even the ultimately successful internationalisation of the English language, were in themselves natural coefficients for Scottish, Welsh and even Irish self-rediscovery. The more the world closes in on us, the more we discover what we have to show it. Eurocrats might wag their fingers at hopes of Scottish reapplication under independence, but Neil could see the European effect as would-be monolithic states were forced to acknowledge their multi-culturism. A Eurocrat would see Spain being hostile to any gesture which might encourage separatism in its borders. Neil saw how much Spain had already devolved where European public opinion replaced Franco rule as a major determining factor. As he wrote in *The boundaries of Understanding* (a *Festschrift* for his colleague Malcolm Anderson, edited by Eberhard Bort and Russell Keat,1999):

> The stronger the European identity, the more it appears there is a need to secure local identities within or below the level of the member state.

Ten years later his final major work *Practical Reason in Law and Morality* (Oxford 2008) (a glorious conscription of so-called pragmatism in the cause of ethics by showing the value of ethics in determining pragmatic agenda) warned:

> Especially in Europe, it seems questionable to attribute omnicompetent sovereignty to any member state of the European Union. It would however, be well wide of the mark to suppose that the EU has itself replaced its members as a kind of sovereign federation or superstate.

> . . . If law depends on there always being a law-giver, dismay and alarm might be the appropriate reaction. Loss of sovereignty equals loss of law – loss, that is, of one's own final law-making authority. For the institutional theory of law, however, this sovereignty argument rests on a fundamental error. The error is that it takes norm-giving to be prior to norm-using. This is completely wrong. The latter is prior to the former.

> To give the priority to norm-giving is to suppose that humans can lead ordered daily lives only if someone lays down norms or commandments telling them how they are to order their lives. If this were true, there could be no natural human languages. But there are such languages, so it is not true. People are able to act in co-ordinated ways without being told to do so. Interactively and spontaneously they can construct and some to share the kinds of mutual beliefs that are at the heart of any common standards of behaviour we have, including common patterns of speech. These can, of course, include co-ordination by common acceptance of a common authority for making further norms and regulating some kinds of tricky situations. Authority, however, presupposes norms that confer it: so not all norms result from authoritative acts.

There are a thousand reasons to mourn Neil MacCormick, but here is certainly a splendid one. Here is cool, clear logic, pointing out to its audience what it knows (however much it may forget that it does). Simple clarity of this kind is what debates on Europe need.

Instead we are dealing with wild winds of superstition worsened by earthquakes of political evasion interspersed with fires of Brutish Nasty and U-PUKE demagoguery. But we went into the 2009 Euro-elections bereft of the still, small voice of Neil, however beautifully preserved in his austere academic Oxonian tome. It and its predecessors will still be there to refresh those who seek them. In place of the insanities gibbered into the public gaze by multi-millionaires in another country, let us return to the wisdom of our own man affirming that law lies in ourselves. The chimera of foreign absolutism taking over (largely manufactured by the foreign absolutists who rule the *Sun* and its junior brethren such as the *Times*) shrinks into proper perspective when we read Neil's 'there's always a reason to refuse absolutism. Human beings are autonomous moral agents – at least, they have the capacity to be such, and they achieve the fullness of their humanity in achieving autonomy and self-command.'

II

I could purr over *Practical Reason in Law and Morality* endlessly. There is, for instance, a beautifully crafted discussion of the Massacre of Glencoe and the Highland Clearances. Neil MacCormick called himself a gradualist, but his gradualism largely consisted in an ecumenism hearing each voice in debate when he could, all the more since he came from Highland and Lowland forebears, and from a multitude of ethnicities beginning with Gael and Norse. His quiet but passionate yearning for justice, his rejection of violence and chauvinism, his love of the law and preachment that it must be made to be our friend, are ideals for the country he served so well. And if we allow ourselves to brave the formidable print embodying his learning, we can see how open he made his genius to the democratic intellect.

By definition Neal Ascherson, journalist, was in the service of lucidity, even if his prose reached an elegance far beyond the capacities of his contemporaries. The 1970s which brought Neil MacCormick back to Scotland (to fill the Chair of Public Law and the Law of Nature and Nations at Edinburgh) took Neal Ascherson to the front page of *The Scotsman* which he transformed into the great cry for devolution. An Etonian himself, he reflected credit on the fine history teaching of that college in ways of which David Cameron seems to have been starved. Ascherson initially made little of his Scottish origins but internationalism dominated his interests from the first. His *The King Incorporated* (1963) was an exemplary investigation of the Belgian slave-state of King Leopold III, a vital book to place before the world when the advent and murder of Patrice Lumumba, the British-French sabotage of the integration of Katanga, and the dubious American provision of the Mobutu tyranny revealed the working-out of Leopold's ghastly tradition and legacy fifty years earlier. Ascherson had won his initial sense of Africa as Commonwealth Correspondent for the *Scotsman* in 1959, and what he saw of Scotland in that brief period may have alerted him to the nature of small nations which stood him in such good stead in studying the Belgians as well as their horror king. He would later show time after time his sense of the dynamics of the smaller states, which gave him invaluable mastery in the Russian satellite states whose perturbations ultimately transformed their tyrant.

The *Scotsman* found its cautious liberal Toryism transformed into full-blooded devolutionism from his return in 1975. He was far too canny to preach to his superiors in Scottish residence, but his unpretentious humour was infectious, and his interplay with the sublime and the ridiculous captivating. Like Neil MacCormick, to whom he naturally gravitated, he luxuriated in Scottish culture, from MacDiarmid to the wayward music critic Conrad Wilson. Instead of subjecting Scots to the superior wisdom of London sophistication, he visibly cheered the gentle humility with which Billy Wolfe accepted defeat on conference motions, and Billy thanked attendant pressman Colin Mackay for supplying a missing page from his major speech. To Ascherson however, Billy Wolfe restored humanity to politics, however simplistic his content.

There were, of course, other varieties of humanity on offer, notably Ms Janey Buchan, MEP, who quickly enshrined Ascherson in her over-worked demonology. The fact that Ascherson had Left-wing credentials made matters worse. The Buchans had by now left the Communist Party behind them, but this had no effect on their readiness to flay Trotskyism when required, and while Neal Ascherson's generous sympathies and untutored prose might leave little common ground with surviving Trotskyites, Janey Buchan could smell out what more guileless noses ignored. Neal at one point alluded to the Sign of the Sorry Head, simply meaning to imagine an appropriate waterhole for hungover party apparatchiks, but Ms Buchan promptly translated this into petty-bourgeois subversion at once requiring its errors and heresies exposed, which she duly did by explaining (a) that it was hopeless to expect any intelligence on Glasgow from the Edimbourgeoisie, (b) that Neal Ascherson was therefore bourgeois and ignorant, (c) that anyone from Glasgow that was anyone in Glasgow, knew that the Sorry Head was the Sarry Heid, (d) that the allusion was to the Saracen's Head which some former Glasgow crusader had affixed to a public house, (e) that whatever they might say in Edinburgh, in Glasgow it would be held that, son (meaning Ascherson), your bum's oot the windae. The Edimbourgeoisie joyfully awaited Ascherson's mode of discourse in reply to these courtesies.

It took a week or two to arrive, but the delay had improved its vintage. At this point the devolution debate was becoming intense. The Buchans were not officially anti-devolution as such, more anti-devolutionaries. They evidently disapproved of devolution on post-Stalinist grounds, but they were fond of Michael Foot, who was its Government sponsor. They compensated for their failure to throw light on their allegiance by throwing heat all around them. Ascherson, on a visit to London, encountered an anti-devolutionist, George Cunningham of Islington, whom the Buchans were unlikely to have supported (he later became a Social Democrat and vanished tracelessly). Cunningham boasted some Scottish origin: having left his country for his country's good, he now proclaimed his readiness to do it further good by blocking devolution, via an amendment requiring 40% in favour of the Bill before it could be implemented. The Speaker should never have permitted so destructive an amendment, dependent as it was on uncertain statistics from an old Register of Voters including persons, however dead or departed, as constituting legitimate percentage totalities whence 40% had to be won. Hence Neal Ascherson, meeting Cunningham at some semi-political occasion, reported to *Scotsman* readers:

> I said 'the cemetery vote' which was rude. He said 'with the greatest possible respect' which is Westminster for Mrs Janey Buchan's 'son, your bum's oot the windae'.

Bliss was it in that dawn to be alive.

But the dawn proved false. Ascherson has looked back on it since, and *inter alia* told the Welsh Political Archive Lecture in 1998 ('The Yes Road: a reflection on two devolution campaigns'):

> . . . in contrast to 1997, the European dimension played almost no part in the 1979 campaign. Labour's rank and file had been divided and reluctant in Harold Wilson's 1975 referendum on Europe while the SNP remained deeply suspicious of the European Community, seeing it as a threat to total national independence – in some quarters – as an international Vatican conspiracy. Their conversion under Alex Salmond to the slogan of 'Independence in Europe' lay many years in the future.

This may require some revision, if not revisionism. As a Catholic, I found little sign of fears of Vatican conspiracies in my days in the SNP (1974-81). It may be that Billy Wolfe's hysterical outburst against the papal visit revealed depths elsewhere to Ascherson though not to me: I could certainly testify to Billy Wolfe's lack of anti-Catholicism on a personal level, since I am one of the best reasons for disliking Catholics that I know and he has always shown genuine affection to me. Neal Ascherson left the *Scotsman* in 1979 and the subsequent civil wars in the SNP may have disguised its Europeanisation from him. The basis for conversion was simple enough. There was always a strong European intellectual presence associated with figures like Michael Grieve (like his father Hugh MacDiarmid), Neil MacCormick and George Reid, and some youthful links were built up with attractive Catalans. The party's loss of all but two seats in 1979 found its first compensation when Winifred Ewing, idolised since her ground-breaking win at Hamilton in 1967 and her defeat of the Tory Secretary of State for Scotland in 1974, won the European seat of the Highlands and Islands. And the arguments of Reid, MacCormick and others to follow the lead of the unscrupulous Irish were translated into action by Mrs Ewing. (There was perhaps a Vatican conspiracy after all, but if there was the SNP joined it.) She relished playing a lone hand (and made short work of interlopers), and told her colleagues at home how she had introduced Ian Paisley to Sile de Valera. Moreover she unquestionably won economic benefits for her constituency. And while she may have exaggerated her Eurostatus as 'Madame Ecosse', she could have claimed Europarliamentary recognition well beyond what her Scottish Unionist colleagues might boast. For the party to have repudiated its Eurostateswoman would have been unthinkable: those who thought it, left. Alex Salmond's 'Scotland in Europe' makes sense from him, but was the logical outcome of the party's filio-pietism. Neal Ascherson's weakness here may have been because his SNP links were chiefly on the Left, notably with Margo McDonald, who was unlikely to waste much conversation on Mrs Ewing's achievements.

Europe did resurface in Ascherson's memoir of Scotland's 1979 referendum when quoting his own diary:

Lord Home was induced . . . to speak to the nation on the box. Incredibly, he urged a No vote in order to secure a stronger Assembly with taxation powers and elected by PR. This did vast damage to the wavering Yes element among the Tories. . .

to which he added:

The historian Chris Harvie, with a retrospective eye on Sir Alec at Munich, commented : 'He began his career by betraying one small nation, and ended it by betraying another'.

But Ascherson's own retrospect pulled no punches:

Again and again, polls revealed that the main block of those who believed in full independence for Scotland were Labour voters, who would never consider voting SNP on grounds of class and party loyalty. In the same way, SNP support included a huge slice, perhaps a quarter, who preferred devolution within the UK to independence, but who judged that a strong Westminster vote for the SNP was 'good for Scotland'. In many European countries social-democrats and nationalists had found it easy to cooperate in movements for national emancipation. In Poland before the liberation of 1918 Jozef Pilsudski had said that 'socialism is the precondition for independence, and independence is the precondition for socialism'. Few people could think like that in Scotland. Hatred between the two main parties, and the neurotic contradiction in political attitudes, formed a knot which seemed drawn tight and hard as a stone.

Neal Ascherson told the Welsh how he perceived the growth in Europeanisation of Scotland's devolutionary politics in the late 1980s and early 1990s:

. . . it wasn't only in the SNP that the European dimension began to matter. The Tory panic over European integration in the later 1980s created a counter-current in Scotland, reinforced by the apotheosis of small suppressed nations in the 1989 revolution – especially in the Baltic. The allure of Scotland as a small European nation among others spread. The Edinburgh summit of the European Union in 1992 was the occasion for a demonstration in favour of a Scottish Parliament which assembled perhaps 15 or 20 thousand people – to the amazement of its organisers.

But in 2006-08 Neal Ascherson raised a somewhat different European analogy:

> . . . the Habsburg Empire in which the core imperial population group – the Germanic inhabitants of Austria – began to lose their identity in the age of rising nationalisms. Robert Musil put this well in his great novel about the last decades of Austria-Hungary, *A Man without Qualities*: 'within the Empire the Czechs knew they were Czech, and the Hungarians knew they were Hungarians, but the Austrians were just . . . Habsburgers?' I thought of Musil when I read a passage from Sir Keith Ajegbo's recent 'Diversity and Citizenship' report. The investigator was talking to a small Year 3 girl in a London school, who was the only English child in her class. When all the others had talked about their origins, she said sadly: 'I come from nowhere'.

He saw an interesting coupling of hate-figures:

> And almost inevitably, the English backlash slowly began. Who are all these eggheads and Eurocrats and Scottish carpet-baggers to tell us who we are and how we should think in our own country?

His essay concluded Tom Devine's *Scotland and the Union* and Ascherson ended it with reflections on the Czech-Slovak divorce, achieved (with little popular support) by politicians who concluded the break would serve their very different interests. And that becomes a danger for Scotland: that an ignorant and unscrupulous politician (say David Cameron) decides his political future is best served by getting rid of the Scots. For if the new Scotland is to succeed, it cannot be by birth from a parcel of rogues. ❒

EPILOGUE

The Word Made Concrete?

Architecture has its political Use; publick Buildings being the Ornament of a Country; it establishes a Nation, draws People and Commerce; makes the People love their native Country, which Passion is the Original of all great Actions in a Common-wealth.

Christopher Wren (quoted in *Parentalia*, or *Memoirs of the Family of the Wrens*, C. Jr. Wren, 1750)

CHRISTOPHER Wren's life (1632-1723) spanned the most turbulent period in modern English history. The fragility of national political organisation was rocked in turn by civil war, regicide, restoration, plague and the Great Fire of London, and a glorious revolution. Yet if any architect's career stands as an exemplary lesson that a nation's social and political life both moulds and is moulded by the spaces it inhabits, then it is Wren's. His great Baroque plan for the rebuilding of London in regular streets and places after the 1666 fire may (in foretaste of the Glorious Revolution) have been rejected because its grand idea took too little account of the English bourgeoisie's feel for their local history and their pragmatic attachment to land and property. Nonetheless his subsequent fifty-one London churches punctuated the ultimate new built seventeenth century order, and St Paul's stands, as Lord Simmons said, as 'a symbol of endurance to a nation so valiant in action, so steadfast in adversity'. Who indeed could forget that image of the cathedral rising in the smoke above the blitzed city on the front page of the *Daily Mail* of 31st December 1940 (more than two centuries after the architect's death), and

Churchill's defiant instruction that 'At all costs St Paul's must be saved.'

The forming of new spaces, and adaptations of old ones as a key to, and a result of ongoing political life is nowhere more apparent than in the story of the devolution of political power to Scotland. Just as in Wren's time in England (and Britain), the last fifty years in Scottish history have seen a revolution in government. It's true that puritan though he may have been, we can hardly claim that Donald Dewar was a real Cromwell to Tony Blair's curly-headed and reluctant Charles – nor for that matter, that Alex Salmond, finally getting to plant his great rump on the throne in Charlotte Square, weighed in as a Jock-dynasty Restoration. The changes in political life in Scotland have not been the result of serious civil disturbances: there have been no beheadings, no slaughters, no gun-running, no humanitarian disasters of mass proportion: it is our contention in *Tartan Pimps* that change was helped along 'by a long, slow literary and academic revolution'.

Throughout this book we have charted the writing of a paradigm shift in terms of the way civil life in Scotland (government, Union, monarchy, constitution, fiscal and industrial policy, law, welfare, history, education, class, religion, geopolitics, race, gender and language) is perceived. The narrative of such a deliberate, gradual and meditated literary turning of the political wheel is by definition contentious, and suffers of difficulty in depiction of the stages of its progression. Nonetheless, over the last fifty years certain concrete markers of progress have left a trace. Take the architecture of Scottish government over that period: 'architecture has its political use' says Wren. Two very different buildings were prepared to house the devolved administrations respectively of the failed 1970s and then the successful 1990s legislations: a contrast of the forms of those buildings can substantiate the history of a revolution in political and civic attitudes through their configurations in sandstone, glass, concrete, steel and timber.

The housing of the 1979 Assembly was to be in a minimal adaptation of an existing building, designed and carried out by faceless civil servant architects of the Property Services Agency (the PSA existed from 1972-93 with a role to manage the buildings and estates of the UK government). The building ultimately completed in 2004 and occupied by the Scottish Parliament was built from scratch and expressly as a parliament in Holyrood (although it incorporates the seventeenth century Queensberry House) by a world famous 'starchitect', the Catalan, Enric Miralles.

The Assembly of 1979 was to be held in a conversion of Thomas Hamilton's Royal High School of 1829, an austere Greek Revival temple-style building on Edinburgh's Calton Hill, the latter a species of national Valhalla bristling with monuments to the greats of history like Hume, Burns and Dugald Stewart. This site may have been unsuitable for the later 90s parliament building for reasons of size and also for the want of technical specifications (TV and radio studios were already a problematic addition to the old building in the 70s, and even the installing of microphones in the debating hall caused great difficulty). Nonetheless the building, since it lay empty after the architectural conversion and failed referendum of 1979, had in some way become symbolic of the unfulfilled nature of the nation's political destiny (marches in favour of devolution typically set out from this point, and the Vigil for a Scottish Parliament, a permanent demonstration, was sited at the entrance opposite St Andrew's House).

It may thus have been unnecessarily antagonistic (in view of its technical inadequacy which he knew of and could have cited) for Donald Dewar to dismiss Calton Hill as a possible site for the new Parliament for the 90s legislation by claiming it was a 'nationalist shibboleth'. (*The Herald*, 7th Jan 1998) Perhaps though given the Donald Dewar Collection of books gifted to the Parliament Library on Dewar's death in 2000 contained the Ted Morgan biography of Churchill, Dewar may have been indeed anxious to avoid the St Paul's symbol of a defiant nation effect on Calton Hill 'at all costs'). Nonetheless, despite the more lowly, less picturesque situation in town of the final chosen site at Holyrood, the architect there made a virtue of such shortcomings, and optimised and emphasised its relationship to the medieval urban (via the Canongate), to the royal history (via the Palace of Holyrood House, of which Miralles had long been a student), and to the land, as he designed his building not as some four square authoritarian – or even Presbyterian – near windowless temple/school, but in organic forms feeding out into Holyrood Park and reaching towards the Salisbury Crags.

This purpose-built 'iconic' parliament completed in 2004 to Miralles' design (the architect himself had died in 2000) sported a timber-beamed ceiling in its debating chamber, designed no doubt to draw the mind back to the hammer-beam roof of the old Parliament House last in governmental session in 1707. But perhaps the most interesting feature of its design is that the seating of the MSPs in this new-build is ordered in a hemicycle, supposedly to 'encourage consensus' and to get away from the adversarial style of politics in the House of Commons in Westminster. (see opposite)

This last point makes for an oddly direct contrast with the Assembly building in 1979. (see page 282) There an explicit instruction was given by civil servants in charge of the conversion of the oval shaped Royal High School assembly hall into the Debating Chamber that the design of the benches for debate be *on the long straight sides only*, and 'without use of curves' (letter from PSA to Scottish Office 17th January 1979). These curves were to be occupied by media and the presiding officers. In this way the direct physically confrontational format of Westminster benches was to be reproduced in the 1979 Scottish Assembly. But surely a knowledge of what in late 70s Scotland was likely to be the make-up of the representative numbers in the Chamber tells us this was in fact no design for a Bagehotian delicate balance between legislature, and executive by cabinet as seen in the House of Commons. In that latter critical schema every single debate between Government and Opposition benches is a debate for the life of the executive (the cabinet) and so, ultimately the Parliament, such that all discussion is of vital importance to the country at large. Instead what we had in the Royal High School was a design where the (non-) discussion would be dominated by near $^3/_4$ of the representatives (Labour, of course) sitting very comfortable on one side in debate with some very sparsely populated benches opposite (all the other loser parties): in effect, a government by praesidium.

This, in 1979, was indeed the Party committee that would, as Michael Fry feared, *control* Scotland, without any need for all that time wasted in debate as seen at Westminster. But by the time Scotland took a second bite at the devolution cherry some twenty years later, things had changed quite a bit. Yet if the hemi-cyclical form of the debating chamber opened in Holyrood in 2004 was designed

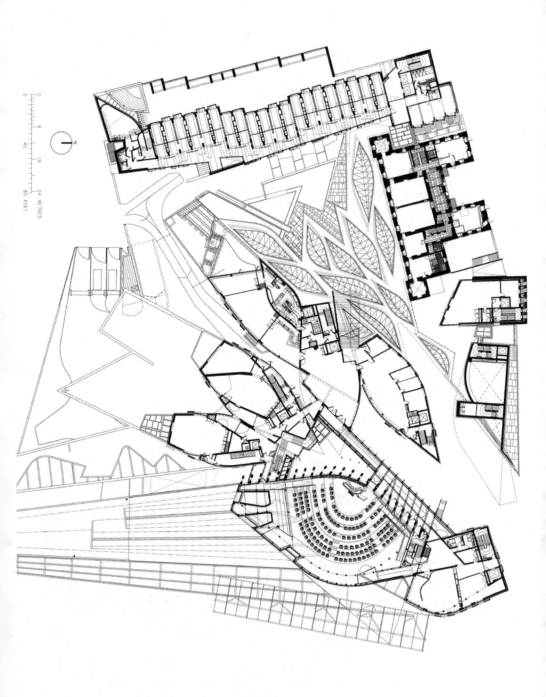

Plan of Holyrood Parliament, Courtesy: RMJM Architects

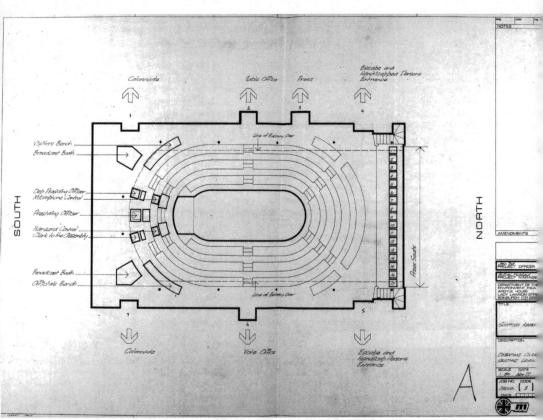

Plan & Section 1979 Scottish Assembly, Courtesy: National Archives of Scotland
SCOTLAND'S IMAGES.COM/ Copyright of the National Archives of Scotland SOE9/399 Plan NO.1 1/125 PSA
Plan A & SOE9/399 Plan NO.1 1/125 PSA Plan C

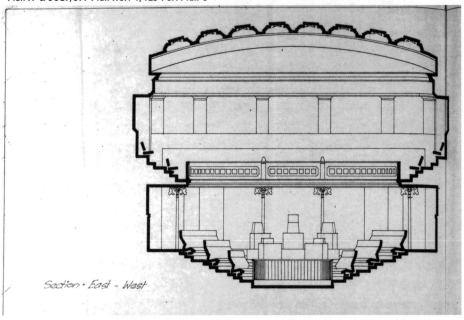

specifically to avoid Westminster style bilateral confrontation, then how would *it* cope with the less transcendent, and more immanent (and imminent) problem of one party domination?

The rest of this book, i.e. everything you have read up until now, represents surely (amongst many other things) a shift to square up to this particular problem. The writings we have analysed, summarised and contextualised map out a debate which took place through individuals and collectives, between institutions, across extended tracts of space and time. There were for sure, specific nodes and nexus points around which we have focussed our study but there was always the potential for infinite extension of the debate to involve other parameters, or to alter the focus of the analysis in hand. Thus this book can be used as a guide to a whole field, and could lead to further interest in a related but hardly touched-upon topic, or a more in-depth study of one particular aspect already dealt with here.

One could for instance, make a contrast of the relative importance and influence of European political thought on the work of Tom Nairn with the corresponding influence of American politics on the thought or policies of Gordon Brown; thus taking further a theoretical counterpoint which sits at the heart of this book. At any rate, the decision to adopt a proportional representation voting system for the Scottish Parliament (which adoption would, at one time, have seemed extremely implausible), and hence to delimit the power of the Labour block in camera, can be read as an outcome of various debates (particularly in *A Claim of Right* and in other publications by the Constitutional Convention) traced through this book. Labour was still by far the most popular party in Scotland after the 1999 and 2003 elections, but with the introduction of this PR system, they had to enter into coalition government with the Liberals, which tempered *to a certain extent* the potentially secretive, cabalistic, and *praesidium-*like nature of their rule.

But only to an extent; it is hard not to conclude that in the first years of devolution this once lively and independent debate exercised through the document and the text, atrophied once it was contained in the formalities of Scottish Parliament. Ultimately, the politicos assumed that they would 'take it from there' and the 'organic intellectual' would naturally defer. Or become Prime Minister.

But where would 'they' take 'it'? Scottish politics was professional-ised, compartmentalised and generally, verbalised into the rituals of governance and parliamentary spectacle. Political writing also changed, almost immediately. The necessarily transient form of political comment and analysis, week by week and blow by blow became an established section in Scottish broadsheets. Some might say that those books that did appear were often slight, instrumentalist or dull, and that the emphasis moved naturally towards documents that described and enacted legislation. Such publications seem to offer only a report-card type take on the day-to-day workings of the parliament; a crit as to whether the population at large are 'happy' with it, and if this or that degree of autonomy has been a 'good thing'. In that sense the hemi-cyclical chamber might only appear as one metaphorical turn in a self-centred spiralling down of debate that is not so much devolution as involution. There is in these publications no consideration, far less operation of the type of intellectual tool collated by *Pimps* and so useful in the analysis of Scottish political history – like 'democratic intellect', 'colonised native', 'uneven development', or even, 'jovial venality' – and thus neither can there be a real putting in context of political behaviours which work either from benefit of these intellectual tools or despite them – eg 'control freaks', BedPan Babies', 'the flagellant Tendency', 'administrative pragmatists', and 'Baronial beermagnates'.

But perhaps it is indeed time to listen to the voices from within the parliament itself rather than the commentary from outside. Shall not the writings, the texts and documents emanating from the constituted parliament now be the true measure of the influence and ultimate importance of these literary debates here claimed as vital? The parliament speaks – or in our case, writes. What then has it learned, or absorbed from the literary and intellectual history as we present it here? Is it just coincidence that the most influential and accomplished documents produced by and for this parliament, both reports and policies, concentrate their efforts on discussion of and legislation for building, construction and the built environment in general?

With the Homelessness Act 2003, the Scottish Government was the first, worldwide, to enact a policy to house all unintentionally homeless people: the 2001 Architecture Policy was also a worldwide first: and the fine prose of the Fraser Report on the fiasco of the building of Miralles' parliament, managed good style, as they say, neither to blame nor exonerate, nor hide the least detail.

In education, possibly the most substantial of the devolved powers, this yearning for the concrete continued. The rhetoric of those first days mirrored the English obsession with 'skills' but took it, if anything, further into a mechanistic recasting of the system around (to some extent) the individual's personal makeup, via 2001's *A Smart Successful Scotland*, *Learning for Life*, *The National Debate on Education* (2002-3), *Assessment is for Learning* and *Curriculum for Excellence* (2004), the latter being a particularly bold and potentially revolutionary reorientation of educational first principles. Nevertheless, there were plenty of Hebrew Old Clothes layered onto the new, not to mention a tension between the holistic and instrumentalist purposes of education. True to Blairite rhetoric, instrumentalist 'business friendly', 'knowledge economy' caricatures of 'learning' were initially dominant, formed (at least spiritually) around the Clydeside vignette of the school disgorging its human contents only for these to immediately shoal into the shipyard next door. At worst these documents with their notions of 'social inclusion' and 'lifelong learning' institutionalised – or certificated – the problem of disengagement in the societal mainstream into apparent non-existence; at best, they formulated what might be called a 'liberal democratic intellect', reflected not in the dignity and autonomy of Davie's professors, but the contribution of 'learning' to the material wellbeing of kids usually cast from the schools straight into an uncertain subsistence in Scotland's housing schemes.

But does this evident striving always to construct a concrete object in its documents represent a real step forward, away from merely intellectual debates and towards working democracy and egalitarianism in practice, or are we metaphorically only witnessing the sclerosis of the mind in the over-institutionalised atmosphere of yet another chamber and another tier (local, regional, *national*, and state) of British government?

The description, in the Fraser Report, of our First Leader Dewar and his cronies, unable to find any place for a new constituted parliament first to meet in order to debate where it would meet, shows that the whole prospect of a politically responsible society moulding and being moulded by the spaces it inhabits had a vertiginous effect.

Certainly this was farce, but then there was never any shortage of theatre; the hemi-circular layout of the temporary debating chamber set up in the Kirk Assembly Halls offered an early opportunity for gesture (or 'iconic') politics when Dennis Canavan, the maverick Labour MP, then Independent MSP, exploited the free seating arrangements to plonk himself behind Dewar. Then we had Tommy Sheridan, clenching his fist as he mouthed the oath. Small, one man shows soon drowned in the careful management speak of the Labour-Liberal Executive and the dryasdust 'oratory' of newly promoted councillors and apparatchiks. But more on them later; a real shock to the system was supplied when Brian Souter invoked the authentic phrasing and vehemence of Scots – that celebrated carrier of bourgeois liberal 'cultural nationalist' hopes in the pre-devolutionary years – in the cause of poofter baiting, snarling, at a press conference that 'We didnae vote for it, and we're no havin' it!'

Was this then, the voice of the people speaking in what Paterson described as 'surprising new ways' – or if you like, Leonard's democracy based on the equality of dialogue? It certainly was not the synthetic Lallans as adored by the *Chapman* reading classes, nor was it the careful modulation of Scottish English as effected by BBC Scotland news-readers (and Scottish politicians); it was an application of Leonard's living language, the language Souter spoke in both the boardroom and the austere gatherings of the Church of the Nazarene. In attempting to scupper the Parliament's first high profile attempt at legislating greater social and personal freedoms, the 'mean dialect' was thus deployed for a mean purpose, and although few talked about it, politicised. Souter understood, clearly, the 'sarcastical vivacity' of Scots speech which Boswell had described to Jean Jacques Rousseau as an astringent against high ideals and cosmopolitan notions.

Decried as a chequebook politician (he had earlier described his bus-riding customers as 'beer-drinking, chip-eating, council house-dwelling, Old Labour voting masses'), Souter compounded this sense of crisis among the old certainties through his unusual partnership with Cardinal Thomas Winning, former star of the anti-Thatcherite consensus of the 1980s. Mr Souter represented a new Scottish business and entrepreneurial avant-garde of savage, American-trained-post-Thatcherite working class capitalists who had decimated the traditional Scottish business classes and owed nothing to old delicacies. Winning however, represented the traditional anti-Thatcherite Scottish left who believed in social justice (but just not for dykes and queers). These large and small 'c' conservative forces were not of the safely foreign brand typified by Thatcher or Norman 'googly' Tebbit. They were reactionary, they were right wing, but they were also home grown. And some of them are now donating to the SNP.

This represented then, not so much a step away from merely intellectual debates, as warmly embracing a culture of narcissistic populism amidst shameless vogueing in the newly intensified media spotlight, the spectre of reserve powers only emphasising the feeling that this new Scottish politics was narrow and insubstantial. Against this backdrop of fragmentation, the replacement of politics *through* the book with politics *by* the (cheque) book, the 'liberal', egalitarian narrative written of in the bulk of Scottish political literature already looked defunct. In fact this would overstate the issue; what was different was that this arch-narrative of the Scottish social democratic commonweal was now challenged by a number of competing narratives, ideals and readings of political questions as they were experienced in Scotland. This meant that *control* – or settled will – was, for good or ill, harder for the Scottish political (dis)establishment to sustain.

But it took said (dis)establishment/praesidium some time to wise up. Initially, Scottish Labour remained convinced that business as usual was not only possible, but the natural (and moral) order of things, as was evident in Dewar's cavalier politicking over the Holyrood site. But the new 'solid state' Scottish politics ran its own course, and it was initially rather troubling. Scotland's Holyrood home brew as casked in the 1999 election left a sour taste and the new building on the site of the beermagnate's former brewery was the principal cause. The bitterness over the mounting costs told of the sense of disappointment in, and distance felt by Scots from the newly devolved politics. Dewar stated that they should build a structure Scotland's parliament deserved.

But almost immediately, the question was raised as to whether it did deserve a starchitectural wonder? Now limited power was in their hands, what had Scotland's leaders done to deserve the cushy new pad in the old town? (The sense that the new parliament building might be something *Scotland* deserved, that its people had merited was rare and barely communicated.)

The Scottish media, with a new political class to tear into (and damn all else to do) exacerbated views of devolution (possibly sponsored and approved by London) as an expensive luxury item foisted on the Scottish people, exhibit A being the Parliament building itself, while simultaneously shoring up the chummy, overly intimate acquaintance between politicians and the fourth estate – never more arch or, you might say, revolting than the chumminess of Jack McConnell and Kirsty Wark. The tone of the debate was noticeably lowered, and the main culprit was *The Scotsman* following the arrival of *Private Eye* bête noir Andrew Neil, swapping his henchman-ship of Murdoch for those other pseudo-Scots, the Barclay twins. He immediately, and to the disgust of many of its journalists, turned the pro-home rule *Scotsman* agin devolution on the very eve of the referendum, then pursued a hectoring and at times, vindictive vendetta against it and its architects. Brillo's frothing led to a gap in reasoned, constructive scrutiny that can only have encouraged Scottish politicians to cultivate friendly faces on the newsstands as a matter of urgency. Amazingly, the Neil *Scotsman* may be the prime culprit behind a situation where the first and fourth estate simultaneously existed in a state of cosiness and alienation.

Besides these profound structural problems, not to mention the decidedly superficial level of analysis and scrutiny by the Scottish political correspondents, the naked mediocrity of the first generation of Scottish Parliamentarians made selling the value of devolution to either hacks or public a real problem. Also unhelpful was the obviousness with which the old Pimps of the Tartan from the four major parties assumed their places in the new system with a sense of maddening entitlement.

William McIlvanney, interviewed on BBC Scotland during election night, wondered where the poets and rabble rousers had gone and made a poor show of hiding his disappointment as the very prosaic party hacks beamed behind their rosettes. As mentioned earlier in this book, the very first result in the 1999 election was called for Tom McCabe, the Labour council leader whose responsibility was to manage the count. Sure, it was Lanarkshire where (you might say) only the lack of a Mediterranean diet and Mafia money distinguishes its political culture from Southern Italy (or New Jersey), but the symbolism was nevertheless rather perturbing. Tom Nairn's expressed hope that home rule would help break the power of the 'peripheric elites' who had previously managed Scotland seemed hollow. Sure, the Tory managers who personified subjugation under the *Magna Margaret* were ousted, but that only emphasised the imperfections in the victorious Labour ranks. So there was home rule. We had it, or a version of it, and yet there they were, those same laconic political managers, apparatchiks, lobby fodder and toon coonmail *arrivistes* all united in their apparent lack of imagination. United, and seated consensually in the sparkling structure sprouting from the Scottish and Newcastle malting pits.

At this point, certainly, there seemed little chance of this disingenuous architecture of Scottish politics – real or conceptual – fulfilling Wren's hope of making the people love their native country. Of course, *we* voted *them* in – following the voting patterns laid down over the majority of the twentieth century and according to the choices offered us, Kirk election style, by each party's selection process (the Scottish Labour Party's process having ironically assured their own ex-maverick Canavan of a landslide victory). It took the Scottish electorate some time to conjure with the notion that they might, if they so chose, break with previous allegiances. In the meantime, the Holyrood scandal consumed the Scottish Parliament and threatened to derail Devolution in its earliest years, as the control freaks of Scottish politics moved to immediately deny all culpability:

> With the honourable exception of Sir David Steel on behalf of the SPCB accepting some responsibility for increased costs, the ancient walls of the Canongate have echoed only to the cry of 'It wis'nae me'.

These are the words of Lord Fraser of Carmylie, who was chosen to lead the inquiry and whose name appears on the subsequent report. His fluent hand shaped one of the better written, if more jesuitical, official post-devolutionary documents. As with Souter, Fraser found playground Scots to be a particularly adroit medium in summing up a negative charge in contemporary Scottish politics. The Tory peer was judicious in ensuring civil servants, the mandarins of Midwinter and Keating's culture of administration, took the blame as murky filters of emerging realities rather than MSPs – nevertheless, his succinct conclusion that 'Not until it was too late to change was there any real appreciation of the complexity of the Architect's evolving design and its inevitable cost' can be read as a cunning and wounding piece of innuendo, a judgement on the adolescence and inexperience of Holyrood's masters, father figures keen to strut their stuff internationally, but too small, too 'parish council' to handle a 'wayward Spanish genius'?

Instead the Scottish *praesidium* settled for the well-worn (or frayed) machinery of semi-secret Scottish government, in which the civil service controlled all perception. Such a mixture of impotence and ineptitude seemed to cement a longstanding (what Beveridge and Turnbull might call 'metropolitan') myth of late seventeenth century lineage, that the Scots simply could not govern themselves. Indeed, Fraser, in protecting the posthumous reputation of Donald Dewar from the wreckage of Scotland's new Darien Housing Scheme emphasised his London-learned credentials:

> It comes as no surprise that Donald Dewar contemplated resignation on the basis that he had misled the Scottish Parliament. Donald Dewar was steeped in the Westminster tradition that there is no greater democratic misdemeanour than misleading Parliament and he clearly carried that with him when he became First Minister in the Scottish Parliament.

And so, rather than desecrate the memory of a lost leader (for any good Scottish Conservative knows the importance of *Hero Worship*) Dewar is redeemed by his lineage as an MP, as opposed to his near-disgrace as one of those snake-oil guzzling MSPs. Thus, Fraser riffed on an already familiar narrative of political commentary in the broadsheets, of London professionals and hubristic Edinburgh amateurs. Nevertheless, the Fraser Report did acknowledge those lamentable administrative hangovers recommending 'that where independent professional advisers have been retained, their views should not be filtered by the Civil Service but should be put to Ministers alongside any disagreement officials may have with the judgements expressed by those advisers', indicating an important change to the way in which power was accessed in Scotland, and how said power *accessed Scotland*.

The electorate showed its underlying, but somewhat indefinable sense of dissatisfaction, by a general disengagement. Nevertheless, three related notions seemed to converge in the 2003 election. A desire to move away from the stultifying greyness of the lobby-fodder first parliament; dissatisfaction with the mainstream parties and a growing distrust of authority, the latter as much to do with foreign wars, global terrorism and the immediacy with which political and social debates, lunatic or mundane, could now be communicated via the internet as any home-grown malaise. Indeed, html played as significant a role in the described changes in Scottish political writing as the changing machinery of government or the predilections of the Scottish literati.

These trends were articulated at the ballot box during the 2003 election, which saw a proliferation of small parties and independents gouging the powerbases of the major parties, yet still failing to make a dent in the Labour-Liberal powerbase. Nevertheless, as a few alert mainstream political commentators saw, it reflected a determination by the electorate to cure and redeem the notion of a Scottish politics. Thus Joyce Macmillan, quoted by Tom Nairn as 'the only rational voice at that time surviving on Andrew Neil's *Scotsman*', predicted of the elections in 2007

> . . . the likelihood of a harder edged determination to vote
> tactically for the parties most likely to break Labour's long
> Scottish hegemony. . .

In hues of dark tan and denim blue, the brief rise of the Scottish Socialist Party as part of the 'Rainbow Parliament' was probably the most colourful and instructive episode of Scotland's new, issue-driven gesticular politics. It saw the militant tradition of the Scottish Left align itself with the post-modernist, post-Faslane and post-Soviet Union left perhaps best epitomised by Rosie Kane, whose open palm scrawled in marker contrasted with Sheridan's clenched fist oath at the swearing in. The Scottish Socialists did not themselves contribute much to Scottish political literature and were in some respects, symptomatic of its post-devolutionary decline; Sheridan did author the rather lightweight political manifesto *Imagine* with Alan McCombes which is ultimately, a Clift Notes version of Marxism that catalogued the faults of Blairism but was evasive on their ultimate solution.

To be fair, as easy reading as it ultimately was, *Imagine* was consistent with the SSP's Militant, activist agenda and desire to disrupt the complacency of the old elites and engage with the popular, through the popular. A more profound document, at least for the shape of recent Scottish politics, was three or so typed pages that typify the neuroses, crisis and schisms of the Scottish hard left in the period covered by this book. 'The Minutes' of the SSP meeting evidence the attempt by Tommy Sheridan to secure the support of his party in denying allegations over his sex life as levelled by the *News of the World*. The minutes were subjected to a fully postmodern dismissal – Sheridan simply claimed they were fake, and a jury, that very Anglo Saxon theatrical invention, by implication, agreed with him. Regardless of which side one takes on the Sheridan case, it was hard not to conclude that the value of the document in Scottish politics had diminished in relation to that of the image (in this case the wronged and slandered Sheridans) and that McCrone's post-nationalist polity was very post-modern in its mistrust of documentary evidence.

But if documents were inadmissible in issues of libel their role in practical governance was if anything, amplified. The growth of policy formulation and related publications became the natural, and increasingly dominant conduit for Scottish political discourse. As mentioned above, some of the flagship policies of the Scottish Executive can be interpreted as concrete attempts to use the intellectual tools developed through years of written debate. Surrounding these big policy documents were solar systems of smaller documents that both scoped prior to, and elaborated after, their drafting. Within months of Parliament's first sitting an entire mixed economy of research and consultancy accrued around the Edinburgh administration, much of it staffed by ex-public servants freed from Scotland's pre-devolutionary administrative apparatus. Their task was often to break down the blank verse of these mission statements into hard outcomes and pen-sketched blueprints for action – or 'delivery' as it is prosaically termed.

The proliferation of a new culture of research and consultancy led inevitably, to a more technical, and specialist discourse in stark contrast to the synthetic and holistic sweep of the literature covered in this book. Whether contracted by the Scottish Executive Social Research unit, or by the various government agencies, consultants worked according to briefs crafted, buzzword by painstaking buzzword. A breeze through the titles of this dispersed, technocratic discourse, of reports, reviews and guidance documents published under collective authorship are instructive: *Statutory Duties to Promote Equal Opportunities and Evidence of their Impact*; *A Scotland Where Everyone Matters*; *One Scotland Many Cultures*; *Assessment is for Learning*; and *The East Dunbartonshire Tenants Survey*. These are not titles that trip off the tongue, nor are the contents of these reports commissioned at national, non-governmental and local authority level easy-reading (and in the case of *One Scotland, Many cultures* demonstrably woolly and muddle-headed), but they contain the rhetorical meat of Scottish governance. They are the software developed around the new constitutional hardware, its binary punch-cards, as purposive and disposable as the bundle of signatures collected in Greyfriars Kirkyard in 1638.

Of course, the Scottish press could have eased this situation by providing an interpretive and critical role. To some extent, they did; commentators such as Ian Bell or Robin Dinwoodie were still worth consulting for accessible analysis of political trends, neuroses and tensions within the new system. Alf Young provided detail, but there was something oppressive (and firmly 'old school') in his dissections of public policy issues that spoke only to a certain (Labour) congregation. But the descent into cheap gossip, innuendo and wafer thin debate in the mainstream broadsheets largely went unarrested.

Big books on politics in Scotland, or even wee, chippy pamphlets were replaced by gazetteers of interest only to those already in the club and a breaking up of the discussion into specialisms and mini-empires that mirrored the new administrative reorganisations. There was no *Scottish Prospect*, or even *Private Eye*. There was *Holyrood* magazine, a trade paper for the parliament no one read that judged politicians purely in terms of their ability to play the game. The *Scottish Left Review* was, by virtue of its title, palatable to only one division of the Kirk, though it did offer a low-key commentary on emerging policy.

The rest of the existing lineup of independent Scottish magazines and press were mostly literary, mostly stuck in the seventies and stuck in the 'Cultural Nationalism' debate. Besides *Radical Scotland*, *Cencrastus* struggled to find its relevance in the years leading up to devolution and wasted away to a sliver before folding, the *Edinburgh Review* was somewhat academic while *Chapman* drew its already close circles even tighter.

At this point, you might expect a publication authored by editors of *The Drouth*, one of a handful of magazines to appear post-devolution, to blow its own trumpet, given the ongoing discussion, in-depth, of the issues raised in this book. This book is in itself, an ample basis upon which the reader can pass judgement on the value and quality of that debate. Other publications, such as *Variant* (on cultural policy), focused on a very particular areas as representative of wider political interests, while new media emanations, such as *Spinwatch*, *Indiewire Scotland* and *Pulse* largely ignored Scottish politics (except where it was grassroots) and (perhaps logically) contributed to the anti-war agenda and the emerging globalisation of political debate. Interestingly, and significantly, the profile of those authoring these new or rebooted publications was considerably less white, less Labour and less tribal (at least in the Scottish sense) than had been typical in Scottish letters.

Amongst the 'old guard' of Scottish political writers fortunes differed. Alan Massie and Arthur Midwinter have continued to be persistent critics of devolutionary divergence from the unitary state and the latter, unembarrassed at his blatant 'spin as scholarship' disgrace over his special report for the *Scotsman* has relished digging into the SNP administration at every opportunity. Newer figures, such as Tom Devine offered Scotland a narrative synthesis it had long needed, but carefully evaded direct engagement in politics. Some publications did stir up trouble in areas once too impolite for discussion.

One of the first major controversies within the Scottish political arena was instigated by the words of a composer and the collaborators on a subsequent book. *Scotland's Shame* as instigated by James McMillan also showed how a native Scottish issue (albeit one that looked longingly or loathingly across the Irish Sea) could be interrogated in a fashion subliminally hostile to the very idea of distinctive entity called Scotland, devolved or otherwise. McMillan in particular, questioned the value of all post-reformation Scottish culture as a desecration of (Catholic) civilisation and even ethnic cleansing (which he graciously retracted). A number of writers, catholic and protestant both contributed : Andrew O'Hagan, who collaborated on the book, answered historian John Haldane's Turnbullandbeveridgesque criticisms of the book's inclusion of views 'from afar' in an interview for *The Drouth*, defending the value of the 'metropolitan' literati's contribution to Scottish affairs:

> 'From afar' is simply code for London, as if being out of Scotland, and being in London, were a sort of sin against natural belonging, as if London life, indeed, were a betrayal of the general Scottish good. . . which leads quite naturally to the rather pious belief that intellectuals who remain in Scotland are honouring some greater truth and living out an honest penance. It's really an exercise in grossest vanity, because Scotland is much larger than its own borders, if only the keepers of those borders would allow it.

Other commentators settled into their silos, but were nevertheless, able to mount perceptive and telling analyses of the latter part of the devolutionary decade, ending as it did, with a Nationalist administration (only just) in power.

In the updated version of the huge Humes and Bryce tome *Scottish Education*, Lindsay Paterson reflected on the eventualities of autonomist thinking in Scotland. As he notes, the education system (arguably the most powerful political lobby in the country) had high hopes of home rule as a process that would resolve its own internal contradictions, in particular the harmful bifurcation between higher education and the primary, secondary and lower tertiary sectors of the system. Paterson's report card is largely positive, seeing many benefits in the new political freedoms and attendant fiscal control (at least in the sense of divvying up block grants). But he goes deeper, touching upon but not name-checking Davie, in placing the cherished mythologies of Scottish education as a 'native' incubator of the democratic spirit:

> Deeper still, the sense that Scottish education was not wholly undemocratic, or unmeritocratic, inspired the common belief that it embodied Scottish democracy itself. Just as a certain kind of Protestant used to claim that democracy was the ultimate fruit of the

Reformation, so also it sometimes seemed in these educational debates of the 1980s and 1990s that Scottish democracy owed a unique debt to Scottish education.

Scottish parliamentary politics certainly owed flesh and blood assets (John Smith for example) to the libidos of certain dominies. More important perhaps, is Paterson's usage of Scottish education as a metaphor for the many constraints and influences, way beyond the much storied Scotland-England axis, that shape Scottish political culture:

> The character of the curriculum and examination systems in the senior years of the secondary school or at university might be a betrayal of certain Scottish traditions. It might be unfortunate that important aspects of it have to be designed with international comparability in mind. But it would be naive to imagine that any independent country could design their structures solely according to inherited traditions. . . if a Scottish government were to ignore this, then it would find that growing numbers of schools. . . would opt for qualifications that were convertible. . . in which Scottish traditions and culture would feature not at all.

Allowing for the particularities of this argument as they relate to the education system, and we see a microcosm of the dilemma facing policymakers in countries bigger and wider than Scotland (but perhaps much more sure of themselves). Against the backdrop of a global market, the threat of cultural obliteration (if such a threat exists) is if anything intensified when a country becomes more 'protectionist'.

Paterson's argument is worth spending some time with as it raised the question of where it might leave the likes of Tom Nairn (like John Smith, son of a dominie). Wouldn't a good Marxist, even a follower of Gramsci, triumphantly seize upon such analyses as proof that nationalist aspirations, particularly those bound into civic, rather than ethnic institutions, are irredeemably bourgeois, irredeemably allied to the interests of capital (because if they are not, the market will simply work to undermine those institutions and make them increasingly irrelevant)? Such lessons (if we take Paterson's word for it) are of course, only learnable in a post-devolutionary environment, where Scotland is increasingly exposed to international trends without the Westminster ozone layer. And the alleged furore in both Britain and USA over SNP Justice Minister McAskill's release of the so-called

Lockerbie bomber, Al Megrahi, only demonstrates how contorted can the manoeuvres of what Nairn calls the 'Big Lads club' become when the interests of capital (and in this case, Libyan oil) are at stake.

At another level, in terms of the big reports and inquiries, such as Fraser and the new Calman confection, there are more interesting questions raised over provenance and intended audience. Who is commissioner and who is the client? asks Owen Dudley Edwards in a scathing attack on the Calman Commission report (*Scottish Review of Books,* 16th August 2009). This is the telling reading of these documents because in the post devolutionary period the potential for internal contradictions in the political system have exploded from Dalyell's famous West Lothian Question to encompass an extremely complex set of institutional interrelations including not only those between Westminster (Lords and Commons) and Holyrood, but there and Dublin, Belfast, Cardiff and Brussels; between the Scottish *Parliament* as a whole and the Scottish minority *Government;* and also between the London and Edinburgh HQ's of the UK parties etc etc. As Edwards says of the Calman Commission, set up by the Labour, Liberal and Conservative parties with the remit of 'anything governmental goes – except independence':

> The three parties of whom the Commission claims independence have decreed that any real meaning of that word may not be applied to Scotland.

This leaves us hanging on the thorny problem of the 'real meaning' of 'independence' not just for autonomists but for devolved unionists too. True independence is not possible in the modern global world, may be the mantra of the unionists, following the same logic of Paterson's non-isolationist analysis, but at the same time they claim independence for themselves of London hegemony in their devolved administration. (eg Scottish Labour leader Iain Gray's stance apparently, but ultimately remaining in his powerless role as opposition leader, *de facto* untested, opposing Brown on the freeing of Al Megrahi). Edwards concludes:

> As for its disclaimer 'The Commission is independent of any political party' when it owes its existence to three, and includes two members from each, the Commission would seem to have a remarkably low estimate of the collective intelligence of its readers. . .

297

It is worth bearing in mind too, that this analysis brings us back to that vexed issue, raised by so many of the writers in this book, of the peripheric elites and the rule of the technocrat. Paterson notes, with a certain grim irony, that the SNP's current strategy is based on overtures to Scotland's co-opted professional middle and business classes; the idea being, it seems, to reassure them they will be as dominant in an independent Scotland as they were in a British province. Given Nairn's insistence on nationalism as a necessary mechanism for overthrowing the power of this group and the 'elite norms of their long counter-revolution'; and given his seeming cooption, at least superficially, by the Salmond government, as the intellectual leading light of big N Scottish Nationalism, it looks as if a major strand of his political thought has reached something of an *impasse*.

The radicalising potential of the independence movement would seem to have been nurtured, then effectively neutered by the very cadre of smart, '79 group nationalists who moved the SNP left-of centre (albeit with some holdouts on issues such as nuclear deterrents and foreign wars, a legacy perhaps, from the radicalising effects of 'Fortress Scotland'). Of course, Nairn does not equate to the SNP, and he has strongly criticised them in the past. But it does raise the question of whether his analysis of nationalism, and the need to support such movements in order to reorient and redress 'uneven development' can be sustained, or taken any further. Certainly his published work since *The Modern Janus* (setting aside *Global Matrix*, co-authored with Paul James) has mostly taken essay form as critiques of open challenges to his synthesis. Prime targets have included the 'No More States?' theories of Rosencrance and Stein, which counsels that those seeking national self-determination must do so within 'metropolitan boundaries'. There are also signs of Nairn looking once more into the spicy ferment of Italian leftist thoughts, having recently published a major essay on the activist-philosopher Antonio Negri.

Rosencrance and Stein's argument for the sanctity of 'metropolitan boundary' would offer a red rag to Beveridge and Turnbull, and these American theorists likely have no real clue as to just how to slack and ill-fitting these metropolitan boundaries are – way too tight in some areas, baggy and frayed in others. But it does seem to some extent, that with the argument for independence made, hardly won (and the recent banking crisis, rightly or wrongly, a gift to unionist parties) Nairn has no new tricks at hand. Instead he retreads and revisits. Leighton Andrews MP hits upon the personal nature of the problem, although his analysis verges on intemperate and is striped with (Labour) party lines and must be dosed liberally with salt:

> All that remains is polemic, convinced of its own rectitude, scathingly unforgiving of alternatives. . .

There is a word for that of course, one familiar to the west of Scotland and ironically associated (at least by French apocrypha) with English ejaculations[2] altogether too strong. Rather, Nairn has perhaps been unfortunate in having to bang on about the same subject so long, having developed a classic argument that, like Hume's scepticism, cannot really find any more to say than what it already has stated, and knows itself to be. Nairn is true to his Gramscian roots at least, in persisting as a latterday Machiavelli, the analyst-activist described in the *Modern Prince* a who aims to provoke action through a particular reading of history, to unify (or perhaps disunify. . .) a people into a national-popular collective. Like Machiavelli, he awaits changes that may lie most realistically, in his descendants' future, but cannot abide a lull in the conversation.

In a critique of Colin Kidd's *Union and Unionism: Political Thought in Scotland 1500-2000*, published in the autumn 2009 edition of *The Drouth* he further presses the case for independence as (as he puts it, and in his italics) '*the sole answer*':

> [Kidd's] cumulative over-praise for Unionism tends to obscure the costs of sustaining such a system. Scots may have liked it, and striven ingeniously to adapt; but partly by downplaying – or even colluding in – the grim costs of the show. That is, in the maintenance of an increasingly preposterous and anachronistic multinational state and monarchy.

A student set to be examined on Nairn and his sayings could write much of this on their arm and pass, easily. But to return to the perhaps vexed issue of Nairn, Salmond and those peripheric elites, he writes:

---

[2] The word bigot is said to be a corruption of 'By God!', as uttered by Englishmen in France.

> As this intolerable structure has broken down since World War II
> peripheral discontent has grown, and taken nationalist form; but not
> enough to help demolish it.

Is this 'peripheral discontent' an admission of the fundamental
problems and contradictions of the SNP's, so far, quite successful tactic
in becoming a party of governance (as opposed to simply aspiration)?
He does not go any further, instead going on to criticise the notion
that Britain could federalise.

> English democracy is of no account to the Union faithful: all the
> pious perceive is the stability and continuity of Union-Britain, an
> inherited Grandeur that has also provided so many jobs for
> outwardly-mobile fringe *intéllos* and politicians, and saved them from
> small-nation obscurity and powerlessness.

This describes, adequately, many of the people mentioned in this
book, but most especially, and quite definitely Gordon Brown, the
number one fellow traveller who took the metro line out of small-
nation obscurity, and the central focus of Nairn's sustained attack in
Gordon Brown – Bard of Britishness, a 'Centurion' in the counter-
revolutionary forces intent on shoring up elite power or, most acidly
(but as Edwards points out above [see p158], mistakenly) 'the Jeeves
of Britain's last days'. Nairn expends a peculiarly individual, non-
vernacular 'sarcastical vivacity' in dissing Brown's often counter-
intuitive attempts to argue for 'British values'. He is never more clear
or accurate than when noting Brown's evasion of the role of the
monarchy in allowing such values to even exist. Unresolved though
in either the *Bard* or recent essays, is the dissonance between Nairn's
perfectly astute criticisms of the messianic Pimp extraordinaire and
his tacit support for the pragmatic, elite-friendly onslaught of the
nationalist project at Holyrood.

Still, Nairn, who is at least for these authors, Brown's Great
Adversary, (and once, great rival for the laurels of 'Scotland's pre-
eminent Gramscian), understands him better than any commentator,
certainly any born (or borne) in England.

> What Brownism calls for, by contrast, is Presbyterian 'realism'; that
> is, teeth-gritted loyalty unto God's Will, as evidence by
> Competitiveness, Market Forces and Heaven's endorsement of an
> imaginary USA. . . the alliance unto death of UK putrefaction and
> global Free Trade. . .

Take a look at any pimps featured here and you will find plenty sons of the manse among them, and many of them who made Scottish affairs an appendix to 'real politics'. They were a literate and hard-headed caste of thousands within Scottish society that made the most of Empire and the Union which made it accessible to them. Through the union 'they' shared a destiny. Through nationalism, says Anthony D. Smith 'we' can all share a destiny. Is the 'Salmond shift' then, part of encouraging 'them' to become 'we'?

Clearly, wordplay of this sort will continue to be essential as Scotland enters decade II of Home Rule. But what about those of us who committed to that other shared destiny, as presided over by her Maj? Gordon Brown is just one who seems uniquely adrift and bereft, cut off from his natural heartlands. His solution to the 'metropolitan boundary' was to embrace it and remove himself to those parts where it might fit better. It still looks however, like he's wearing his Dad's suit to a shotgun wedding.

Raiding Nairn's reading list, we come across a particularly interesting passage from Gramsci's *The Modern Prince* that seems to explain why Brown has become so painfully isolated.

> The modern prince, the myth-prince cannot be a real person, a concrete individual; it can only be an organism; a complex element of society in which the cementing of a collective will, recognised and partially asserted in action, has already begun.

Against such a reading Brown's failure can be characterised as a failure to recognise that as a putative 'myth-prince' he should not even exist (yet). Gramsci explains why (and though he didn't know it, also explains Nairn);

> . . . the Prince did not exist in historical reality, did not present himself to the Italian people in a directly objective way, but was a purely doctrinaire abstraction, the symbol of a leader, the ideal condottiere; but the emotional, mythical elements contained throughout this small book [*The Prince*] are recapitulated and come to life in the conclusion, the invocation of a 'really existing' prince.

In Scottish politics we seem to have travelled rapidly along the trajectory of myth-prince to misprint to the missed pimp. The worried stoop of said myth-prince/pimp communicates his isolation from the only collective will he truly understands; he may never recapture the command of it he showed as a writer during the 70s and 80s. In those days it was organic, living and lively; by the time of that post-Blair infatuation, when the English/British press were amazed at Brown's active engagement in the word, it had ossified into risible, Union Jack-flash artificialities. He has busted his flush before the end of the book has been written.

Mentioning which, the books Brown published on the eve of his ascension to the throne in Downing Street (much more real, he might think, than the Salmond-*cloaca* in Charlotte Square) are instructive. The first, *Courage: Eight Portraits* is clearly literary voodoo on his own behalf (calling on the *loas* of RFK and Nelson Mandela to aid and abet him), while *Britain's Everyday Heroes* sees him fully commit to the desperate gambit ridiculed by Nairn in *Bard of Britishness* (and not even seen as credible by Nairn's many pro-Brit detractors). This latter book seems particularly lightweight and silly compared to his earlier works and perhaps it is this, rather than any *Hansard* or BBC-recorded folly that best sums up his sad slump into a 'doctrinaire abstraction'.

* * *

. . . the People will have to watch it closely.
But that will be easier to do when we surround it.
Alasdair Gray

This last word, written in 1992, the year of John Major's election victory when a real Scottish parliament seemed distant, goes to the Scottish novelist who wrote to us in the aphoristic language of civic mottoes, one who through the democratic technologies of the printed book and the poster-painted mural, attempted to build and illustrate the nation during its 1960s-70s doldrums.

Why Scots Should Rule Scotland is a somewhat thin analysis and Gray parses Scotland's political predicaments (and why they even matter) much better elsewhere (*Lanark, 1982 Janine, Unlikely Stories,*

Mostly). But almost his last words in that short pamphlet express perfectly the central question of Scottish autonomy. Or devolution. Or Home Rule. Or Independence in Europe, or whatever alternative word structure you think best describes a better *political* structure for Scotland and its people.

The question of structure has been a distinctive feature or Scottish political debate over the last century. It provides the crucial link between the independent artists of no-or-various-parties (Leonard, Lochhead, MacDiarmid and of course, Gray) found in our selection here, and the two magnates, Brown and Thatcher, who dominate this book. Leonard and Gray are in particular, imaginative artists who have worked hard to bring something to our understanding of the Scottish democratic structure, from the virtual reality championed by Midwinter and described by Kellas, to the fact of a parliament building that can be embraced, surrounded or potentially, besieged by the people who paid for it.

It is this pull towards the concrete, some might say substantial, others mundane, sphere of politics that explains why Leonard and Gray's 'silent partner' James Kelman, sits absent from these discussions. Oddly enough for a book about books, our conclusions about the literary dimension to the new Scotland is spatial. Think of it as the new St Paul's rising out of the beerpits surrounded by a commons, populated with petitioners looking, in the manner of Kafka's nameless victim, for the Law and its Doormen. If Gray has worked to map the extent of these commons, and Leonard sought to articulate the thoughts and feelings of its people in a language that is authentically of them, then Kelman has attempted to draw their attention to other horizons. Kelman has frequently engaged in the great debate about structures, but his tack has been to ignore the very notion of parliaments in favour of direct democracy, grass roots activism and libertarian left systems of organisation. They are, (if we may paraphrase) in the manner of Knoxian theocracy, methods unfettered by temporal mercies, timeless, as necessary in a devolved or independent Scotland as one tied with London. Kelman's contribution is an important one, in some respects more so than any of those mentioned here. but it is at heart existential, anti-constitutional in approach. Kelman, we would argue, had other things on his mind.

Scottish politics, as the books selected and interrogated here show, has frequently been something that happened when we were making other plans. You could characterise it as 'politics by proxy', as an appendage of London, or Moscow, or even an appendix of some future PM's PhD. Some cases in point: Tom Johnston wanted to take on the nobility, and inadvertently created the intellectual space for interrogating Scottish class dynamics separately from those in England. Hugh MacDiarmid held out for communism and ended up puffing on Harry Lauder's pipe. (Gaelic scholar John MacInnes recounted to one of the present authors how on a visit to the dying MacDiarmid in his cottage at Brownsbank the poet responded to a question about his career in poetry by extending his right arm full length and gazing on his pipe held out there with, as MacInnes described it, Marxist-Leninist critical objectivity, while declaring 'I have achieved everything I set out to achieve'. This vignette of the delightfully arch MacDiarmid feigning a singlehanded Communist rewrite of the long Scots 'see oursels' egalitarian tradition can only be truly appreciated in all its meretricious absurdity when we know [as MacInnes did not] that the pipe subjected to the severity of this long-armed poetico-political scrutiny had in fact formerly belonged to Sir Harry Lauder.) George Davie had an axe to grind about the Scottish unis, but inadvertently took a pick-axe to long-buried notions of 'native democracy'. Gordon Brown wanted to go to London, and set the colleagues he left behind sliding down the slippery slope to a heterodox form of Home Rule. Thatcher wanted to English Reaganomics, and drove the Scots to the comforting familiarity of a covenant. Somewhat incredulous of a capitalised 'People', Tom Leonard wanted to explore living language, and presaged new forms of political dialogue. . .

We could go on. These of course, are the meanings *we* have derived from our own list, and it is only *our* list. The reader should feel free to make up their own – a fun activity for the pub or the dinner party or even a political meeting.

With Scottish politics there are always books, and always a seemingly 'bigger' topic for them to contend with. Even Gray was talking about what, to him, seemed to be the inevitable truth of an independent or 'home ruled' Scotland as a poorer country, one where its parliamentary elites (for such they are now) may be more tempted towards corruption than those in richer, fatter countries, and so had to be watched more closely. Look if you will, to the MPs' expenses scandal of 2009 and draw your own conclusions about that, but what Gray was 'truly' (rather than 'really', in the Presbyterian sense) talking about was that a modern, west-European country such as Scotland will always create elites and vested interests, and against them a notion, perhaps rather facile, of a popular will and the frenetic exchange of ideas that will always shift faster and more fluidly than an establishment. Or even a (dis)establishment.

And now we have the interesting situation where our political energies are fixed upon a new bespoke outfit in Holyrood that still smells faintly of sour beer and urine-treated Tweed (north and south thereof). We are still also, embraced by somewhat slackened metropolitan boundaries. The SNP government have resurrected their plans for a new referendum that could remove these altogether. In any case, it seems likely that Scottish politics, which for the last ten years has been bottled in a shiny new parliament, will once again open up into a much larger, less easily defined space for debate and argument. Will books be the conduit? Or will websites, blogs and Facebook? There is no credible answer to that yet, but what is certain is that now we *have* our own St Paul's, we must indeed 'surround it'.

Holyrood Parliament and Royal High School, Courtesy: Andrew Lee

BIBLIOGRAPHY

Gordon Brown
Gordon Brown (ed.) *The Red Paper on Scotland* Edinburgh Univ Press
  1975
Gordon Brown, *Maxton* Mainstream 1986
  *Where There Is Greed: Margaret Thatcher and the Betrayal of Britain's
  Future* Mainstream Publishing 1989
  Global Europe: full employment Europe HMSO 2005
Gordon Brown and Douglas Alexander *New Scotland, New Britain*
  Smith Institute 1999
Gordon Brown and Robin Cook *Scotland: The Real Divide – Poverty and
  Deprivation in Scotland* Mainstream 1983
Gordon Brown and Henry Drucker *The Politics of Nationalism and
  Devolution* Longman 1980
Gordon Brown and James Naughtie (eds.) *John Smith: Life and Soul of
  the Party* Mainstream 1994
Gordon Brown and Tony Wright (eds.) *Values, Visions and Voices, An
  Anthology of Socialism* Mainstream 1995

Margaret Thatcher
Sir Keith Joseph *Monetarism is Not Enough* The Centre for Policy Studies
  1976
The Rt Hon George Younger et al. *The Authority of Government Group
  Report* 1975
J. Campbell *Margaret Thatcher Volume 1: The Grocer's Daughter* Jonathan
  Cape 2000
J.Campbell *Margaret Thatcher Volume 2: The Iron Lady* Jonathan Cape
  2003

Tom Nairn
Tom Nairn (ed.) *Gordon Brown – Bard of Britishness* Institute of Welsh
  Affairs 2006
  Atlantic Europe? The Radical View Amsterdam: The Transnational
  Institute 1976
Tom Nairn 'The English Working Class' *NLR* no. 24 March-April 1964

'The Nature of the Labour Party' *NLR* 27-28 (September-October, November-December 1964)
The Left against Europe Pelican 1973
The Break-Up of Britain Verso 1981
The Enchanted Glass Radius 1988
The Modern Janus: Nationalism in the Modern World Verso 1990-1999
After Britain Granta 2000
Pariah Verso Books 2002

Tom Nairn and Angelo Quatrocchi 'Three Dreams of Scottish Nationalism', *New Left Review* I/49, May/June 1968
The Beginning of the End: France, May 1968, Verso, 1998

The Idealists

Marinell Ash *The Strange Death Of Scottish History* Ramsay Head Press 1980

Craig Beveridge and Ronald Turnbull *The Eclipse of Scottish Culture* Polygon 1989

George Davie *The Democratic Intellect* Edinburgh Univ Press 1961

Owen Dudley Edwards (ed.) *A Claim of Right for Scotland* Polygon 1989

Michael Fry *Patronage and Principle* Aberdeen Univ Press, 1987

Christopher Harvie *The Lights of Liberalism* Viking 1976
Scotland and Nationalism Routledge 1977
A Voter's Guide to the Scottish Assembly 1979
No Gods and Precious Few Heroes, Scotland 1914-1980 Edinburgh Univ Press 1981
Mending Scotland Argyll 2004
A Floating Commonwealth: Politics, Culture, and Technology on Britain's Atlantic Coast 1860-1930 OUP 2008

Tom Johnston *Our Scots Noble Families* Forward Publishing 1909 (new edition Argyll Publishing 1999)

Tom Leonard (ed.) *Radical Renfrew* Polygon 1990

Hugh MacDiarmid *A Drunk Man Looks at the Thistle* William Blackwood and Sons 1926

T.C. Smout *A Century of the Scottish People* Fontana Press 1986

The Pragmatists

Neal Ascherson *The King Incorporated: Leopold the Second and the Congo* Granta 1963

Henry Drucker et al. (eds.) *Scottish Government Yearbook* 1976–1992

Michael Keating and Arthur Midwinter *The Government of Scotland* 1983

James G. Kellas *The Scottish Political System* Cambridge Univ Press 1973

Neil MacCormick *Practical Reason in Law and Morality* Oxford 2008

David McCrone *Understanding Scotland: the Sociology of a Stateless Nation* Routledge 1992

John P. Mackintosh *The Government and Politics of Britain* Hutchinson 1970

Lindsay Paterson *Education and a Scottish Parliament* Dunedin Academic
  Press 1989
  The Autonomy of Modern Scotland Edinburgh Univ Press 1994
Lindsay Paterson (ed.) *Scottish Affairs, 1992 –*

Other Works Cited
Aristotle *Politics*
  Poetics
Walter Bagehot *The English Constitution* 1867
Eberhard Bort and Russell Keat (eds.) *The Boundaries of Understanding*
  (a *Festschrift* for Malcolm Anderson) International Social Sciences
  Institute 1999
Norman Buchan *Macdunciad* illustrations by Gale Famedram Publishers
  1977
G. K. Chesterton *The Wisdom of Father Brown* 1914
Amy Chua *World on Fire* Arrow Books 2004
Reginald Coupland *Welsh and Scottish Nationalism: A Study* Collins 1954
Abraham Cowley *Poems* Cambridge 1905
Tom Devine (ed.) *Scotland and the Union 1707-2007* Edinburgh Univ
  Press 2008
  Scotland's Shame Mainstream 2000
Owen Dudley Edwards, Rhys Ioan Gwynfor and Hugh MacDiarmid
  Celtic Nationalism Routledge and Kegan 1968
Frantz Fanon *The Wretched of the Earth* McGibbon & Kee 1965 (first pub.
  in French as '*Les Damnees de la terre*' in 1961)
Ernest Gellner *Thought and Change* Weidenfeld and Nicolson 1964
Duncan Glen (ed.) *Whither Scotland? a prejudiced look at the future of a
  nation* 1971
Ernst Gombrich *Story of Art* Phaidon 1950
Antonio Gramsci *Quaderni del Carceri* Einaudi 1948-51
Alasdair Gray *Lanark*, Canongate 1981
  Unlikely Stories, Mostly Penguin 1983
  Why Scots Should Rule Scotland Penguin 1992
H.J. Hanham *Scottish Nationalism* Harvard Univ Press 1969
Jaroslav Hasek *The good soldier Schweik* 1912
Thomas Hobbes *The Leviathan* 1651
Eric Hobsbawm and Terence Ranger *The Invention of Tradition*
  Cambridge Uni Press 1983
David Hume *Political Essays* Cambridge Univ Press 1994
Tom Johnston *History of the Scottish Working Classes* Forward Publishing
  1921
Elie Kedourie *Nationalism* Hutchinson 1960
J. R. Kipling *Barrack Room Ballads and Other Verses* Methuen 1892
Tom Leonard *Intimate Voices* Galloping Dog Press 1984
Liz Lochhead *Mary Queen of Scots got her head chopped off* Penguin 1989
Macaulay *History of England* 1848
John MacCormick *The Flag in the Wind* Birlinn 2008 original edition
  1955

Hugh MacDiarmid (ed.) *Golden Treasury of Scottish Poetry* MacMillan 1940

John McEwen *Who Owns Scotland?* EUSPB 1977

Charles McKean *The Scottish Chateau* Sutton Publishing 2001

John P. Mackintosh *The British Cabinet* Stevens and Sons Ltd 1977

Machiavelli *Discorsi sopra la prima deca di Titio Livio* 1531
  Il Principe 1513

Andrew Marr *The Battle for Scotland* Penguin 1992

Kingsley Martin *The Crown and the Establishment* Hutchinson 1962

Karl Marx *The Eighteenth Brumaire of Louis Bonaparte* 1852

Arthur Midwinter *Local government in Scotland: Reform or Decline?* MacMillan 1995

Karl Miller (ed.) *Memoirs of a Modern Scotland* Faber 1970

Vince Mills (ed.) *Red Paper on Scotland* Research Collections @ GCU, 2005

John Milton *Paradise Lost* 1667

Robert Musil *A Man without Qualities* 1930-42 (first published in English 1953)

Plato *The Republic*

G.J. Renier *The English: Are They Human?* Williams and Norgate 1933

Johnny Rodger and Gerard Carruthers (eds.) *Fickle Man: Robert Burns in the 21st Century* Sandstone Press 2009

Walter Scott *Old Mortality* 1816
  The Black Dwarf 1816
  The Letters of Malachi Malagrowther 1826

Rev. Robert Simpson *Martyrland: A Tale of Persecution from the Days of the Scottish Covenanters* 1890

T.C. Smout *History of the Scottish People 1560 to 1830* Collins 1969

David Stenhouse *On the Make: How the Scots took over London* Mainstream 2004

E.P. Thompson *The Making of the English Working Class* Victor Gollancz 1963

A.D. Wightman *Who Owns Scotland?* Canongate 1997

C. Jr Wren *Parentalia (Memoirs of the Family of the Wrens)* 1750

INDEX of NAMES